The Fighting Submac
Machine Pistol, and Shotgun

ACKNOWLEDGMENTS

First, I'd like to dedicate this book to my wife, Eleanor, a wonderful wife, mother, and companion, and to Catherine, who is a blessing for us both.

Any book like this represents a lot of work and assistance by more than the author. While only I can take the blame for any weakness in the end product, many people rendered me great service in making this book possible. I wish to thank them for their efforts and make it clear that I appreciate their kindness and consideration.

- *Debbie Gallop*, my long-time secretary who, charged with the task of rendering this text by sections onto a computer disk, learned far more than she ever wanted to know about this subject, I am certain.

- *Kent Lomont*, who was able to supply me directly or via John Ross with many of the weapons tested in this book and who always represented an optimistic, positive force in the project. In addition, Kent was able to add many insights of his own when evaluating these weapons because he has, no doubt, seen more and done more than almost anyone else alive today in the field of automatic weapons.

- *Shawn McCarver,* who offered an experienced view and sophisticated evaluation to my comments about what I was learning in my experiments.

- *John Miller*, who allowed me to visit with him and test his collection of weapons as well as providing me with insights about them and other weapons in light of his many years of military and police experience.

- *John Ross*, a good friend who kindly gave me unlimited access to his wonderful collection and even indulged me by buying some weapons that I am certain he really did not want to until he shot them and discovered that I was correct about their being good firearms.

- *Chief Edward Seyffert*, a good friend who went along on numerous testing trips to evaluate weapons and in the process froze in the winter and sweated in the summer as we tested various examples. He never once questioned why his friend wanted to test all these odd weapons.

- *Leroy Thompson*, who listened as I developed this concept for this series of books, offered his insights about the weapons tested, helped with photos, and generally rendered great assistance to me at all times.

The Fighting Submachine Gun, Machine Pistol, and Shotgun

A Hands-On Evaluation

Sten Gun
Great Britain

M1921
Thompson
United States

MP5
Germany

Owen SMG
Australia

Timothy J. Mullin

PALADIN PRESS • BOULDER, COLORADO

Also by Timothy J. Mullins

American Beauty
The 100 Greatest Combat Pistols
Testing the War Weapons: Rifles and Light Machine Guns from Around the World
Training the Gunfighter

The Fighting Submachine Gun, Machine Pistol, and Shotgun: A Hands-On Evaluation
by Timothy J. Mullin

ISBN 1-58160-040-2
Printed in the United States of America

Published by Paladin Press, a division of
Paladin Enterprises, Inc., P.O. Box 1307,
Boulder, Colorado 80306, USA.
(303) 443-7250

Direct inquiries and/or orders to the above address.

Visit our Web site at: www.paladin-press.com

CONTENTS

FOREWORD

This third volume in T.J. Mullin's definitive work on the world's military and paramilitary weapons deals with perhaps the least understood of individual weapons: the submachine gun, machine pistol, and fighting shotgun. Although the combat shotgun has traditionally been an American favorite in wartime, the submachine gun and, especially, the machine pistol have achieved far wider acceptance in Europe and the Third World. This has changed to a marked degree as the mission of U.S. military forces, especially those assigned to special operations, has changed during the last decades to include hostage rescue and other missions requiring enhanced close-range firepower. Although the U.S. Army's Rangers and Special Forces and the U.S Navy's SEALs have been the foremost proponents of the submachine gun, in Latin America, many European countries, and some Asian ones, the submachine gun is the primary weapon of paramilitary internal security forces and some elite raiding units. The fact that the pistol-caliber submachine gun lends itself to being suppressed has made it even more ubiquitous in the special operations arsenal.

Because of strict legal controls on civilian access to fully automatic weapons and the rarity of many such weapons, far fewer shooters will have the chance to actually test most submachine guns or machine pistols themselves; hence, this work will allow them to come as close to a hands-on test as possible without having access to the actual weapons. Once again, as with the previous two volumes (*The 100 Greatest Combat Pistols* and *Testing the War Weapons*), this one should be an invaluable reference for military or police armorers, as well as for anyone else who may need to know how an automatic weapon actually performs as opposed to the bare statistics available in *Janes Infantry Weapons* or other such works. I've already recommended all three volumes of Mullin's works to one fiction writer and to another motion picture writer in hopes that they might start getting their weapons usage right!

As a former infantry officer and federal agent, Mullin brings the proper real-world experience to balance his strong knowledge of firearms history, thus allowing his analysis of the various weapons in their historical and tactical context to focus on what makes each unique as well as where each fits in the developmental history of modern small arms. Both the shotgun and the submachine gun have often been incorrectly viewed as strictly "spray (or pump) and pray," weapons best suited to throwing a lot of projectiles into a constricted area. Both weapons types can, indeed, be used to fill an area with a "curtain of death," but each may also serve other tactical needs as well. Hostage rescue units, for example, would not overwhelmingly choose the Heckler & Koch (H&K) MP5 if it could not be fired with the precision necessary to place a shot exactly on a hostage taker.

Even more misunderstood is the machine pistol, and I think it is this weapon about which I learned the most from this text. In reading Mullin's evaluations of these highly specialized weapons, I have certainly come to take them more seriously and have learned to use them more effectively when I've had occasion to fire them. Additionally, I especially like the first five chapters in which Mullin sets forth the tactical doctrine for the use of the submachine gun, suppressed submachine gun, machine pistol, and combat shotgun. These chapters establish the proper mind-set and intellectual framework for reading the subsequent evaluations.

As with each of the preceding volumes in this landmark series, I think you'll read this volume cover to cover and then place it on your reference shelf to refer to again and again. That's certainly how I use each of the volumes in this series and why I look forward to each new one so avidly.

Leroy Thompson
St. Louis, Missouri

PART I

The Military Role of the Submachine Gun

The submachine gun (SMG) has had a very short life as a valid military weapon. Arriving on the scene in 1918 with the introduction of the Bergmann M1918, the SMG was made obsolete in 1940 by the development of the M1 carbine. As military weapons go, a 22-year life span is quite short. The Brown Bess musket was a standard military weapon for more than 200 years, and the Colt Government Model M1911/11A1 was the standard military weapon of U.S. forces for more than 70 years.

Further, not every military organization in 1918 decided that the SMG was a valid weapon. In fact, most viewed it then somewhat like more advanced thinkers do today: as a police weapon not truly suitable for military use because of its limitations. In the 1920s, Britain shunned it, and before 1940 the United States bought only a few. In Germany, development continued on the SMG concept in the 1920s, but most sales were to small Third World nations or China, where the weapon was popular. France had basically no development of SMGs, nor did the Soviet Union until the mid-1930s. Switzerland, traditionally a place where German gunmakers flee, worked on the design, but even the Swiss did not buy them (although they sold them to both sides in many a small war). In the United States, 15,000 Thompson SMGs were made in 1920–21, enough to fill all demands through 1940.

Things stayed this way until the Spanish Civil War began in 1936. The Soviets sent advisors to this war, as did the Germans and Italians. Each side saw that the SMG was an effective weapon in the hands of poorly trained troops, and the rush was on to make more SMGs. The Germans led the way to SMGs that followed a more modern construction approach with the MP 38 SMG, where previously they basically remade the M1918 Bergmann style when they made the MP 28, MP 34, and the Erma SMG. The Italians turned out the M38, which was a masterpiece. The Soviets adopted a series of guns that are now mostly forgotten. France, Britain, and the United States ignored it all.

During the invasion of Poland and the low countries in the late 1930s, the Germans used the SMG to great effect, and in Finland the well-trained Finns equipped with the M1931 Suomi SMG cut the Russian invaders to shreds. The Soviets and the Western allies rushed to obtain more SMGs. In the United States, manufacturers made numerous SMGs, but the real achievements were making the Thompson faster and cheaper and developing the M3/M3A1. The British designed the Sten guns, and the Russians developed the famous PPsH-41 and PPS-43 SMG. By then, however, these guns were obsolete because the M1 carbine was more accurate than any open-bolt SMG, fired a more powerful cartridge, and was lighter. Still the production lines were up and running, and SMGs by the millions poured out of the world's arsenals.

The benefits of the SMG were that it provided a high volume of fire, was effective at short range, and was cheap to make. In a day when only bolt-action rifles existed, such short, handy—albeit heavy—guns with a large capacity and the ability to fire rapidly were very tempting. The disadvantages of the SMG were its lack of accuracy resulting from the open-bolt firing mechanism, its short range because of the cartridge, its ballistic limitations, and its weight. As the ranges decrease and the need to carry weapons over long distances goes down, the respect afforded a SMG goes up, which is why

It looks like some mid- to late 1920s "industrial relations specialists" from the Southern Illinois coal-mining region to me. Note the two M1921 Thompsons with rare 100-round drums, which must have been quite the negotiating instruments for contract disputes. Who needs the National Labor Relations Board when you have a Thompson?

SMGs are seen as effective police weapons today, much like they were viewed in the 1920s and 1930s.

As we head into the 21st century, the question of whether the SMG has any valid role in today's military must be asked. A few years back, the answer was clear: No! But in recent years, there has been a resurgence in the use of the SMG among military units. Why? If you look at these units you will see they have been charged with nontraditional tasks, mainly counterterrorism or special warfare operations. Generally such operations are more of a police-type function than a military operation in the normal sense. One consequence of that fact is that the action tends to occur at very close range and in urban areas or at night. All these unusual characteristics tend to minimize the deficiencies of the SMG and enhance its good points, such as low noise level, ease of suppressing the weapon, low penetration, and small size.

However, ignoring these unusually tasked military units, are SMGs found today in any modern military unit that has gone on to the second generation of post-World War II (i.e., 5.56x45mm) weapons? Except for some old equipment still in inventory, such as the M3A1 SMG for tankers, the answer is no. With the advent of such weapons that weigh no more than a typical open-bolt SMG but that have effective ranges of one-third to one-half again as much as an SMG, the need for the SMG in a traditional military unit has disappeared. For this reason, we must view SMGs as interesting relics of the past, much like we view cap and ball or flintlock rifles, which in their day were also effective military rifles. So it is with the SMG in military circumstances.

Author firing the M1921 Thompson SMG. Note the aggressive stance used: high elbow and foot placement add recoil control and on-target accuracy. A similar stance is used for proper combat firing and on auto loaders or revolvers.

The Silenced Submachine Gun—Its Development and Use

During World War II, the need for a weapon that could be used to remove enemy sentries without alerting the entire community on one hand or requiring very close-range knife or piano wire attack on the other became evident. Getting to within 50 yards of a person is often not difficult to do without detection, but getting within touching distance is something else entirely.

Silencers for firearms certainly were nothing new. Maxim had been making them before World War I, but other than occasional use on M1903 Springfield sniping rifles, it seems that little use was made of them. Perhaps the general noise level on World War I battlefields negated their usefulness. During World War II, however, it soon became obvious that such devices could be very useful. Early efforts to use civilian suppressors on semiautomatic pistols and rimfire rifles soon established that the idea was good, but something with greater effective range than a pistol was desirable, and .22 rimfire rifles are not very useful except for very specific purposes. However, it soon became apparent that the pistol-powered SMG was an ideal vehicle because it used a subsonic projectile (generally to avoid sound wave booms), could be effectively used at greater distances than a handgun (except in expert hands), and was a viable weapon for more generalized use as well.

Early attempts to silence an SMG seemed to be centered around the Thompson, which was an unfortunate choice because it was expensive and already quite heavy and long. Early prototypes were used by British Commando forces. In 1941 the Sten SMG came on the scene, which was a much better candidate for a silencer. Soon the MK II Sten SMG was developed, and the suppressed SMG came into its own, with a specific model, the MK II (S), being developed. It used quite an effective suppressor, which lowered the 9mm ammunition to subsonic levels, offered good protection to the weak hand from heat, and was not too long or heavy because of the short 8-inch Sten SMG barrel. A separate bolt was designed, and fiber wads were used to limit bolt clatter. Since the Sten SMG was a selective-fire weapon it was used as a semiautomatic carbine, thereby limiting problems with the suppressor. But, of course, it could be used in the full-auto format if necessary.

The Sten MK II (S) set the standard for silenced SMGs, and it was widely used (as those things go) during World War II. German forces apparently were quite impressed with the examples they captured, but despite attempts by Germany's premier commando leader, Lt. Col. Otto Skorzeny, to get Germany to make it, its leaders declined. U.S. forces developed the silenced M3 SMG, which was also quite good, albeit heavier than the MK II (S) and not nearly as user friendly.

At the conclusion of World War II, the old wartime guns stayed in the inventory and were used for many years. As late as 1970, silenced M3 and Sten Mark II (S) SMGs were used in Vietnam, but, of course, new weapons had been developed in the intervening 25 years and they also were also occasionally seen. Among Western developments, the suppressed Sterling, which offered excellent suppression levels even though firing from an open bolt, and the various Ingram M10/11 SMG/suppressor combinations are well known. At the tail end of the Vietnam War period, H&K introduced its MP5 SD model. The MP5 has become the standard special operations SMG in many Western military and police special operations units. Its popularity is due in large part to its closed-bolt operation system that makes it easy to use, as well as its high accuracy, generally good performance, and, most critically, its gas-bleed-type suppressor, which allows standard military ball loads to be used and yet still remain subsonic exiting the barrel/suppressor unit. For large organizations, the convenience of avoiding the need for specialized ammunition is highly desirable.

During this same time frame, many suppressors came on the scene that could be adapted to existing SMG designs. While a few were really not any better than the Maxim units designed before World War I (not surprising given the actual principles involved with suppressors), a few were quite good and adopted by military and police special operations units.

On the other side of the fence, among the communist forces a specialized silenced SMG, the Chinese Type 64, was popular, and it appears that it was equally as good as the Sterling. Similarly, many designs recently have been encountered in the former Soviet Union that appear to be the work of numerous designers who were attempting to build suppressed weapons for Soviet special operations personnel. Exactly how effective they are is impossible for me to say given my lack of experience with them, but Soviet weapons are generally quite good, although rarely up to the standard of really top-quality Western designs. It also is unclear to me how many of them were made in quantities and how many of them are mere prototypes. It does show, however, that the Soviets thought highly of the concept of suppressed SMGs.

The question remains: how useful really are suppressed SMGs? All of us who have encountered them no doubt find them interesting, and it is quite pleasant to be able to shoot a weapon without wearing earmuffs. Similarly, the ability to fire a weapon in areas where the noise would otherwise preclude firing is also quite nice. Then, of course, they make ideal "dog and cat" guns for urban officers on night-time patrol in small towns across the United States, as some people who will read these lines know quite well. But for real-life military or police operations, are they worth procuring?

For specialized heavy-weapons police units, whether they are hostage intervention or heavy-duty arrest teams, I think suppressed SMGs are well worth the price of admission. Generally, such teams work at close range and in urban environments, and frequently the sound of gunfire can alarm residents or cause a large gathering of hostile people, which creates more problems than existed before the operation started. A raid that precipitates a riot does no one any good. Additionally, weapons are commonly used inside buildings. The blast can be deafening and quite disorienting. My ears still ring today from the blast of an Uzi SMG fired immediately to my rear during the course of one such urban operation. I suppose the noise coming from the front would have had the same effect, along with the added danger of a missile strike, but I do rather wish my colleague would have had a suppressed Uzi, especially when I lie in bed at night in a quiet house with my ears still ringing loudly. There is no known cure for this problem. Plus, as noted, the noise and flash can be disorienting, and suppressors will minimize both the blast and flash. The first time I shot an M66 4-inch .357 Magnum loaded with 125-grain jacketed hollowpoint (JHP) Federal ammunition in the dark, I thought my revolver had exploded. I remember distinctively jumping back in alarm—hardly the best tactics in the middle of a raid.

My conclusion for police operations is that, if an SMG is called for, a suppressed model should be selected—as long as the overall length is not greatly extended. Perhaps the best example is the H&K MP5 SD or its U.S. commercial equivalents. They give you everything the standard model gives, albeit at a slightly longer overall length. Since the barrel is drilled, the velocity is lowered; thus, I suggest using standard or greater velocity ammunition so that power is not reduced to unacceptable standards. While you may get a ballistic "crack," it is the blast and flash you are attempting to reduce. Using subsonic ammunition in such suppressed weapons with ported or drilled barrels will cause the velocity to be reduced to levels in the 650 to 700 feet per second (fps) range. At that level, you are basically launching nonexpanding .35-caliber projectiles, very similar to target wadcutters. Performance on target is rather dismal, as might be expected. If +P+ ammunition is used, you get standard (1,150 fps) velocity, which, while not awesome, is at least acceptable, especially with rapid repeat shots impacting the target area.

The area of military operations is another where the use of the suppressed SMG is helpful. Unfortunately, the suppressed SMG has a very limited role here because of its lack of power and range. But for certain functions, it is excellent. I have a friend who blew up a critically important bridge in Mozambique, and he claims he would not have been able to get close enough to it to place his charges without the use of his suppressed Sterling SMG. With it, he was able to shoot the sentry guarding the area in the head and get to the bridge, place his charges, and disappear without being discovered. Lest anyone think this is far-fetched, bear in mind that the Sterling has a muzzle noise like that of a heavy-duty acoustical tile stapler and that water was rushing by the scene all the time, drowning out noise. Generally one shot can always be taken without alerting people, sometimes even more, if circumstances and conditions are correct. Israeli counterterrorist operatives used the suppressed Ingram M10 very successfully on the raid on Entebbe, Uganda, in July 1976 when they rescued an airliner full of people being held hostage by Arab and German terrorists.

However, except for such specialized uses and occasionally for night operations, where the range is typically short and low noise and muzzle flash are critically important, the suppressed SMG has little real military use. Certainly it should be available for raiding parties, prisoner snatch groups, and perhaps even ambush teams, but it need not be available to every platoon as part of its standard table of organized equipment (TOE).

Suppressors themselves, when attached to standard caliber service rifles and light machine guns (LMGs), have some use, mainly on sniping rifles on operations where concealing the muzzle blast will help prevent snipers from being discovered and perhaps on LMGs at ambush sites. However, they are typically long, heavy, and expensive; so again, except for occasional tasks, they are best omitted from the standard/platoon TOE. A suppressed, short-barreled rifle or pistol might be a dandy weapon for downed pilots, but realistically the idea of the downed pilot harvesting wild game to sustain himself while walking back to friendly lines does not seem very realistic to me. I could see it for brush pilots in the wilderness, but if the plane is lost or wrecked, the pilot likely welcomes the noise if it will alert others to his whereabouts.

Although it is likely that anyone who has ever used a suppressor likes it (if for no other reasons than it allows one to shoot in areas where it otherwise might not be feasible and it saves wear and tear on one's ears without resorting to bulky, heavy muffs), suppressed weapons, especially suppressed SMGs, have little legitimate military application today, except for very specialized roles. However, the opposite is true for the police use, where the suppressed SMG has quite a legitimate role. In fact, I would conclude that any time an SMG is really necessary in police work, it should be suppressed.

The Machine Pistol—Its Unique Characteristics and Use

The first autoloading pistols were all burst-fire weapons, apparently, and designers soon discovered that they had such a high cyclic rate with the perceived use of the weapons that they were ineffective. Disconnectors soon appeared to permit them to fire one round with each pull of the trigger.

Thereafter, autoloading pistols, except for malfunctioning weapons and occasional rare exceptions, did not fire bursts. Of course, their rarity and the fact that the majority of specimens that were encountered were defective ones caused many people to decide that burst-fire, hand-held weapons were worthless as fighting weapons.

I believe that a lot of this perception is attributable to three factors: (1) the unsuitable firing stances used by early-day shooters, (2) the fact that many of the weapons offering selective- or burst-fire features were made either by second-string manufacturers or in rather obsolete designs, and (3) a lack of an opportunity to use the weapons. Any time it is difficult to find examples of an item, where they can be used only under carefully proscribed and artificial circumstances and frequently only briefly so as not to alarm the entire neighborhood, you will not get much development.

I am certain that most people will admit that their first encounter with a true machine pistol (by this I mean a weapon designed to be fired without a buttstock that was made as an integral part of the weapon, not an SMG) was probably with a World War II "bring back" Mauser Schnellfeuer pistol. They likely loaded it up, fired a few rounds, and worried all the time that someone was calling the local sheriff's office to report someone firing a machine gun. This is hardly conducive to a proper developmental approach to the weapon and its use.

Think for a moment: if the National Firearms Act of 1934 (NFA) had not been passed (or if it had been declared unconstitutional, as it no doubt would have been had not the solicitor general lied to the Supreme Court in 1939), many manufacturers would have no doubt developed selective-fire versions of their weapons. Prior to 1934, there was a surprisingly flourishing business in converting Standard Government Model Colt .45 self-loaders to selective fire. I have also seen similarly converted Luger pistols. No telling what else was converted during the time and long ago consigned to a hole in the ground.

Unfortunately, gun publications of the period did not chronicle this development as they would do today, because most manufacturers were concerned with hunting and target shooting, not personal defense. Of course, that was no doubt due to a lack of concern for personal defense in a day when criminals expected to be resisted and shot!

In any event, the NFA with its $200 tax, the equivalent of 10 weeks or more of wages for a normal working man at the time, coupled with the 1986 ban on making new machine guns, greatly limited this whole area of development. I do not believe that government-sponsored research will ever lead to any real developments in this field simply because it takes a lot of creative people working on their own time, with their own money, and without bureaucratic restrictions to develop anything truly useful in any field. Just think how much differently computers would have developed if similar laws had been applied to them. I am certain no little laptops would exist!

With this in mind, the issue becomes, what use does the machine pistol actually render to the shooter today? The key distinction between a standard self-loader and the machine pistol is the rate of fire. Both actually cycle at the same rate. Because of its disconnector the standard pistol requires that the trigger be manually released and then depressed before the next shot is fired; the machine pistol automatically provides this function. Typical machine pistols have quite high rates of fire because of the short travel of the slide and the power of the cartridges. In actual tests, they seem to measure between 2,200 RPM with the H&K VP 70 to 1,200 RPM with the Glock 18 or Browning P35. Actually, when later weapons are fired in bursts of three shots the ear cannot distinguish between individual reports. This cyclic rate issue becomes an interesting aspect when we consider that in actual tests with an M3 SMG I shot 350 RPM, Ed McGovern shot 600 RPM with a Smith & Wesson K-frame .38 revolver, and I have gotten a 425 RPM reading shooting either a standard P35 or Government Model Colt. However, any way you slice it, the typical machine pistol fires faster than the conventional self-loading pistol by a two- or threefold factor.

Fast-firing weapons can be viewed in two fashions: either the weapon fires so fast that the bullets are exiting the barrel before the weapon begins to rise, thereby allowing the shooter to keep his rounds on target, or the weapon recoils so much that the rounds are all off target after the first one is fired. German designers typically follow the high cyclic rate theory, and this is why they have such weapons as the H&K VP 70. Other makers, such as Star, have adopted rate reducers on a rate system so the rate of fire is about 325 RPM, and thus the shooter can respond to the recoil and pull the weapon back on target before the next shot is fired. Firing on fast semiautomatic at 425 RPM allows the shooter to control his weapon and produces good groups, so the slow-fire full auto is even easier to control. The shooter needs to concentrate only on the target, not worry about controlling the trigger action. Both the high cyclic rate and low cyclic rate machine pistols are very rare creatures, I believe, because of the oppressive laws found on the subject. All machine pistols are rare, of course, but the most common seem to run at about 1,200 RPM.

In actual tests, these weapons seem to fire the first round at the aimed point and the next round 24 inches up from that point when used with a two-hand hold fired at 5 yards. Of course, the more you practice with the weapon, the better you get; and some, such as the polymer-framed Glock M18, seem to hang in place on long bursts, although the first 2 to 3 rounds follow this same pattern.

The key to effectively using the machine pistol is to first understand what it is. This means you understand how it is to be used tactically. Failure to understand this will result in the weapon's being misused and the shooter's losing a very valuable tool. The machine pistol should be viewed as a small hand-held shotgun firing projectiles that are more deadly than any found in a shotgun because of their weight and caliber. It is designed to allow the shooter to saturate a target with missiles at close range in a very short period of time, much like a sawed-off shotgun. As with the shotgun, the projectiles are scattered over the target area, thereby improving the chances of hitting a major organ as well as inflicting the maximum amount of shock because a large number of wounds are being inflicted almost at the same time. Viewed as a hand-held, concealable, sawed-off shotgun, the machine pistol becomes the single most deadly hand-held weapon available at close ranges (under 20 feet), if used correctly. Unlike the sawed-off 12-gauge shotgun, it can be fired a number of times in 3- to 5-round bursts, its projectiles are bigger with a greater ballistic coefficient than the shotgun cartridge contains, and it can be reloaded more rapidly. Additionally, if a more distinct target is present, it allows long-range, pinpoint accuracy. For example, I can hit a man target at 200 yards with a Glock M18 on semiautomatic—try that with your sawed-off 12-gauge loaded with heavy shot!

The key to maximizing these good qualities is understanding how to shoot it properly. Obviously firing it like a conventional pistol offhand with a mere hand hold will not work because the recoil of subsequent shots will cause all rounds to go wide and high. Instead, the shooter must use as strong a hold as possible (I prefer the Weaver, but other stances will also work) and then be very aggressive about the stance. The shooter should lean in to the weapon, in much the same way as a person plunges a bayonet into a target. By flexing the knees deeply

Note the author's aggressive stance as he fires the Glock G18 machine pistol. This extreme forward stance is necessary to control the weapon effectively, unlike the normal handgun shooting method used for other firearms. The forward stance is also helpful for fast, accurate semiautomatic work.

and adopting an aggressive stance, you put all of your body weight behind the weapon and limit the muzzle flip. Taking a high hand position also minimizes the potential for muzzle flip. A good test of your stance is to have another person attempt to push you back or to the side. With the proper stance, your movement should be minimal. Next, realize that as the weapon fires, you will not be able to see the sights. They will be a blur. If you are accustomed to using the sights, this can be very disturbing. Instead, pick out a point on the target and focus your eye, and hence all of your energy on that point. For instance, focus on a particular button. By doing that, you will focus all of your energy on directing the weapon's muzzle to that area.

As with any shooting activity, skills rapidly decline if not used and perhaps more so with the machine pistol because it requires more skill to use it effectively than almost any other firearm, except perhaps the sniper rifle. The person who is assigned the machine pistol must plan on firing it enough times to learn the tricks of the weapon (about 1,000 rounds in one day seems about right) and then shoot it enough to stay good (say a couple of hundred rounds once every two weeks). By doing that, the shooter can retain the unique skills called for, and he will be rewarded with the single most effective close-quarter weapon around.

The Combat Shotgun

The combat shotgun is used by U.S. forces and occasionally by British units but is almost unknown everywhere else in the world. Occasionally, if the United States gives its military allies combat shotguns they will use them, but usually as soon as the U.S. advisors leave, they will discard the shotguns for SMGs or something else.

The combat shotgun has had a long and honorable role in U.S. service, but it was not until World War I that mission-specific shotguns were widely available. Before that time, men merely took sporting shotguns and shortened the barrels. During World War I, the M97 and M12 Winchester 12-gauge shotguns, as well as others, were adopted specifically for the military. The barrels were chopped to 20 inches, a ventilated handgun was installed, a bayonet lug was included, and slings were added. Apparently these were well received by U.S. forces, who found them very helpful for grenades thrown at them by the Germans while the grenades were still in the air. The standard load was a 12-gauge, brass-cased, 2 3/4-inch load of nine 00 buckshot. The Germans thought so much of these weapons that they threatened to execute U.S. troops found with them. This threat was neutralized by the U.S. response to retaliate against German prisoners. Today, I assume the U.S. Army would simply withdraw these effective weapons.

After the war, shotguns continued in the inventory, and although mainly used for guard duties, no doubt they were occasionally used in Nicaragua, China, and other trouble spots frequented by U.S. forces in the period between the First and Second World Wars. However, no real development of the combat shotgun took place, and, as a consequence, when the United States entered World War II, the shotgun looked much like it did in 1917. Other than by guards, there did not seem to be too much use of the combat shotgun in Europe during World War II, but perhaps that was because of mobile warfare, greater range than occurred in World War I trench warfare, and the general issue of the M1 Garand rifle.

On the other hand, the combat shotgun was well received and used as frequently as possible during the island and jungle campaigns in the Pacific theater. The shotguns selected were again modified to accept an upper handguard to prevent burned fingers, a bayonet lug was added, the barrels were shortened to 20 inches, and slings were added. Once again, brass-cased shells were issued.

This reflects one of the major problems with the combat shotgun: until the advent of plastic shells a few years ago, ammunition was either all brass cases or paper. The brass cases worked fine but were extremely expensive to make and heavy, but they did avoid the swelling problem associated with paper shells in humid climates. Many people today do not remember the problem of shells swelling because they have only used plastic shells. But before plastic shells, this was a real problem for hunters—and in the military, where conditions are frequently worse than while hunting and continue for weeks at a time, the situation was worse. Frequently it got so bad that the shells simply would not fit. At that point, the shotgun got discarded for the SMG, Browning Automatic Rifle (BAR), carbine, or rifle. Bill Jordan, formerly of the U.S. Border Patrol, tells the story of using a shotgun on the islands until his shells got so swollen they would not fit. He then had to discard the shotgun and start using a Thompson SMG.

While great strides were made in airplane and bomb technology during World War II, shotgun technology was static, and we ended World War II with the same shotguns and ammunition we went into World War I with in 1917. During the Korean War, shotguns were not used much, possibly because of the ranges involved, although a gentleman who frequented the same gun store I went to when I was 11 years old used to tell stories of using a shotgun while riding on top of tanks. He told how he would shoot North Koreans who would hide in the drainage ditch on the side of the road. While the tank would pass, the North Koreans would jump up and attack the tank with a bomb. The tank rider simply shot every North Korean he saw lying in a ditch to preclude it. Since the ranges were short and the vehicles high (which allowed many North Koreans to be found), the shotgun was ideal for this use.

During the Vietnam War, there were early reports of the shotgun's being used by U.S. advisors, and at one time there was a proposal to arm village defense units with shotguns to allow them to protect themselves from the Vietcong. Many combat shotguns were sold during the period and shipped to Vietnam, but I have reports of people seeing them stacked up in warehouses awaiting issue because either the South Vietnamese did not trust their own people with the weapons (one of the reasons the former leaders are now dead, "reeducated," or running shops in Los Angeles or Paris), or they preferred issuing M1 carbines, SMGs, and M16 rifles to the villagers.

Early Vietnam War issues were merely World War II weapons using brass or paper shells. Soon, however, the plastic shell came into being, and for the first time, inexpensive, reliable shotgun shells were readily available. But because of the lack of interest in shotguns, the weapons remained basically the same as they had been in World War II. This is odd because in a lot of places Vietnam offered the ideal shotgun terrain.

I think the main drawback to its use in Vietnam

A U.S. Navy SEAL deploys with the M870 Remington 12-gauge shotgun.

was the lack of a real military shotgun. All the units available were sporting weapons modified for military purposes. Because the demands on sporting and combat shotguns are different, such modified weapons always fail ultimately. They are either too slow to load, too difficult to clean properly after a dunking in the swamps, or simply break down under heavy use. In a lifetime of use, many hunting guns may be used for not more than 90 or so days with perhaps an average of 20 rounds a day through them. A military weapon may be on the field for a year or more, and many fire thousands of rounds in that time.

Naturally, what should have been done was to develop a magazine-fed, semiautomatic 20-gauge shotgun with similar durability and field-stripping capability as an AK-47. The cost of one F4 fighter could have accomplished that, I am certain, and the carry-over to the law enforcement market would have made a fortune for the manufacturer. Just about the time it looked like such an item would be developed, the "assault rifle" hysteria popped up. Therefore, I am not encouraged about its being developed even now, especially in light of the trend to pistol-caliber carbines in police circles to help small-statured officer candidates qualify.

Other than the U.S. forces who had shotguns in inventory and more or less used them, depending upon the circumstances and commanders at the time, only the British showed any similar interest. The reason for this disinterest is rather a mystery to me, given the supply of shotguns on the Continent. Perhaps it was the supply of pump guns, but Fabrique Nationale (FN) did make semiautomatics. The British also used the semiautomatic Browning autoloader in Burma. Reliable reports of a long-barreled 12-gauge auto shotgun with a 10-shot tube magazine have survived. When the guerrilla war broke out in Malaya (now called Malaysia) in the late 1940s and early 1950s, shotguns became

British soldiers during the Malayan "Emergency Days" with the Remington M870 shotgun (left) and the Bren light machine gun .303 (right).

common. In fact, the British contribution to this field was the so-called Malaya load that consisted of standard buckshot mixed with small-sized shot. By doing that, the chances of hitting the enemy at least somewhere were improved, and in the rotting jungles of Malaysia, almost any wound that did not get proper care would cause a severe problem. Reports of shotguns being used in Kenya also exist, but for the most part, the British have not developed along this line.

Today U.S. forces view the shotgun more as a security tool than an infantry weapon, although I would imagine that if ranges were short, one would see U.S. troops with shotguns that came from "someplace" patrolling.

Except for the previously mentioned British Malaya loads, shotgun loads have traditionally been nine 00 buck pellets in a 2 3/4-inch 12-gauge case. In recent years, the pellets have been harder, which causes them to deform less and get slightly more range. Oddly enough, the military has never explored the area of smaller gauges or the use of smaller-sized buckshot. This is surprising in that police researchers have found that smaller-sized shot with more pellets (such as #1, #3, and #4) often gives better results and that 20-gauge shotguns are much easier to shoot and only give up perhaps 5 yards in range while losing nothing in lethality below that to the 12 gauge.

As we approach the 21st century, I fear that the shotgun as a military weapon for front-line infantry troops may be a technological dead end. This is indeed unfortunate because there is much room for improvement in this area, and had we applied as much energy and time to the combat shotgun as to fighting knives and bayonets, I think much more effective shotguns would exist.

What's Really Needed in a Good Submachine Gun?

To determine what is the best SMG, you first need to decide what qualities you want in the weapon. The nearer the SMG gets to that standard, the more likely it will be a good SMG.

Much depends upon the purpose for having your SMG, of course. Originally in a day and age when rifles were long, bolt-action weapons and machine guns were water cooled, belt-loaded guns for the most part, the SMG was designed to give the shooter a handy weapon that was useful at 200 yards or less, gave excellent area saturation, and was as light as a standard rifle with lighter ammunition than that used by a rifle.

By the time World War II came along, it was also thought that SMGs should be easily made, with a limited amount of machine time or fitting necessary, so that they could be turned out by the millions and issued to a wide variety of people, many of whom had very marginal weapon skills. For such purposes, keeping the costs down frequently was more important than including other features that would have made the SMG a better weapon.

By the end of World War II, it was obvious that rifles now could be made that were lighter and shot a more effective cartridge than SMGs and that they would be only marginally more expensive (or in some cases even cheaper) than many SMG designs. The role of the SMG then shifted to police operations where the short-range characteristics of the SMG were seen as a benefit, not a drawback. This is odd when it is recalled that British military authorities in the 1920s stated that the SMG was a weapon suitable for "police operations only." It now appears they were correct, although in the middle of World War II it certainly did not appear to be an accurate prediction.

In reviewing what features are desirable in an SMG, it is obvious that many of them are conflicting in nature and that no one weapon has them all. Cost, which seems to be such a critical concern for manufacturers, of course, is of no concern to the end user. I will thus ignore that point and leave it up to the designers or manufacturers to figure out how to make our "ideal SMG" cheaply or leave it up to the taxing authorities to get the money to buy them. Certainly no one concerns himself with the price of a jet fighter as long as it does the job. If we spent what we pay for one jet fighter, approximately $40 million, we could buy close to a half-million SMGs at $85 per copy, which is what AK-47 rifles cost today and which, I believe, represents a good standard for cost comparison. Thus, a fighter wing would pay for all the SMGs anyone is ever likely to need and would, no doubt, deliver a lot more in results.

CALIBER

The first issue that needs to be addressed is caliber. Most commonly encountered SMGs today are in 9x19mm, 7.62x25mm, or .45 ACP, but the 7.65mm Luger, 9mm Mauser, and .38 Super used to be common. And even today the .40 S&W and 10mm are available. Although the 9x19mm is certainly the world standard today for new development, it is not the best choice in my judgment because it does not have the power level truly desirable in a shoulder-fired, antipersonnel weapon. The 9mm Mauser got greater velocity with the same bullet size and weight, and I think the 10mm loaded with fast-stepping 135-grain bullets may very well be the best SMG cartridge available.

Although I like .45 ACP, the ammunition is likely too heavy, has a short range, and offers limited penetration for military use. For police work, where such concerns are not critical, the .45 ACP may well be an excellent choice, given available weapons. However, I still prefer the fast 10mm cartridge.

Despite these comments, it is only fair to say that 9x19mm and 7.62x25mm are likely to be the most commonly developed or encountered SMGs today. Neither is perfect, however, as they lack velocity or bullet weight and size. They are on the low end of power for an SMG, because they were originally designed to be used in handguns. Although the high-velocity 10mm is quite a handful in a pistol, in a 5 1/2-pound shoulder-fired weapon, it is not excessive.

BARREL

The SMG is frequently shorter and more convenient to handle than a rifle because of its barrel length and stock design. Because the SMG fires a pistol cartridge, it does not need the long barrel necessary in a rifle to burn the powder to give the cartridge its power and to avoid its blast. Although the 16-inch barrel on the AK-47 is quite short in comparison to the more common military rifles of today, which range between 18 and 20 inches, the SMG is more likely to have a barrel under 11 inches. Such older designs as the M31 Suomi have longer barrels, but the Uzi at 10 1/2 inches and the Sterling at 8 inches are much more common. Additionally, that is all that is really needed to maximize the performance of the cartridge yet avoid the blast effect. Although very short barrels (as found on the Ingram M10/11 services) are actually too short to be comfortable without a suppressor or other extension being used, the SMG can have barrels between 6 inches (which would be long in a combat handgun) to a foot in length without the weapon's seeming awkward.

Many SMGs have collapsing or folding stocks and thus can be very compact. However, almost every such stock is uncomfortable to use as a shooting platform. Unless size is absolutely critical, the shooter of the SMG is better off with a fixed, full-sized stock of some type, even though they are more difficult to store, make exiting an airplane more difficult, and do not look as "neat" as a folding unit. Still, shooting is the most important function, and you must be guided accordingly.

Stocks can be made out of wood or a synthetic material. Given the costs involved and the availability of strong, easily molded material, I would recommend the synthetic material for all furniture on the SMG.

As an aside, it would be a good idea to cover all places where skin may contact the weapon with a neutral type of material to avoid freezing or burning the face or hands on bare metal, a common problem with many designs. Another feature missing from most SMGs is a good-sized trigger guard or winter-style guard. They are now seen on better rifle designs, and an SMG likewise should be capable of being shot with mittened hands.

Before leaving the barrel issue, it might be useful to discuss the desirability of barrel removal. With a rifle cartridge power weapon, rapidly removable barrels are not common because of the high pressures involved. With the lower pressure SMG, it is no trick to have a removable barrel. Such barrels make it easier to clean your weapon, always a concern in battlefield environments. All other things being equal, detachable barrels are a good feature. It can be like the Suomi, the Sten, the K45, or the AUG, but all make maintenance much easier than a Thompson or H&K MP 5.

BAYONET/SUPPRESSOR ADAPTABILITY

Another feature to be considered is whether the SMG should mount a bayonet or be threaded to accept a suppressor. Many SMG designs over the years have taken a bayonet, and although such things frequently make the bearer feel more aggressive, I remain unconvinced that they are worth the weight and expense. Among all my friends, I am the only one I know who ever stabbed someone with a bayonet (on my M14 rifle), so I think the likelihood of ever really using them (except to intimidate prisoners as mentioned by Roy Dunlap with the Beretta M38 SMG) is pretty slim. I would pass on it and save the expense and weight. Having the barrel threaded to accept a suppressor is handy, except, of course, in the military such suppressors are not likely to be encountered: the balance of the weapon is adversely affected when the suppressor is installed, and the overall length is likewise altered in an adverse way. Given the cost of doing this (and remembering that the threads must be correct or the alignment of the suppressor may be affected), I think I would pass on this feature as well. Instead, I would buy dedicated units for either military or police use and thereby get a better performance in a handy package.

BUTT TRAP

Any stock on an SMG (as on a rifle) should contain a butt trap to hold cleaning gear and small parts that may be needed. Naturally, the butt trap needs to be wrapped to avoid knocking, but it is an excellent idea to have such gear with any weapon in the field.

LOCKING SYSTEM

The SMG, due to the power of the cartridge, does not require any sophisticated locking system. Although locking systems have existed—such as the "Blish" found on the Thompson, the Hungarian locking system found on the M43, or the one on the H&K MP5—really simple, blow-back, unlocked systems seem quite adequate to the task. I would imagine that if you took the locking rollers out of an MP5 bolt it would work equally well, although it would no doubt fire faster due to the lightweight bolt.

SLINGS

One critical element on the SMG that is commonly overlooked is the setup of the sling swivels. On many SMGs, they are added seemingly as an afterthought, whereas the proper use of the sling will greatly improve the use of the weapon, not to mention making it easier to carry in the field.

Slings should be placed properly to allow the weapon to be carried in the "ready" position and not rattle when on patrol. Many have metal-to-metal contact, requiring massive amounts of tape to be placed on the swivels to avoid this noise problem; if they were designed properly, this could be avoided. Additionally, some are simply placed in the wrong location to begin with if the weapon is to be carried in the "ready" position, yet the sling is used to minimize the weight of the weapon carried in the field. Another common fault with sling systems, and one I find somewhat unsettling, is that they are so complicated it takes an engineer to figure them out. An example of this type is the German H&K sling system, which I find far too complex for practical use, although a lot of people seem to like it. Slings should follow the KISS principle, I believe.

Sling mounting points that are welded in place avoid rattles yet allow good use if placed properly. Some are simply located in the wrong position. If the sling has no hard plastic or metal fixtures on it and the welded fixed mounting points are properly located, this arrangement is quite acceptable. The sling should be located toward the top of the weapon to allow the weapon to be slung over the shoulder to distribute the weight, yet the sling should not interfere when mounting the weapon to fire.

SIGHTS

Selecting the sights involves four issues, actually: the type of front sight, type of back sight, color of sights, and what, if any, protection should exist for the sights. Typically front sights on older European models are pyramid type, but I find these hard to see and use. Over the years, I have determined that I get much better results from a standard blade-type front sight. This blade, of course, needs to be painted some contrasting color to allow swift pickup. Coming from the background I do, I have always found painting the sight white quite helpful, but if I lived or operated in a colder climate, white paint would make much less sense. In such an environment, fluorescent orange might be better. However, whatever color is ultimately selected, it should be different than the background it will likely be used in, and clearly it should not be merely dark-colored metal, as is commonly used.

Rear sights can be open or peep. Open sights can be the typical European V notches or, better, a square notch. Both are harder to use than a good-sized peep, which allows quick pickup in dim light, and the sight will blur anyway once a burst is fired. Having used all types, I found the peep unit much quicker than any other type of rear sight on the pickup in actual use.

Whatever type is selected, however, the sight should be adequately protected from blows. All too many SMG designs have no protection against damages. Whether a stout set of wings is used with the top open or a good circle of metal is used is not critical, in my opinion. Both have drawbacks and advantages. If pushed, I suppose I prefer the wing protection because it prevents the sight from getting too dark on some days and mud from filling the hole if the weapon is dropped. However, if wing-type sight protection is used, it is critical that the blade be painted a good contrasting color, or otherwise you will pick up the wings or the blade instead. I have done it when shooting clay pigeons with my SMG, so I know.

Optical sights, such as the low-power units found on the Elcan or AUG, offer some potential if developed properly. I would have thought such optical units slow until I started shooting clay pigeons with them and discovered that a scope of 3X or less actually was quite useful. I got good results with my 16-inch barrel AUG on such flying clays also, due mainly to its optical sight. This seems to be a promising field for development if the proper units are used and the shooter avoids the temptation of turning the SMG into a sniper rifle.

HANDLES

The charging handle on a properly designed SMG, as with the design on a rifle, should be available to either hand and further allow the shooter to maintain his firing grip while cocking the weapon. This means, at a minimum, the cocking lever should be angled up to permit the left hand (assuming a right-handed shooter) to grasp it and pull it to the rear. The handle should be available for the strong hand also, so I am not convinced that merely putting it on the left side is the best solution. A top-mounted handle like on the Thompson SMG M1921 actually is quite good. It is also nice if it does not require too much of an effort to withdraw it, and the ratchet-type system that helps the bolt prevent premature firing on the Uzi is a good feature. Bolt handles should be big enough to be grasped easily yet small enough not to dig into your body or collect vegetation. It is also nice if the handle has enough serrations on it, so it does not slip out of a sweaty palm. I have had that problem with the side-mounted bolt handles on the Thompson M1 SMG model.

PISTOL GRIPS

Most SMGs now have separate pistol grips, but not all did in the past. Although we commonly expect it, actually integral-grip SMGs are quite handy and avoid another projection that can strike something and break off as you hit the dirt. I suppose the pistol grip model can be made strong enough, however; thus, except for fashion, there really is little to prefer one design over another. If anything, the integral-gripped model seems slightly faster on the clay pigeon range.

MAGAZINE RELEASE AND SAFETY LOCATION

The magazine release and safety location are often seemingly added as a last thought on many SMG designs. If approaching the matter from the beginning, it obviously helps if the magazine can be released with equal ease with either hand. The button or lever should be easy to operate with mittened hands and brute movements. Further, the mechanism should be sheltered from inadvertent dislocation. As much as I like the Suomi SMG, I must say that the magazine release is hard to operate. The magazine housing, cut as it is with grooves to help locate the magazine in the proper position, is very difficult to use in mild weather in good light. Trying to insert a new drum or magazine in the dark with cold-stiffened fingers must have been quite a challenge. On the other hand, the H&K MP5 magazine release is a centrally located lever that can be pushed easily, and the magazine housing is a large, beveled unit that helps guide the magazine into position. Although some people may think that such magazine housings not contained in the grip are old-fashioned in light of the Uzi "hands find hands" principle, the size of the double-row cartridge, the thick metal magazine, and the plastic furniture on the grip all make the Uzi grip much fatter than is totally comfortable for my size-9 hands.

Many SMGs have such marginal safeties fitted that the trained shooter simply leaves them off and places the bolt to the rear when a sudden shot appears. As this is akin to leaving the chamber empty on a .45 Government Model pistol and loading it only when an emergency actually presents itself, this seems like a very poor substitute for a proper safety design. I know I would not tolerate carrying my Colt Government Model in this fashion, and I use a Sten or similar design SMG in this fashion only because of the inherent design flaw.

Most SMG safety systems are simply too marginal to be trusted. This is quite odd when you consider that most of us trust the safety system on an M16 rifle without any qualms. A properly designed SMG should have a dependable safety that can be flipped off with the thumb or finger rapidly and reapplied equally quickly, is not likely to be brushed off by accident, and only allows the weapon to fire when the trigger is positively pulled to the rear. Certainly achieving this with open-bolt SMGs may not be easy, but with a closed-bolt weapon, it should not be any more difficult than with a rifle-caliber weapon.

Magazines on SMGs can be inserted from the bottom, the left or right side, or the top. Obviously, the top-mounted type allows gravity to help feed the cartridges and permits you to get a closer ground position for when you start using a 30-round magazine in your SMG. Oftentimes it requires a quite high prone position. Still, the top-mounted magazine requires off-set sights, making it difficult to fire from the left shoulder.

If the magazine is placed on the left or right side, balance will be affected—you cannot put 30-rounds of ammunition on the side of a weapon and not affect the balance. Still, such side-mounted magazines allow for a low prone position, permit gravity to help out to a degree, and avoid the off-set sight problem. However, for some people, the magazine release will be hard to operate and does snag in the bushes and on door frames more easily than I like to see.

Bottom-mounted magazines require well-made magazines because you get no help from gravity and they cause you to take a high prone position. As you go to the larger-caliber cartridge, such as .45 ACP, the problem gets worse, but if the magazine capacity is kept to 25 rounds or so or the magazine curved slightly, it is not critical. You will not be able to take the extreme low prone position common on the rifle range, but in all honesty, except on a trimmed range, I have never been able to use prone anyway. I find that the grass is almost always too high for me to see through. Instead, I get behind something such as an earthen mound, a vehicle, or a wall to allow me to see over the intervening grass to fire at my target. With that in mind, the problem of the high prone position of the bottom-mounted magazines seems of minimal real-world importance. By accepting it, I get an easier-to-handle magazine release system and better balance and avoid off-set sights.

FINISH

The finish on an SMG is as important as that found on a pistol. Although blue finish was common on both in years past, today any SMG should take a page from the Glock pistol and use a Tenifer process. It will make it dark, shine resistant, and durable. Traditional blue wears off and rusts, paint chips, and parkerizing will also wear off and rust. Darkened stainless steel or Tenifer traditional steel seems to be the way to go in this area. Unfortunately, no current SMG (except the Glock G18) has it.

MODE OF OPERATION, CYCLIC RATE, MODE OF FIRE, AND USE

The last area that needs to be considered is actually one that is quite involved and has a lot of cross elements. This is mode of operation, cyclic rate, mode of fire, and philosophy for use. As earlier noted, the SMG really does not need any sophisticated locking system. The real question is should it fire from an open or closed bolt? The open-bolt method allows the shooter to avoid cook-offs and no doubt was cheaper to make in years past than the closed-bolt SMG. Still, cost is not a critical issue when you are talking about SMGs and the general costs involved in actually deploying the weapon. I do not believe anyone actually fires an SMG enough to get a cook-off. Although such things might well occur with a belt-feed machine gun, I think a cook-off is unlikely to ever occur with an SMG. To obtain this "benefit" you saddle the shooter with a weapon that uses a heavy bolt that runs forward before the cartridge is fired. No one can do his best work with such a disadvantage inflicted upon him. The shooter will do better with a closed-bolt gun, and since hitting targets is the key issue, it is best to use a closed-bolt SMG.

Because such closed-bolt guns tend to have a faster cyclic rate because of the lighter bolt, you need to decide whether you wish to follow the fast-cyclic-rate German school, where you try to fire the weapon as fast as possible on the theory that the bullets have left the muzzle before the weapon begins to rise out of point of aim because of recoil, or the British/U.S. school of moderate, if not slow, rate of fire that permits the shooter to better control the recoil impulses and thereby keep the cone of fire small.

A lot depends on your view of the SMG. Some view it as a short-barreled, self-loading carbine, less powerful than a rifle, but retaining full-auto fire for rare emergency situations that involve very close targets or ill-defined targets of short duration. Others see it as the equivalent of a buckshot-loaded shotgun but capable of throwing more ballistically effective patterns at a greater range than would be feasible with a smooth-bore shotgun. In the latter case, the ability to fire a rapid burst at extended ranges is critical.

Although it appears to me that the first approach made a lot of sense in the early days of the SMG, when rifles were long, heavy, and manually operated, today with such shorter self-loaders as the M4 and AK-74 available, such a need no longer exists in the military community. Of course, for specialized functions such as raids and sentry removal, the subsonic suppressed SMG still provides a great potential weapon; for average field use, it was superseded by the M1 carbine in 1940. For police work, on the other hand, when low penetration yet surgical precision (not to overlook low recoil because of the large influx of nontraditional law enforcement types into many agencies) is crucial, the traditional self-loader, short-overall-length SMG role still provides a useful function.

In the military environment, the view of the SMG as a more ballistically effective, long-ranged pattern-throwing weapon makes sense. It is only fair to note, however, that many of the small-caliber weapons will throw patterns equal in size to SMGs, and the smaller calibers are ballistically superior to the traditional loads fired in SMGs. On the other hand, when you compare the more effective loads sometimes used in SMGs (such as the heavy ball or AP) with the less effective smaller rifle cartridges, the advantage goes to the SMG.

Because I believe the SMG is tactically obsolete in today's military, except in specialized tasks, I tend to prefer the self-loading, short-overall carbine role for the SMG and the slower rates of fire. This is an area that could use much development: rate reducers, as seen on the FN-D, and various Spanish machine pistols have allowed the rate of fire to get under 325 RPM, creating an easily controlled weapon. Certainly, such rates of fire coupled with a trained shooter are better than the various burst limiters frequently encountered that serve only to complicate the weapon system while adding very little benefit. I particularly find 3- and 4-shot burst devices worthless, although I must say that the 2-shot burst group on the H&K MP5 are somewhat interesting. Better, however, would be the flywheel FN-D style rate reducer with standard semiautomatic fire availability and a trained shooter.

Having gone over all these points about what is needed in a good SMG, I found it painfully obvious that no existing weapon has everything that is needed, much less desirable. Of course, some are a lot better than others, and naturally a person must prioritize his desires in a weapon so that the most critical elements are obtained before less critical elements are selected. Yet equally obvious if a new weapon is to be developed, there is no reason for not requiring all the desired elements to be there in one package because none of them is beyond our technological reach today. If as much effort was made in developing a truly effective SMG as goes into developing a modern combat aircraft, I am certain much better weapons would be developed. As it is, the poor infantryman is left with designs and concepts that were old hat when Hermann Göring headed the German air force and claimed he could crush Britain by bombing from the air. No nation today would equip its military or police forces with airplanes or radios of that vintage, and it is amazing to me that we still encounter such designs in the small-arms field.

PART II

Australia

OWEN GUN

The story of the Owen Gun, as it is typically called, is about an outstanding SMG that almost didn't get developed. In 1939 when Australia entered World War II, its army had no SMG and apparently felt no need for one—until events in Europe proved the worth of the SMG in battle. The Australian military scrambled from then on. At first Australia looked to the United States for the Thompson SMG, but such weapons were heavy and, worse, expensive. Then along came the British Sten SMG, and for a while the Australian military authorities thought that the British would supply SMGs to them, but Britain had no SMGs to spare. About that same time, the Japanese entered the war, and all of a sudden, the enemy was close at hand, not on the other side of the world, and Australia had a real problem.

Australian military officials were so poorly informed about what was needed in an SMG that they originally wanted a design to shoot the low-powered .38 S&W round, which was the cartridge used by their service pistol. Sounder heads prevailed, however, and the 9x19mm cartridge was selected, which turned out to be a fortunate choice.

The Owen SMG was developed by an Australian gunmaker for use in World War II.

An Iban native tracker with an Owen SMG during the Malayan "Emergency Days." Note that this is a refurbished 1950s model with the safety at the end of the receiver; the author's Owen was issued during World War II and lacks this extra safety. The buttstock on this Iban's Owen is also the latest variation.

A native Australian designer created the Owen Gun. The history of this weapon and its development is well detailed in the book *The Owen Gun* by Wayne Wardman, which readers can consult for more historic information on this fine weapon (self-published in 1991 in Cuptin, Australia).

When they first see the Owen SMG, many people are put off by its appearance and some of its unusual characteristics. First, unlike most weapons, it is not blued. Rather, it is painted with a green camouflage pattern because it was designed for the field, not for the drill field. Today, we are all used to the idea of camouflage-painted weapons to break up distinctive outlines, but in the 1940s, it was an unusual treatment, especially coming directly from the factory.

The Owen uses a top-fed magazine. To the ill-educated, this looks ungainly. In fact, that location makes shooting from the prone easy and allows the shooter to change magazines rapidly. The sights are offset and seem awkward, but when you throw the weapon up to your shoulder for the first time, you will find the sights right on. Of course, if you are a lefty, then you'd better get something else. The barrels come out with a quick change button. Some commentators think this was to allow the rapid change of barrels due to overheating, like on a light machine gun, and they say this is a silly feature. Not true. The feature allows the shooter to rapidly remove the barrel and clean it from the rear. In the days of corrosive ammunition when hot water was the standard method of cleaning the weapon, this feature must have been cherished. I know I like it when I shoot corrosive ammo in my Owen. It would also be appreciated if you lived in the jungle.

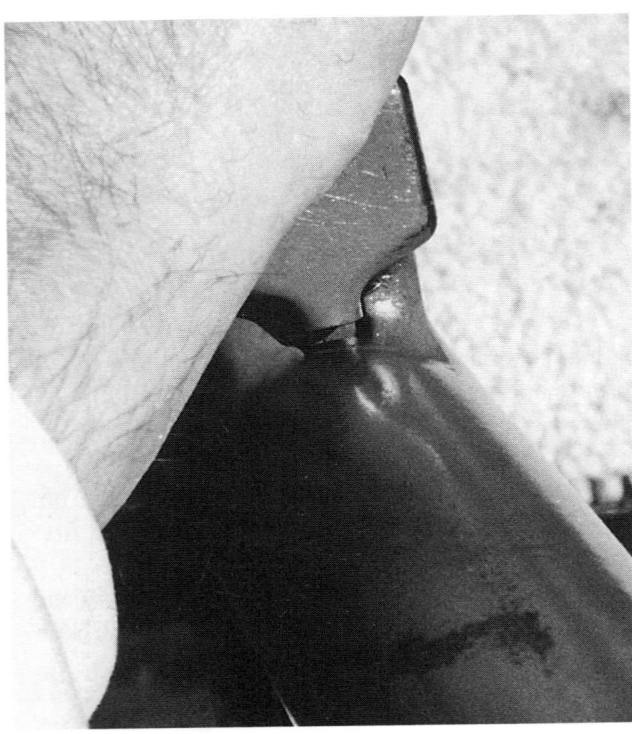

The magazine from an Owen SMG can be removed very quickly by pushing with the palm while grabbing the magazine with your fingers and pulling up rapidly.

Right-side viewof an early-model Owen with finned barrel and metal buttstock.

The cocking handle on the Owen is nonreciprocating, unlike most designs of the time. This avoids the distraction that comes from watching the cocking handle go back and forth from the side of your eye as you shoot. Even better, however, is the sealing system used on the bolt because its design prevents dirt and debris from getting into the system. The seal system and the top-mounted magazine, which combined a double-feed magazine along with gravity, were what always contributed to the reputation of the Owen Gun as one of the most reliable SMGs in the world.

The barrel contains a muzzle break, which is probably superfluous on a 9mm SMG, but it certainly does not hurt. The rear sight is a fixed peep, which is very fast to use. It lacks adjustment, but you can adjust the point of aim off the front sight. I certainly like it better than many of the open sights found on German SMGs of the period.

The lower frame of the Owen is cut away to allow dirt and mud to fall out. The front and back pistol grips are handy to hold and give the shooter greater stability. The selector/safety system will sometimes fail when worn and allow the weapon to shoot bursts even in semiautomatic, but the cyclic rate is low enough that firing single shots is no problem. I do not trust any safety on an open-bolt SMG and would urge you not to either. It is better to leave the bolt closed and pull it to the rear when you need to shoot, as opposed to the bolt slipping forward past the safety, firing the weapon. The bolts on the Owen SMGs are quite hard and thus tend not to wear the notches round, but even so I urge caution.

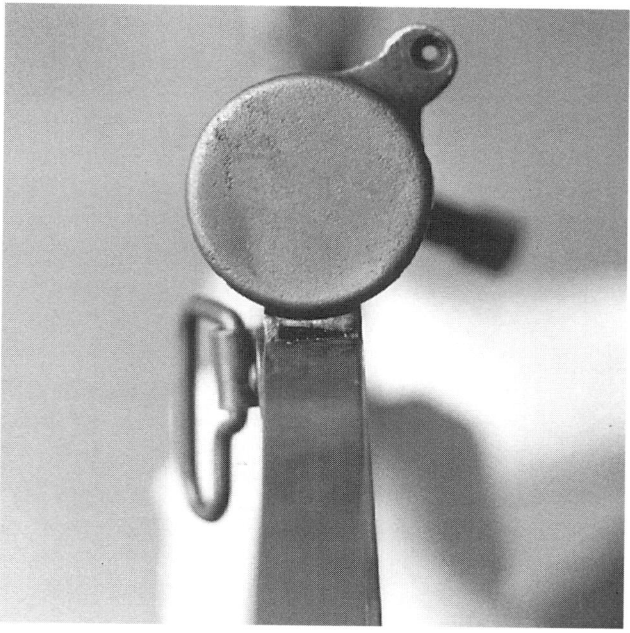

The offset rear sight is simple but allows good accuracy out to 200 yards. The rear swivel will rattle on metal and needs to be taped.

The sling swivels are neatly placed to allow the weapon to be carried over the shoulder. This is especially helpful in light of the heavy weight of the Owen: more than 10 pounds loaded. I have never carried an Owen on a night patrol, but if I did I would tape the swivels to avoid the noise of metal-on-metal contact.

The buttstock of the Owen comes in two patterns: solid metal and wood. I prefer the wood, but I am not sure it makes any real difference. It just seems to hit my face better. Your face may be different; try them both and decide.

The Owen is much longer than is commonly encountered today and close to twice the weight of an MP5. It looks ungainly and odd, but it is easy to handle and very reliable. I rate it as the best SMG in the world made prior to 1946, and it presses hard on the heels of more recent weapons. That's not too bad for an unknown designer who had few resources and a limited background and who was tasked with building an emergency weapon in a time of grave crisis.

AUSTEN

During World War II, the Australians had three basic submachine guns: the Thompson, the Owen Gun, and the Austen.

The Thompson, an American SMG, was very expensive and available only from overseas, but it caught the bulk of the early fighting simply because it was available. Two native designs, the Owen and the Austen, were also manufactured. The Owen Gun, which was a private enterprise weapon, is detailed in the previous segment.

The darling of the Australian military was the Austen. Made in about half the numbers of the Owen, the Austen apparently was best loved by the military ordnance personnel who were hostile to the

The author firing the Austen 9mm SMG. The excessive length of the stock is evident in this photo.

This photo of the Austen broken down into its major components for field stripping shows the influence of the Sten and MP38–40 on the Australian SMG.

Owen. The Austen can best be thought of as a combination of the main body of a Sten, the folding stock of the German MP40, and the front grip design of an early Thompson.

As with the German MP40, the folding stock on the Austen has a tendency to wobble, which causes accuracy to be degraded. Additionally, the metal struts on the stock hit your cheek, which reduces accuracy. The stock lock is not particularly easy to collapse to permit the stock to be either folded or unfolded. Because of the front pistol grip, care must be taken when folding the buttplate down. Pinched fingers are common when using this type of stock.

From here forward, the weapon adopts the Sten mechanism. As on the Sten, the safety consists of merely turning the bolt handle on a slot on the stock. Not only is such a safety slow, but, if the weapon is dropped, the bolt can easily jump out of the slot and fire. Although I would not use any safety on an open-bolt gun, such safeties are slow and difficult to disengage. Generally, the bolt can be retracted and fired faster than the safety can be removed from either a Sten or Austen. Additionally, the handle design is such that wet or cold hands tend to slip off too easily for my taste. Although merely pulling to the rear is not a problem, the finer motor skills necessary to pull the bolt back and then twist it down and out of the slot are time consuming.

The cyclic rate on the Austen is equal to that found on the Sten, and both are easy to fire. Single shots are easy to get off, although a selector does exist. Whereas the Sten is held around the barrel extension (not the magazine) to fire it, the Austen has a vertical foregrip. Many people like this feature, and I suppose it does make it easier to hold because the side-mounted magazine projects out into the normal grip that is taken. However, I am somewhat doubtful about how it will hold up. A foregrip was added on the MK V Sten, but it quickly became apparent that the device should be taken off when used in the field. I can easily see the Austen grip having the same problem, as well as getting caught on all the vines

Close-up of the action of the Austen SMG shows the bolt closing on a loaded round to fire it.

Removing the magazine from the Austen. Note that the release button is not well protected and is easily depressed.

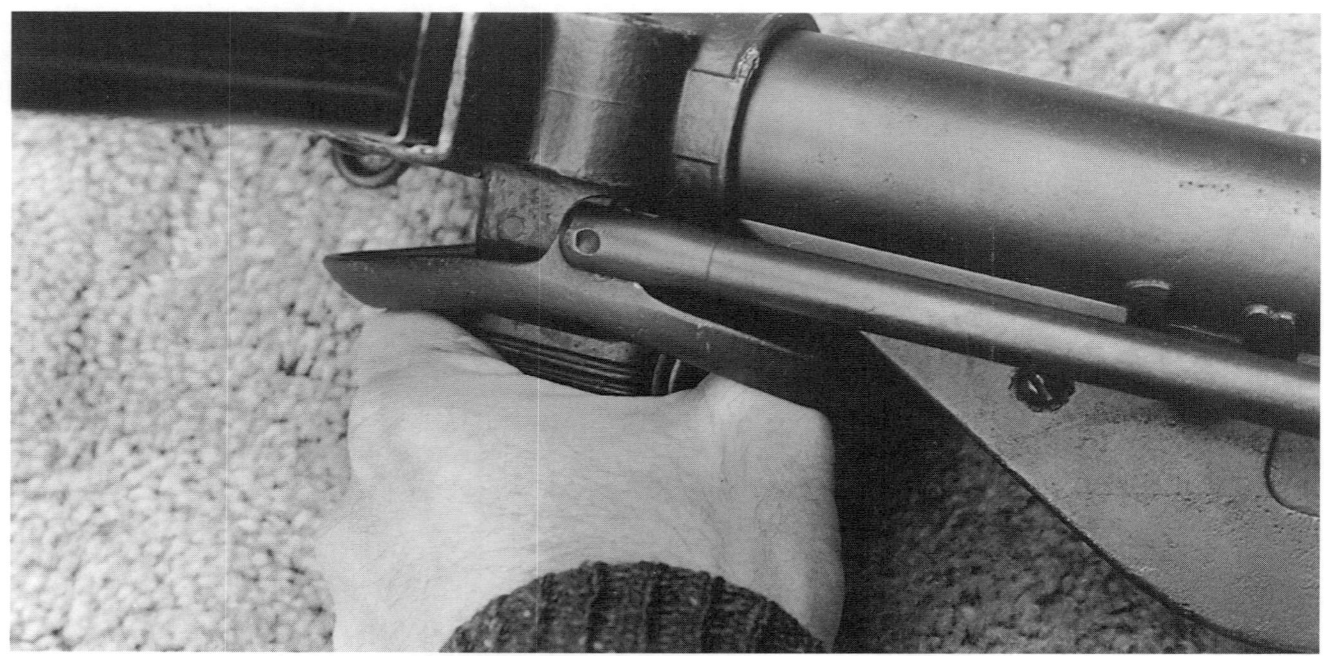

The forward grip area on the Austen is quite cramped, especially with the stock folded.

found in the jungle environment Australian troops fought in during World War II.

The Austen came on line late in the war and was not widely used by Australian forces, largely because of the Thompson SMG and M1 carbine from the United States and the excellent Australian Owen. If none of those had been available, the Austen might well have been accepted. Still, it was not as easy to use as the Owen, it had the unfortunate single-column feed system of the Sten, and the folding stock was not as important to the Australian infantryman in the jungle as it was to the motorized German soldier. When the war ended, the Austen was stored away while the Owen was refurbished for further battles. That in itself speaks a great deal about the Austen.

Although many think of the Austen as a "refined Sten," I am not so certain. I think of it, at best, as a "Sten variant" that might not even be as good as the original.

Austria

MP34

In the early 1930s, Steyr developed the MP34 SMG. Rapidly adopted by a number of countries, it was fairly common during World War II. It was sold in some numbers chambered for .45 ACP for the Latin American market but is commonly found in 9x19mm. It reflects a tradition of old-world gunsmithing involving high-polished metal, good blue jobs, machining, and heavy construction methods in a very solid stock. The MP34 is a nicely designed SMG with an excellent design feature allowing quick and complete access to the top of the weapon for easy cleaning. But especially when we see what was developed a scant seven years later with the Sten gun, it really was a lot more involved than it needed to be under the circumstances.

As with many SMGs developed during the

Author with the test target shot at 25 yards with the Steyr Solothurn MP34 at full-magazine capacity burst to test controllability. The example is a .30 Mauser version.

period, it has a heavy, ventilated barrel jacket that, unfortunately, is expensive to make, very heavy, and prone to getting clogged with mud. The Beretta M38, which is a very similar design, has this same jacket, yet a few years later, the Beretta factory determined the barrel could be shortened and the jacket dropped. These modifications made the weapon less elegant but no less efficient. The Steyr MP34 has a bayonet lug to allow the soldier to affix a bayonet, and while many laugh at such things, I must say I rather like a bayonet for guarding prisoners and whatnot. Roy Dunlap said nothing was better than an M38 Beretta with bayonet attached for guarding Afrika Korps prisoners in 1942 North Africa. He should know; he was there.

The MP34's bolt handle is smooth and prone to slipping from weak or cold hands and, unfortunately, is angled in such a fashion that it is difficult to withdraw with the left hand when firing to the right. The sights are European pyramid-style front and a small V-notch rear, both of which are difficult to use. When firing begins, they rapidly blur out completely. Painting the front sight would make it much better. The front sight is protected by wings, and, further, it appears to be sturdy in size and staked firmly into position.

The stock is rather straight in design without as much drop as one commonly encounters, and this is actually all to the better when firing the weapon. It is a very stable platform to fire the weapon from, although it does make it less compact than many designs. Still, shooting ability is the key concern for a weapon, not its ability to be stored in small places. On the left side of the stock a selector appears. The safety uses the typical bolt-turning method common to the Bergmann M1918 and similar weapons. Such safeties are slow to engage and disengage. I generally ignore them and simply pull the bolt back when ready to fire, but I also tend to walk with my hand or palm holding the bolt handle forward to avoid a stumple that could cause the bolt handle to fly back far enough to pick up a cartridge but not catch the sear, which can result in an accidental firing. I suppose that they might be useful if you had fired a few rounds and wanted to move across an open field without dropping the magazine out so you could lower the bolt but did not wish to run with a cocked SMG in hand. Other than this scenario, it is hard to see why anyone would use such a system; certainly it would be too slow for jump shots encountered when on patrol in the woods or jungle.

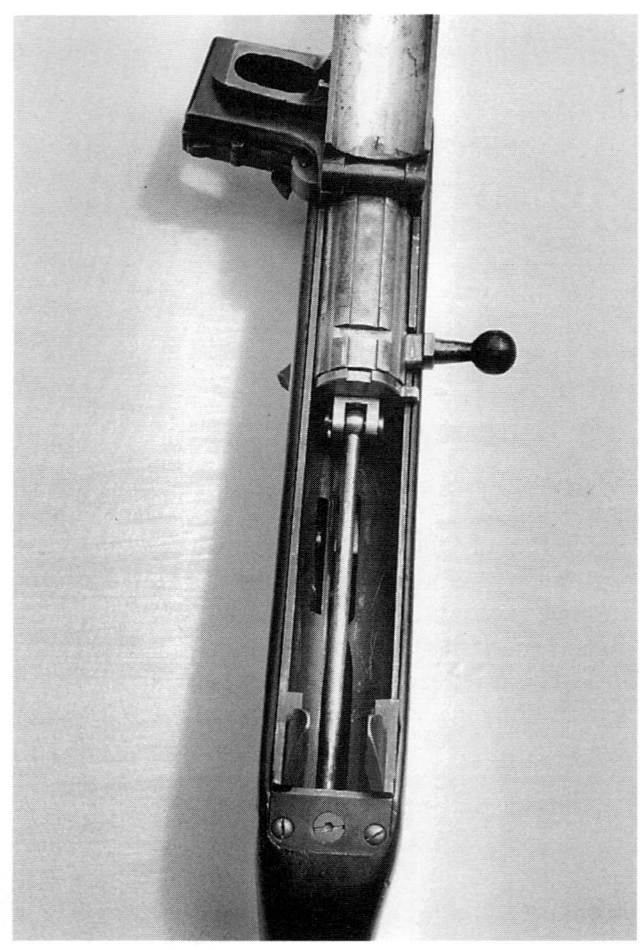

Top view of the Steyr MP34 with the top cover open. This makes it easy to maintain the weapon. The rod attached to the bolt depresses the spring on the SMG butt, much like the system on the FN FAL. Note that the magazine housing doubles as a loading tool—inserting the magazine in the bottom and stripper clips into the slot allows the magazine to be rapidly loaded. The bolt handle is rugged and can be operated by either hand, which is handy.

As with most SMGs, the trigger guard is too small and should be bigger, especially if you are using mittens. Why this point was not noted by a Central European arms manufacturer of long experience is a mystery to me. At least Steyr got it right with its current AUG!

As always, cyclic rate depends on the ammunition used. The MP34 fires faster than the MP18, from which its basic design stemmed, but it

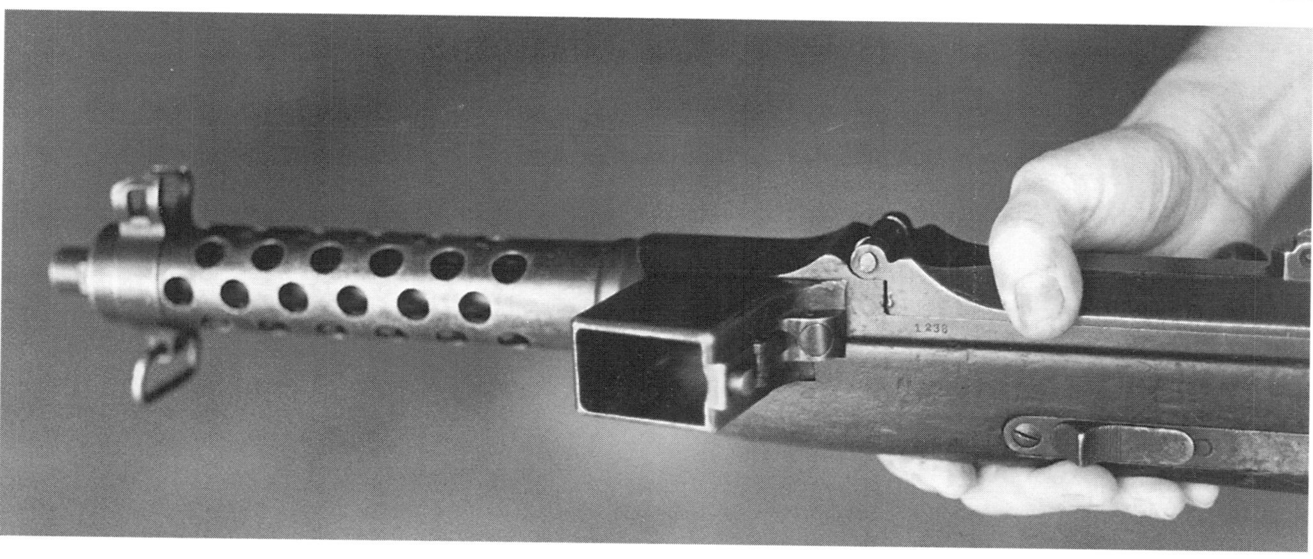

Side-mounted magazine housing and safety.

is not terribly high, unlike some later Soviet designs that will hit 1,000 RPM when hot ammo coupled with old springs is encountered. Still, smoothness counts for more than mere cyclic rate—the M31 Suomi tested was hitting 925 RPM, yet after the third shot always seemed to hang in there without much in the way of muzzle rise. The stock design, coupled with the general smoothness and muzzle design of the MP34, allowed easily controlled bursts to be fired.

The magazine release is not terribly well protected and, of course, is side mounted. Additionally, it is not straight out to the side, as on the MP28 or similar clones (such as the Lanchester), but at a slight angle to the receiver. I suppose this was designed for greater feeding reliability, although it does make for an odd appearance. Still, side-mounted magazines typically perform well. And even if they are somewhat ill-balanced, especially as the rounds are fired, they work well if handled properly with the magazine resting on the forearm of the left arm rather than being used as a handle for the shooter to hold. When done in the latter fashion (as commonly seen on TV or in the cinema), malfunctions are created, typically since the magazine is pulled down out of the proper location and occasionally even twisted in position, neither of which improves functioning. On the 9mm versions, you can use the magazine housing as a loading tool for charging magazines. This feature is missing on the .45 ACP versions.

Although the MP34 has many typical features of a first-generation SMG that make it reliable, dependable, and easy to shoot, it is also very expensive to make. However, its design, which allows quick access to all the parts by flipping up the top of the receiver, makes it much easier to maintain than similar SMGs of the period. For that reason, it may be considered a more convenient design than the MP28, MP35, and similar pre-1939 designs.

AUG 9x19mm

Closed-bolt 9x19mms are all the rage now for police service, primarily because of the inability of many police entry teams to handle the open-bolt SMG properly. They find the closed-bolt version is easier to shoot accurately and makes it less likely for them to have any accidental (or negligent) discharges.

In police entry operations the ability to put rounds on targets when innocent bystanders may be nearby and the ability to maintain the weapon in the field are paramount; therefore, low-cost features that are so critical in the military environment are absent from police models. Naturally, these police SMGs are used as semi-carbines for the most part, but then that is actually the proper use for all SMGs, with full-auto fire

Right-side view of the AUG 9x19mm.

being reserved for highly unusual circumstances that call for a high volume of area fire.

In the world of closed-bolt SMGs, the primary one is the H&K MP5. This weapon has been adopted by so many "high-speed teams" that it has become almost the expected choice. Military special operation teams have also selected this weapon, mainly for its ability to use a sound suppressor effectively. The use of lower-powered pistol cartridges in the military is an accepted trade-off for the low noise; whereas in police service, the low power of the rounds, with accompanying lowered risk of excessive penetration, is the primary reason for selecting the SMG over a standard rifle.

The MP5 has many fine features, but, of course, it is much more involved to maintain than a more traditional open-bolt SMG. Seeing the success of the MP5, other manufacturers have attempted to enter this rather restricted market, with the new Ruger SMG being only the latest example. Both of the primary competitors are variations in military rifles that started out as 5.56x45mm weapons. The Colt CAR 15 9x19mm uses the M16 format, fires from a closed-bolt locking with bolt-weight only, and uses a spacer in the magazine well to accommodate the smaller 9x19mm magazines.

The Steyr AUG uses a similar spacer that fits into existing 5.56x45mm rifles, and then a spare barrel chambered for 9x19mm can be installed. Because the Steyr AUG barrel is rapidly detachable, the existing 5.56x45mm Steyr AUG can be altered to fire the 9x19mm caliber. It fires from a closed bolt and retains all the standard controls and sight system, but, of course, it is blowback in nature, not using any locking system.

The three key features of the AUG are, of course, its selector/safety system, its short overall length, and its sighting system. Taking the selector/safety system first, the AUG is a selective-fire weapon with a very convenient push-button safety. By pulling the trigger halfway back on the selective-fire weapon, semiautomatic fire is

The author firing the AUG 9x19mm SMG. This SMG handles surprisingly fast when compared to the H&K MP5 or other more conventional SMGs.

available. Firing full-auto merely requires a full pull to the rear. With 5.56x45mm weapons, the recoil of the cartridge prevents this system from working well for me, because it is subject to inadvertent firing. Additionally, the recoil of the 5.56x45mm cartridges was such that effective full-auto burst-firing was limited. With the lower felt recoil and blast of the 9x19mm cartridge, however, the performance on full auto was much better, and it was possible to avoid the inadvertent firing in full-auto mode that results from accidentally pulling the trigger all the way through the cycle rather that merely halfway, which is what gives semiautomatic fire only. The safety, being a push-button type, is much faster than the lever-type found on the MP5.

The AUG, being a bullpup design, is always short, but with the 16-inch, 9x19mm barrel, it is even shorter than normal. The overall length of the AUG 9x19mm SMG version is no more than that of an MP5 basically. It is handy and "lively" feeling in the hands, with the weight between the hands rather than being concentrated in the muzzle.

The excellent sighting system of the AUG is an integral 1.3x scope that looks like a carrying handle but really is not. The sighting system when used on the standard AUG is somewhat deficient past 300 meters because it is so difficult to hold over a target. With the reticle design of the AUG in a 9x19mm SMG, which is unlikely to ever be used past 200 meters because of the power level of the cartridge and its trajectory, the sighting system is fine. I found with the AUG 5.56x45mm rifle that I could hit clay pigeons thrown from position number seven (straight ahead) quite readily. In fact, the sight system did not slow me down, but actually made it easier to hit the targets. I see no reason why a person would not get identical results with the same sights on a 9x19mm weapon.

In testing the 9x19mm SMG, I found that the conversion unit installed readily in the weapon. The magazine was located quite a ways to the rear, and the button to release the magazine was more difficult to use than the magazine release on the 5.56x45mm version. This may have been because of my unfamiliarity with the 9x19mm unit, my familiarity with the 5.56x45mm unit, and my fear of hitting the AUG 5.56x45mm button, which would have released the entire magazine conversion unit, not simply the 9x19mm magazine.

I found the lowered blast of the 9x19mm unit quite nice on an AUG. The muzzle is so close to the face that it is always something of a disagreeable experience to fire them, especially without muffs if under cover or in a building. The ability to rapidly fire follow-up shots or quick bursts was also quite a bit higher than with the same weapon in 5.56x45mm because of the lowered felt recoil. I, of course, realized at the time that I was likewise putting substantially lowered power on the target area.

Overall, I would rate the 9x19mm AUG quite highly as a closed-bolt police SMG. It may be easier to maintain than the H&K MP5 because of its lineage from the 5.56x45mm AUG.

Although some may think the sights are weak, extensive tests over 20 years have found them satisfactory, and in my shooting test, they performed adequately on close combat/immediate reaction courses of fire.

The magazine release is not located in the most convenient place or manner, but the selector/safety system is far easier to use than that on the MP5. Additionally, the trigger guard of the AUG is such that it can be used with mittened hands, something difficult if not impossible to do with the MP5.

Although I like the 9x19mm AUG, I think that the caliber is weak for an SMG or semi-short carbine and that the 14- or 16-inch 5.56x45mm with SS109 ammunition for military or 40-grain SP "Blitz" ammunition would be better for police work. If a suppressed weapon is needed, then certainly an effective suppressor could be installed on a 9x19mm AUG barrel, and for military units already armed with the AUG, such a system would be better than inserting a different weapon system into the inventory. This is what often happens in the U.S. and British militaries, where the service rifle commonly used operates and feels different from the suppressed MP5 used on some operations.

GLOCK 18

Although common in many areas of the world, the Glock 18 is a rare bird in the United States. Because of what many view as unconstitutional laws, the Glock is restricted to law enforcement and military units in the United States because it falls into the post-1968 foreign-made machine gun category.

The Glock 18 resembles the standard G17 in many ways, but subtle design changes have made it impossible to fit the slide from a G18 onto the receiver body of a standard G17. Still, externally the G18 looks like a G17, and it will fit into all standard G17 leather.

The main difference, of course, is the selector lever that appears on the left side at the rear of the slide. The G18 is a true burst-fire machine pistol. It does not fire in limited bursts, like the Beretta M93 and H&K VP70; nor was it designed to be used with a stock, as is the case with both of the other weapons.

When the selector is flipped into the semiautomatic position, the G18 operates just like any other semiautomatic Glock pistol. When it is flipped into the full-auto position, a spur projects through a hole in the slide. This spur then hits the disconnector as the slide closes, allowing the firing pin to be tripped and thus firing the weapon. This is a simple and seemingly foolproof safe system for getting burst fire in the design. Although the G18 slide will not fit on a G17 frame, the design is such that a similar selector system would work on any of the Glock line.

Despite lacking the burst-limitation devices many people find useful and a stock, the G18 is an amazingly controllable weapon. In actual tests, I have found that I could place 5-shot bursts on a playing card at 5 yards using a good Weaver stance. Because of the high volume of fire, coupled with good controllability, I would say that the G18 is probably the single most effective hand-held weapon available at 5 yards or fewer in the world. It certainly becomes an ideal choice for the lead man, on an entry team, or anyone else who may need to confront armed assailants across the width of a standard room.

Although I typically can fire accurate, fast semiautomatic fire, I cannot fire anywhere near as

Left side view of the Glock G18 SMG pistol.

Author firing the Glock G18 in burst-fire. Note the case immediately above the slide.

fast with a semiautomatic Glock as I can with a Glock 18 in the burst-fire mode. In actual tests, I was getting perhaps 300 RPM at a minimum on semiautomatic and close to 1,100 RPM on full auto with the G18. The consequences are that you are literally hitting the target with a shotgun-like effect only with 9mm projectiles of 115 grains rather than light-weight buckshot. Such target saturation can be truly devastating in a close-range confrontation, quickly closing down the opponent's systems.

The plastic frame on the pistol,which many people believe accounts for its light recoil, is likewise present on the G18. In fact, the recoil impulse is amplified in a machine pistol because the impulses come so much faster. In testing a burst-fire P35 and a Glock 18, it becomes readily apparent that the G18 is far superior in this area of control and on-target impact.

In some areas of the world, if you can buy the pistol, it makes no difference if it shoots bursts or not, and in those areas, the G18 is common. For example, my friend from Switzerland took two for self-defense on a recent hunting trip to Africa. I am told they are quite popular in Latin America also. Certainly, they have been adopted by a number of European police and military teams. The Rome police are said to carry the G18, although I must admit I did not notice it when I as there in 1994.

As with any burst-fire weapon, you must use special techniques to master the weapons if you are to get the best of it. Aggressive, forward-leaning positions are needed. Single-hand firing on full auto is not likely to get good results. Unless you anticipate a long-range shot with your pistol, it would be best to carry it in the full-auto mode and change to semiautomatic if a long-range shot is indicated. If you are in a situation where an unanticipated use is likely to be demanded of your weapon, it is probably going to be most effective in the burst-fire mode: such attacks generally take place at close range, where the devastating target saturation effect of the Glock 18 is at its best.

Although rare in the United States, the G18 is an excellent weapon, and it is regrettable that such weapons can be obtained only by law enforcement agents rather than the law-abiding citizens who pay their salaries and employ them. Does this type of restriction seem as odd to you as it does to me? I am certain Patrick Henry and Thomas Jefferson would find it odd too, and no doubt would have a pair of G18s under their coats if alive and active today!

Chile

FAMAE 9mm

Chile is not typically thought of as an arms-making center, but it has produced weapons of various descriptions for its own military and police forces since the early 1800s. Most, of course, have been copies of European designs, and the FAMAE SMG falls into that category as well.

Basically, the FAMAE is a modified Sterling pattern. Looking at the FAMAE and noting its similarity to the Sterling, I was quite hopeful that it would be a similarly good-quality weapon. Although the Sterling SMG is perhaps overengineered for its needs, the FAMAE cheapened various aspects of it and managed to produce a much less impressive weapon. This seems odd to me because the handwork in the Sterling SMG, which results in its costing so much, should be less in Chile, where the labor is much cheaper than in the United Kingdom. Hence, it would seem logical, to me at least, to accept the detail and hand-fitting to get the reliability of the Sterling if a similar pattern was to be made in Chile.

Obviously, designers think differently than end-user infantry types, and they all seem to be driven to make their weapons as cheap as possible. When clearly none of them could possibly compete with a wartime Sten for costs, to go on the cheap seems odd to me. And if the weapon they make is not better than a Sten, what have we gained by the exercise? A country would be better off to simply buy surplus stocks of Sten SMGs (which are available to this day in quantity) than go to the expense of designing and manufacturing an SMG that costs more and does either the same or less than a Sten MK II or III.

The front sight of the FAMAE is a well-protected blade that needs to be painted to allow quick pickup, but it is otherwise acceptable. It does lack adjustment for windage and elevation, but that

Left side view of FAMAE 9mm SMG. The trigger area shows that the selector and grip areas came from the Sterling SMG. One difference, however, is that the grip is not as full or comfortable as on the Sterling.

absence can be lived with if care in zeroing at the factory is taken. The rear sight is a fixed, two-position peep, which I always prefer to an open notch. Interestingly enough, unlike the Sterling, the FAMAE uses a 100-meter fixed peep in both positions, but the second one is patterned after the rear sight found on the suppressed Sterling with numerous small holes around a center peep to allow more light in for night work—quite a clever design feature.

The front of the FAMAE is not covered by a tube, as on the Sterling, and the barrel is exposed, which can lead to burned hands if the weapon is fired extensively. Actually, it is unlikely to be a serious problem and does save weight. The front has a spoonbill-type compensator on it that I rather doubt does anything and could easily be discarded.

Magazine capacity on the FAMAE is 45 rounds, rather than the Sterling's 34 rounds, and as a consequence, the FAMAE's balance is poorer. Both the FAMAE and the Sterling will operate with Sten magazines, which is a nice feature not typically found on SMGs. The magazine release button is a little stub and could easily be accidentally depressed. Of course, because the magazine is a side-mounted unit, it is not likely to fall out like it would with a bottom-feed design. It could, however, cause the magazine to drop down far enough not to feed properly but not far enough to be noticed. Of course, one should always tap the magazines and then pull on them to ensure proper seating. The longer magazine made going through doors and other confined spaces more difficult than with the Sterling with its shorter magazine.

The bolt handle is positioned like the one on the Sterling, but on the tested FAMAE it seems to be only loosely attached to the bolt. Once when I got a jam, I was reluctant to kick it open with my combat boot, something I would not hesitate to do with the Sterling. The receiver appears shorter on the FAMAE, and when I was firing Egyptian ammunition, the bolt went to the rear far enough to jam in the rear position by kinking the spring. This would not have occurred with a Sterling. The endcap on the tested FAMAE was quite loose, with the detents shallow and spring catch weak. I expected at any minute for it to come undone and for the bolt and spring to come back into my face. That was hardly conducive to good accuracy on target.

The rear sight offers numerous small holes to help collect light for shooting, much like the sight found on the suppressed Sterling SMG.

As with the Sterling, the FAMAE grip felt good in the hand, and the selector/safety switch fell to hand nicely. Of course, it cannot be easily used by a left-handed person, and one wonders why it was not made ambidextrous by the Chilean makers.

Cyclic rate appeared to be similar to that encountered with the Sterling fired on the same day except that, because the weight on the front end was less on the FAMAE, it tended to pull to the side on extended bursts more than the Sterling did. It also did not seem to be as smooth an operation due, I believe, to the bolt's bottoming out on the rear of the receiver tube, unlike the bolt on the Sterling, where it never hits the end of the receiver and thus "floats" inside the tube. The jarring is thus absent.

However, the FAMAE has one feature that would cause me to throw it away immediately if it were issued to me: the stock. Unlike the Sterling stock, which is very rigid yet at the same time quick to collapse once the trick is mastered (albeit perhaps quite costly), the FAMAE uses a wire-type stock similar to that found on the M3/M3A1 or MAT 49. So in addition to having a wobbly steel rod, which also strikes the cheekbone when firing, the FAMAE does not stay extended. You pull it out,

When shooting the FAMAE, the author was upset by the collapsing stock, which caused the rear end of the receiver to strike his face and almost break his glasses.

and a small notch in the steel rod serves as the locking points for the spring-activated locking point on the underside of the receiver. Unfortunately, the stock will wobble and allow the metal block that goes into the notch to jump out of position. Thus, when the shooter shoulders the weapon and leans into the weapon using the proper stance, the pressure put on the stock causes it to collapse. This, in turn, causes the shooter's face to go forward and hit the end of the receiver at the same time the weapon is recoiling. It happened when I fired, greatly upsetting me and almost causing me to break my glasses. I was unable to shoot the FAMAE from the shoulder unless the stock was taped in the open position. In the field, I would use it only long enough to get a better weapon from a fellow soldier or fallen enemy. The stock, even when firmly (or semi-firmly) taped in the open position wobbled, bruised the cheekbone, and was cold on the face on the January day I tested it (and no doubt would have been hot if tested in August). But worst of all, I worried about its collapsing on me again.

A good guide to evaluating SMG designs is to ask if the SMG is better than a Sten. If the answer is no, then pass on it because there is no reason to select something that is not as good yet is more expensive. The FAMAE 9mm SMG fails this test: it is neither as good as the Sterling it was developed from nor as cheap as a used Sten.

China

THOMPSON M1928A1 (MODIFIED TO .30 MAUSER)

Apparently after the end of the Chinese civil war in 1949, the Chinese Communist forces had a large quantity of Thompson SMGs that had been provided to the Nationalist forces by the United States through its Lend-Lease Act or other means, but .45 ACP ammunition was in short supply, especially when compared to the available quantities of .30 Mauser ammunition. Or the Chinese, who had always favored the .30 Mauser, wanted to simplify their supply problems. The Russians had given them large quantities of PPsh 41/PPS 43 SMGs, which took the .30 cartridge, so they decided to rechamber available Thompson SMG to the .30 cartridge. The weapon I tested was a modified Thompson.

Of course, the overall length of the .45 ACP and .30 Mauser is equal, so there was no problem with length. But, naturally, you encounter the problems of barrels, bolts, and magazines. In this case, the Thompson's barrel was simply sleeved with a .30-caliber tube. Otherwise, it remained the same, even to the Cutt's Compensator that, because it was designed for .45-caliber bullets, does little if anything with .30 cartridges (assuming it actually does anything with .45 bullets). The sights remain the same, which is unfortunate because the M1928A1 tested had the less-desirable, fixed-peep unit rather than the fully adjustable Lyman unit. At 50 yards or so, the sights made no difference, but the long-ranging ability of the cartridge is unfortunately compromised with such sights.

The bolt head was reduced in diameter to accept

Right side view of the Chinese modified Thompson M1928A1 SMG 7.62x23mm.

the smaller .30 Mauser cartridge. An interesting adaptor was designed to fit into the magazine well and use PPS-43 magazines, which are slightly modified by cutting a notch about 1/4 inch down from the normal location. As a consequence, Standard PPS-43 magazines will not fit into the modified Thompson and feed, although the modified-for-Thompson magazines will work in a normal PPS-43 SMG. The magazine release, as might be expected, is centrally located and relatively fast to operate. Although not as well protected as the release on a PPS-43, it is acceptable. If anything, it is faster and easier to use than a standard Thompson magazine release. The standard Thompson release, of course, should not be touched when using the modification or the adaptor might come out.

As the weapon is otherwise the same, there are few surprises when using the Chinese-modified .30 Thompson. Interestingly enough, in the pre-World War II period, apparently some test examples of .30 Thompsons were made by BSA; it would be interesting to see how they compare. As always, the Thompson feels heavy in the hands and somewhat "dead" as opposed to "lively." This naturally impacts your ability to get on your targets quickly. Because of the weapon's weight, which is slightly heavier than the larger-bore example, and the light recoil of the .30 Mauser round, recoil is lighter than that found with .45-caliber variations. Thus, controllability should be better, but, unfortunately, the rate of fire is much faster. Although I lacked a PACT timer to get a definitive answer, it appeared that using Bulgarian factory ammunition it was between 1,000 and 1,200 RPM; I could not get single shots off when the selector was on automatic. Generally, I can do this readily with any weapon under 1,000 RPM. I could get doubles off easily enough, so I conclude it was under 1,500 RPM: when guns get to that level, I find doubles difficult, with triples being more common.

In an actual test of controllability, I fired off-hand at an 8 x 24-inch plate at 15 yards. I fired a 30-

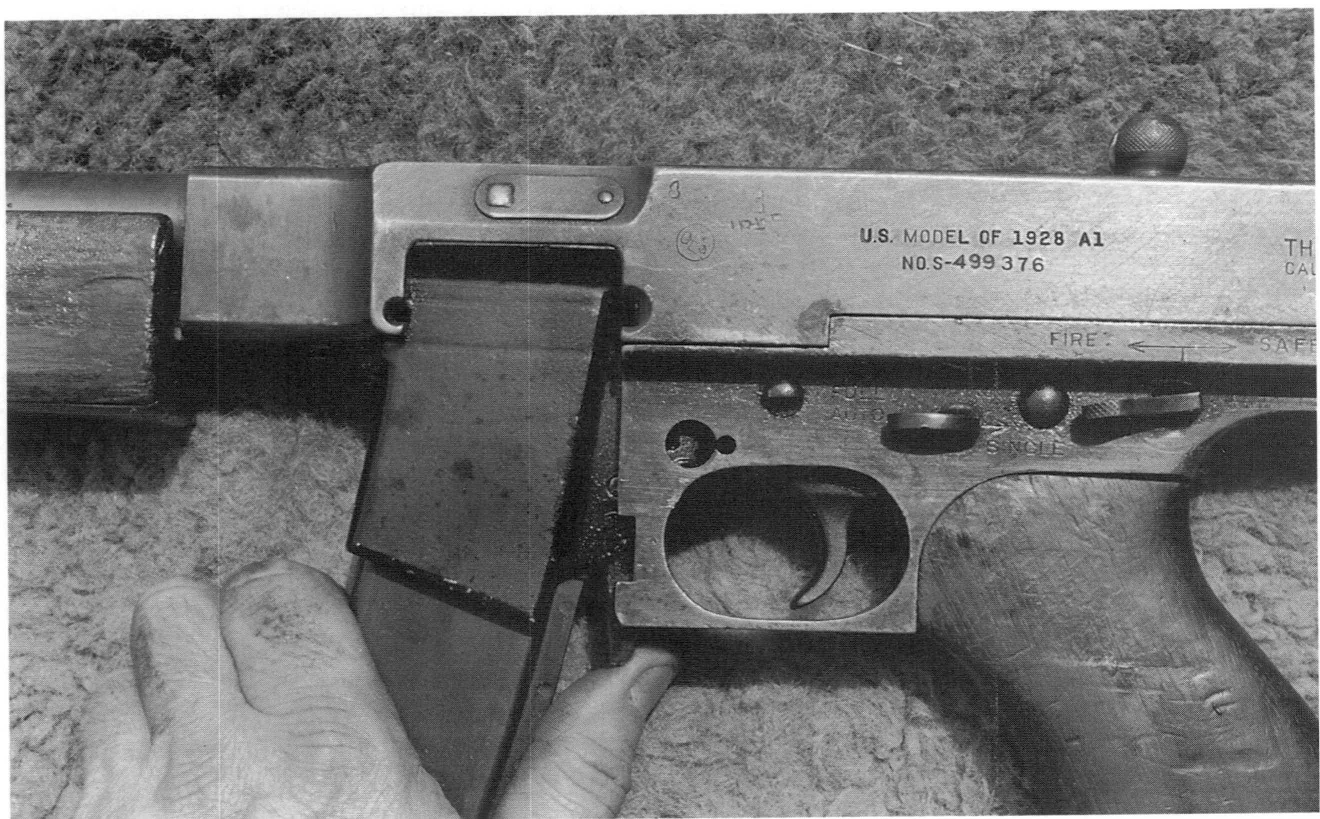

Removing the magazine from a Chinese-modified M1928A1 Thompson SMG is faster and easier than on a standard Thompson. Note the central release lever.

In actual tests by the author, the modified Thompson performed only 75 percent as well as the excellent Australian Owen SMG.

round burst and got 21 hits on it. This compares to 28 hits out of 30 done the same day under identical circumstances with an Owen SMG. The modified Thompson did only 75 percent as well as the excellent Owen. Of course, the .30 Mauser rounds dented the plates in a much more aggressive manner than the ball 9x19mm rounds did. No doubt this would be a benefit in cold weather when heavy clothing and web gear limit penetration; although, steel-cored 9x19mm cartridges would obviously do as well as the .30 Mauser rounds, if not better. When I compared the .30 Thompson to the PPS-43 fired with the same ammunition on the same day, it was clear that the Thompson was more controllable, but it is substantially heavier and less pleasant to use than the PPS 43. Of the two, I would prefer the PPS 43 because it is lighter and more lively in the hands and has a quicker safety.

The Chinese-modified Thompson shows some excellent ingenuity and was an interesting weapon to test. If given a choice of the .30-version versus the .45 for military purposes, I certainly would give some serious consideration to adopting the smaller caliber. What really would be nice is one in 9mm Mauser or 10mm, which would give the shooter lighter ammunition plus better stopping power over the .30 version while retaining the otherwise excellent penetration.

Czechoslovakia

ZK 383

This SMG is rare in the United States except as a post-May dealer sample because only a few have been brought into this country. The ZK 383 was the standard-issue SMG during World War II in Bulgaria and was also widely used by German SS units. No doubt most were lost on the Russian front. A few were sold in Venezuela and Brazil, and the one I tested had a Venezuelan crest on it, likely sold prior to the Communists taking power in Czechoslovakia in 1948.

The sights on the ZK 383 are rather typical of Central European guns: a pyramid front type protected by sturdy wings and a tangent V-shaped rear. It is graduated out to 800 meters, which seems rather odd to me given the power of the 9x19mm cartridge the weapon shoots and the open-bolt design. I find such pyramid front sights and V-notch rear sights very difficult to use on rifles, and on SMGs they become a total blur after the first shot. The cocking handle is on the left, which makes it convenient for either hand, and the magazine is similar to the one on the Sten gun in that it feeds from the left. The magazine release is a large button on the left side. I would imagine that changing magazines must be difficult for a left-handed shooter. I found that I could hold the weapon on my shoulder with my right hand at the forearm and reach around with my left shooting hand to disengage the magazine without difficulty. But when I pulled the magazine out, I pulled the weapon from my shoulder. I could not get the magazine out with my right hand at all when firing off my left shoulder. Perhaps a natural left-handed person could do better, but this design is not really suitable for the 11 percent of the population that is left-hand dominant.

The author with a Czechoslovakian ZK 383 9x19mm SMG.

The weapon has a selector on the left marked "1" and "30" to allow for selective fire. I assume that the designer meant for it to be kept on semiautomatic mainly and used as a carbine. Certainly, you cannot change its operation quickly, given its location. The barrel is covered by a thick jacket. When I fired the ZK 383, it never even got warm. Such jackets, while protecting the barrel from accidental contact with the hand, are unnecessary because of the improbability of firing an SMG in combat long enough to create a burning-hot barrel, which can be a problem with light machine guns and perhaps sport shooters. All the jacket does on an SMG is add unnecessary weight and expense.

The weapon has a fixed wood stock, one of three unusual things I found on the ZK 383. On

The fire-selector switch on the ZK 383, marked "1" and "30," is poorly located because it cannot be adjusted without the shooter's removing his hand from the pistol grip. Typically, such weapons should be used as self-loading carbines, but it would still be better to be able to flip the switch down without having to release the grip. Placing the bolt handle on the left was an excellent idea, however.

The wood stock is one of the more unusual features on the ZK 383.

most rifles and SMGs of the period, I find the comb so low that I am forced to take my cheek off the stock to properly align the sights. Obviously, this is not the best solution because it causes you to lose one of your points of alignment, thus affecting accuracy. On the ZK 383, due to the height of the stock comb and the straight nature of the stock, I actually had to force my face down on the stock to see the sights, which should help accuracy. It was an unusual experience for me. The buttplate is a rather standard metal plate type.

Another unusual characteristic of the weapon is the integral bipod. It is permanently affixed to the weapon and can be quickly pulled down from the horizontal and put to use. Such a bipod allows the shooter to take a firm firing position, and perhaps in a foxhole, trench, or other prepared position, it would be very handy. However, on a 9x19mm open-bolt SMG, it seems rather a waste of time and money to build it, not to mention to carry it. I do not know about German SS or Bulgarian army troopers, but had the ZK 383 been issued in the U.S. Army, no doubt you could follow the troop trail by watching for discarded bipods lying in the mud. When the U.S. military put a monopod on the BAR, it was immediately thrown away, and friends who carried the gun in World War II and Korea tell me that many people discarded the bipod on the BAR as well. A bipod on an SMG seems the product of fuzzy thinking. I can almost accept the concept on 5.56x45mm rifles, which are made out of plastic and are very light (such as the SIG STG-90), but even then I am uncertain. It would be better to tuck an airweight Smith & Wesson in your breast pocket.

The last unusual feature of the ZK 383 is the multiple cyclic rate. By removing the weight in the bolt, you can make the cyclic rate go higher. According to the reference books, the rate without the weight is 700 RPM; with the weight it is 500 RPM. Unfortunately, I shot this weapon before I had access to a PACT timer, so I cannot confirm that. I did notice a slight difference in rates, but it was insignificant. In my experience, such parts always get lost, and the designers would have done better to simply keep the bolt heavier and the cyclic rate at 500 RPM. I do not think the average soldier knows enough about cyclic rates to make an informed decision, and the removable weight is just one more thing to lose, one more thing to have to build, and one more thing to go wrong. If the weight were going to be put in, at least it should have had a place in the stock toe or butt to store it when not in the gun so that it would not rattle on night patrols.

Overall, the ZK 383 is an interesting weapon that shoots well. It is more like a heavy self-loading carbine than anything else. In a closed-bolt semiautomatic version it might have been more successful because it would have weighed less. As is, it certainly is not in the Suomi class.

VZ 61 SKORPIAN .32 ACP

The Skorpian machine pistol is common throughout much of the world, but not in the United

The first thing that strikes you about the VZ 61 is how small it is. Although it is as big as an N-framed S&W revolver, it is a machine pistol, not a revolver. The magazine is located in the front of the trigger guard, rather like on the old Mauser M96 and its successor pistols. This makes it easy to change magazines and, more critically, allows for a small pistol grip. When you use double-column magazines of 9x19mm or larger/longer cartridges and put them in the grip as you do with the Czech 23 or Uzi SMG, the firing grip can get quite broad and uncomfortable, especially for shooters with smaller hands. Because the VZ 61 is frequently found in the hands of females and small-statured males with nonmilitary backgrounds, the smaller pistol grip is no doubt appreciated.

The VZ 61 SMG with its stock fully extended.

States. Very few of them have been imported into this country because they do not fill a common role in the law enforcement community. Any use of machine pistols is rare, and .32 ACP weapons are typically scorned in U.S. law-enforcement circles. Through the kindness of Dan Stelmach, I was able to test his Yugoslavian-built copy of the VZ 61.

The VZ 61 fires from a closed bolt, which always helps accuracy in practical terms. The barrel is short, and there is a tendency for the nonshooting hand to migrate to the front of the muzzle area. However, if the shooter will place his support hand in front of the magazine and firmly place his fingers in the lighting cuts on either side of the magazine, he can maintain a firm grip. At the same time, the magazine will not be pushed out of position, as can occur when the magazine is held by the nonshooting hand, thus causing malfunctions. The magazine release is a simple button and can be reached easily by the nonshooting hand. The magazine release lacks a protective shelf around it, and I imagine that it frequently gets depressed by rubbing on the shooter's body, thereby dislodging the magazine. Of course, the VZ 61 is not likely to be slung around the neck on a patrol like a more conventional SMG, so perhaps this is not really a problem.

To collapse the stock on the VZ 61, push in with your thumb as indicated and push the stock forward.

To cock the VZ 61, pull the knobs on the side the rear and release quickly.

The safety is located on the left side of the weapon and would be difficult for a left-handed shooter to use. Oddly, the center position marked "0" is safe, the rear position marked "1" is semiautomatic, and the full forward position marked "20" is full auto. The safety lever itself is small, feels somewhat fragile, and had more sharp edges on it than I would prefer. I was also not certain you could carry it on safe and rapidly flip the safety switch off to the rear for semiautomatic fire, so I assume the designers meant for the shooter to push it forward to burst-fire mode. The cyclic rate was slow enough that single shots were possible, but generally two or three shots would be fired unless great care was taken. I assume in an emergency that would be the pattern also. With short, 2- or 3-shot bursts, the VZ 61 is very much like a low-recoil 12-gauge shotgun firing 000 buckshot, except that, of course, the .32 ACP bullets at 71 grains are ballistically superior. Additionally, the VZ 61 itself is handier, shorter, and has a lower recoil than a 12-gauge shotgun. Last, it can be reloaded much more rapidly than a typical tube magazine shotgun.

The VZ 61 has a well-protected, post-style front sight that offers adjustments for elevation and a rear notch-type sight that is also well protected. They are preset for 75 and 150 meters. In my tests, I found them to be hitting low, but that situation was easily remedied. I was able to hit chest-sized metal plates from the kneeling position on semiautomatic fire at 200 yards with the VZ 61, which would have been impossible with a combat shotgun. The rear sight notch needed to be widened and cut deeper for quick pickup, and naturally the front post needed to be painted a contrasting color because the black front and narrow shallow rear sight are not ideal.

The stock is a friction fit in the folded position with the butt loop fitted over the barrel. A push with the palm will dislocate it, and it then snaps into the open position. To unlock it, the locking piece on the left side must be pushed in. Unfortunately, it locks only at one place, and the locking surface is small.

The magazine is removed by pushing the button to the right with the thumb: forward is full auto; middle is safe; rear is semiautomatic.

This photo shows that the bolt on the VZ 61 is to the rear and the case in the air, yet the muzzle is level because of the low recoil.

As a consequence, it wobbles both up and down and side to side. This does not enhance accuracy.

The VZ 61 is easy to strip, and all the important parts are accessible for easy cleaning. A straight blow-back weapon, it has no involved cleaning requirements so even minimal maintenance should keep it running a long time. The weapon is typically blued, not the most durable of finishes. I suppose most VZ 61s are not used in the field under rigorous outdoor conditions, so the blued finish is not a serious drawback. However, in my experience with the weapon in Europe, I found that it does get rather scratched and brown with long use.

The trigger pull had more stick and slack in it than would be desirable, but it was not as bad as the ones found on many open-bolt SMGs. You will never confuse it with a rifle trigger, however.

The VZ 61 is meant to be shot from the shoulder, but it can be shot single-handed. It is light enough to hold at shoulder level without difficulty by anyone who is reasonably proficient with weapons. It can also be shot using a two-hand Weaver stance without using the stock. The best use, however, is with the stock from the shoulder or tucked against the hip area by the arm to help give support.

Although the VZ 61 is a light, handy, interesting weapon, I do not believe it is as good as the H&K VP 70 or the Star MMS pistol with stock. Both offer a superior caliber in the same size package. Still the .32 ACP is not to be sneezed at, and the way to view the VZ 61 properly is as a shotgun of 4- to 7-shot capacity firing 000 buckshot but in a much handier package. And when you think about it, that is not such a bad weapon system.

Denmark

MADSEN M50/53 SMG

The Danish military entered World War II with few submachine guns but obtained some Suomis from Sweden during the war. After the war, the need for Denmark's rearming was obvious: those weapons that had not been stolen by the Germans or liberated by resistance fighters were clearly obsolete.

The Madsen company had a long tradition of making fine firearms, and some of the earliest machine guns were Madsen products. Looking at the postwar needs of the military, as well as with an eye to overseas markets, Madsen developed the M50 SMG, which was later updated slightly to the M53 SMG. Although most models were made in Denmark, Brazil also made copies in .45 ACP.

Guatemalan rebels armed with Madsen M1950 SMGs in 1954.

The Madsen M50/53 offers some very interesting features. Its barrel can be removed readily from the receiver, so cleaning is easy. The weapon has a short overall length, and the stock folds without too much difficulty. The stock is wrapped in leather to prevent the face from touching the metal, which would otherwise be cold in the winter and hot in the summer. This is a nice touch, although as the weapons age, the leather covering deteriorates—or perhaps all the samples I saw just weren't maintained well.

The front sight is a fixed post, but it is not well protected and it should be painted white. The rear sight is a peep unit that is fixed, but it does offer a rather interesting adjustable aperture. Thus the shooter can open it up to the widest location for nighttime work or close, fast targets and close it down for more distant targets. Although it is not adjustable for windage or elevation, it does seem sturdy. However, my experience with all such fixed sights is that they are never exactly right, which is always disturbing. Obviously, the Madsen M50/53 SMG was designed for only 200 meters or less (typically a lot less, I guess), but still, anything that requires you to hold a little off is simply unacceptable in my mind.

The receiver on the M50/53 is a "clamshell" type, and by removing the barrel nut, both the barrel and the whole receiver can be opened to permit easy cleaning. This is a nice feature, especially in dusty or muddy locations. However, the weapon is made entirely of metal, and I found the firing grip to be rather uncomfortable. It did not get too hot to hold in my tests, but I would imagine that it would be painful to handle if the climate was hot. And, of course, the opposite would occur in a cold climate—except the trigger guard is large enough and positioned properly to allow the shooter to wear mittens or gloves.

The weapon is a typical blow-back SMG, and that generally results in a lower standard of accuracy than is the case with closed-bolt SMGs, such as the H&K MP5. Unlike on the Uzi, the magazine is well forward, and the magazine well is small. Therefore, reloading at speed is difficult. One of the most common SMG problems with open-bolt guns is that inertia can cause an accidental firing if the weapon is dropped. On the Madsen M50/53, a paddle near the magazine housing must be depressed before the bolt can go forward or backward. This design prevents an accidental firing if the weapon is dropped because there is no inertia pulling the bolt to the rear. Unfortunately, it also means that you must always hold the weapon with both hands. Although the occasions that call for one-handed firing may be few and far between, such necessities as guarding or searching prisoners always arise, and with the Madsen M50/53, once the weak hand is removed from the magazine housing area, the weapon is incapable of being fired. I suppose I would tape it in the forward position if I were issued a Madsen M50/53, but then I would need to watch the inertia firing problem carefully. The Uzi with its ratcheted top cover seems to be a better solution.

The Madsen M50/53 lacks a dust cover, and the bolt handle is small. In cold or rainy weather, it can slip from your hand, causing a discharge if brought far enough to the rear to pick up a cartridge but not far enough to hit the sear notch.

The Madsen M50/53's safety is flat and hard to operate. I would be reluctant to depend on it because my hand could slip off the button if it got wet or otherwise slippery. However, I generally do not depend on safeties on open-bolt guns of any type, so this is not a major drawback for me.

The bolt is released when the nonfiring hand depresses the lever in the rear of the magazine housing. Little pressure is needed to depress it, but the system does preclude one-hand firing, which could come in handy in some situations.

The Madsen M50/53 is a nonselective fire gun in most examples (at least I understand a selective-fire version was made, but I did not have one to test), but the cyclic rate is low enough for anyone to fire single shots without difficulty.

The Madsen M50/53 is an interesting example of immediate postwar SMG design. Although it has some good design features, such as the adjustable operature on the peep sight, the overall package falls well below what is available from other manufacturers.

Finland

SUOMI M1931, M37/39

The Suomi M1931 SMG is one of the early so-called first-generation SMGs. That is generally taken to mean that the weapon is made out of machined steel parts, as opposed to pressings, and has a wood stock. Today, this SMG rather looks like a weapon that is attempting to be a rifle when in fact it shoots only a pistol cartridge. At 15 pounds loaded with its 70-round drum magazine, it is very heavy for an SMG, according to modern standards, and is likewise long. But it is this same weight and length that make the M1931 such a fine weapon from a shooter's standpoint. In Finland, where the weapon was designed and first adopted, it was used to fire matches at 300 meters, and it got good results because it is a good SMG. It was also the star of the 1940 Winter War with Russia. My image of that war has always been a white camouflaged Finnish soldier gliding through the woods on skis attacking Russian positions with his Suomi SMG.

During World War II when it became obvious that the Swedes needed an SMG, they looked around for a good design. Obviously, the Germans were not likely to be a good source. The Swedes bought some Thompson SMGs from the United States, but that was not a dependable source. Sweden needed a locally produced model, so its military leaders looked to Finland. There they found the Suomi and modified the stock slightly and trimmed the barrel back to a shorter length. The weapon became lighter and handier but lost little of its fine accuracy.

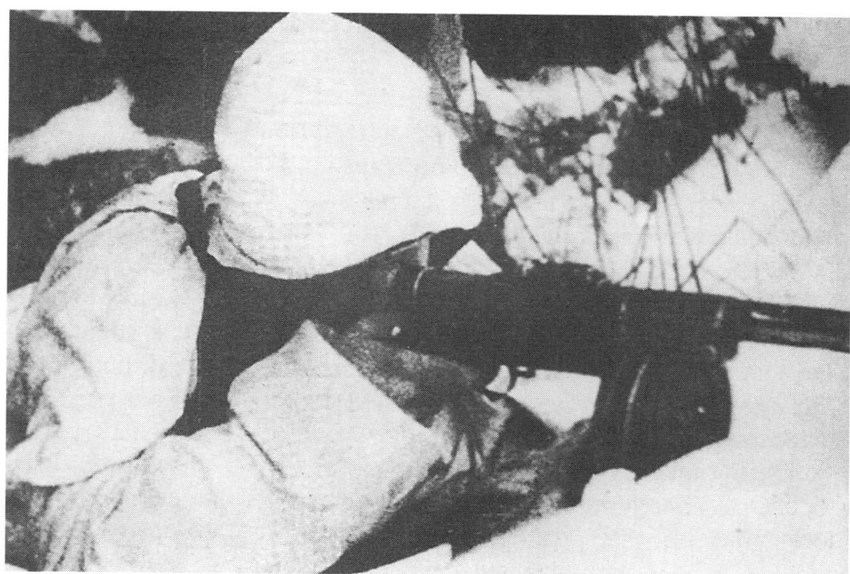

Finnish soldiers with Suomi M31 9x19mm SMGs with drum magazine during Finland's Winter War with Russia.

A female Italian resistance fighter with a Suomi M31 SMG during World War II. It would be interesting to know how the Suomi got to Italy. Was it smuggled through Switzerland?

The Swedish M37/39 Suomi uses a fixed front sight that is rugged enough not to need any protective wings. The rear sight is a three-step notch and has wings. You can set it for 100, 200, or 300 meters—and they mean it when they say it will hit at that distance. With my Suomi gun, a M37/9 version made in Sweden, 300-yard chest-sized plates are a reasonable target. Try that sometime with a Sten MK II and see if you think the Suomi and Sten are equals.

The Suomi uses a very finely designed solid stock. Occasionally, complaints are heard about stocks breaking at the pistol grip area, which I would imagine is slightly weak, and combat skiing no doubt results in a lot of falls. Fortunately, it has never happened to me, but, then, I do not ski with my Suomi SMG in hand. The comb on the Suomi stock is very good. It keeps the stock high on your cheek, allows you to get a firm and rapid sight picture, and directs the recoil straight back.

The Suomi has a bolt-cocking lever on the right sight that does not reciprocate with the bolt. Unfortunately, it does crowd your shooting hand somewhat and can cause some discomfort when your right hand is holding on to the pistol grip near the top. It is not easy for a left-handed shooter to operate, given the cocking handle location.

The safety is centrally located, which is always nice, and is combined with the selector. Pushing it halfway gets you to semiautomatic; all the way forward out of the trigger guard gives you full auto at about 900 RPM. The trigger guard is really too small, in my opinion, especially considering it is used in a very cold part of the world where mittens are common. Why designers put such small trigger guards on weapons, knowing full well that they will be used out of doors in very cold weather, is a mystery to me. The selector tends to get pushed all the way forward to the full-auto position. It is difficult to stop it midway at the semiautomatic position unless great care is taken.

The cyclic rate is 900 RPM. Generally, I prefer slower guns, but the Suomi is so smooth in operation that I find it very controllable. After about the third round in a burst, the weapon just seems to hang there. Because of the cyclic rate, it is difficult to fire individual rounds when set for full auto, but since it has a selector you really don't need to worry about that. Keeping it set on semiautomatic and cocking the bolt when ready to fire is the best policy—in effect, using the Suomi as a handy, low-recoil carbine.

The magazine release is centrally located, which is always nice, but the lever is so small that leverage is slight. This makes exchanging magazines more difficult than it needs be. Additionally, the magazine must be fitted carefully in the slots in the receiver. That type of magazine fitting is always slow because so much care must be taken to fit the magazine properly. SMGs really should have a flared magazine housing like International Practical Shooting Confederation (IPSC) match guns have so the shooter can load magazines rapidly without

Top: Finnish version of Suomi M31. Bottom: Swedish version of Suomi M31.

The author firing the Suomi with Vector ammunition.

having to "thread the needle" in the magazine housing. This is especially so when you consider that many SMGs do not have their housings in the pistol grip and are frequently used at night, unlike match pistols.

The Suomi swivels are nicely located on the side of the weapon, but the front needs to be taped to avoid noise during night patrols. The Suomi disassembles quickly, and the barrel can be quickly removed to allow easy cleaning with hot water. I am certain many Finnish soldiers appreciated that feature when cleaning their weapons after a busy day shooting Russians in 1940.

The M31 is heavier and longer than the M37/9, but both use the same 70-round drum or 50-round 4-column magazines. I prefer either to almost any other SMG in the world. They are easy to shoot and dead reliable. They may be heavier than desirable, but they balance well. I've found that frequently a heavier, well-balanced gun will carry better than an ill-balanced, lighter weapon. In my judgment, the Suomi ranks in the top three SMGs ever made, along with the Owen and Star Z-63. Although it is comparatively rare in the United States because of its point of origin, you can never go wrong selecting the Suomi SMG to carry and shoot.

France

MAS 38

The MAS 38 SMG is light, handy, and short in overall length; balances nicely between the hands; and has an excellent dust cover, good sights, and a straight line stock to minimize muzzle rise. What it lacks is a proper cartridge: the 7.65mm French long caliber selected is simply insufficient for an SMG cartridge. Had this same weapon been made in 9x19mm, it would have been a wonderful weapon, being much lighter and handier than similar weapons of the time period, but the unique and unfortunate caliber selected doomed it.

That is not to say that the MAS 38 was not used; it did see service in the early parts of World War II. Then during the occupation it took on the role of a police SMG. Later, after the Germans were gone, it was the standard SMG in the early days of the Indochinese and other colonial wars. Throughout all of these actions, it proved to be a good design, hampered only by its cartridge.

At first glance the stock seems straight, but it is actually sloped slightly downward. As a consequence of that slight angle, sights fitted to the top of the receiver can be mounted without projecting upward too much, unlike with such straight-line stocks as the M16 rifle. The front sight is a dark, pyramid-shaped unit that seems quite sturdy despite the fact that it is unprotected. Interestingly enough, it has a slot cut in it much like the excellent sights on the 8mm carbine that accommodates a thick front sight to allow quick pickup, yet the slot permits the shooter with more time to center it in the peep for good accuracy. The rear sight is a very nice unit, consisting of two peeps, that folds down into the top of the receiver when it is not being used.

The French MAS M1938 7.65mm SMG with the bolt open and ready to fire.

French police officer armed with MAS 38 SMG searches the rooftops of Paris for a criminal in the 1950s.

Although it is not protected by any wings, it appears to be affixed firmly enough to avoid being knocked out of position, especially considering the fact that it is supposed be lowered when not in use. Naturally, if the sight is raised when the weapon is dropped on its side, it might well get bent or broken, but I think that is unlikely. Because the sight folds down into the weapon, the sight should not catch on clothing and web gear when the weapon is slung across the chest. Even though the shooter must remember to raise it into position before firing, all things considered, I think it is a quite elegant solution to the problem of protecting the rear sight on a weapon that is flat on the top, such as the MAS 38 SMG.

The magazine well has a dust cover that can be raised to cover it when the weapon does not have a magazine installed in it. Although this may be useful in peacetime storage situation, it could easily be left off, whereas the dust cover on the ejection port attached to the bolt handle is quite helpful because a lot of dust would enter there otherwise, potentially disabling the weapon.

The MAS 38 does not have a quickly removable barrel, which makes it more difficult to clean when hot water is used, as is required with corrosive primers. Nevertheless, it is a no-nonsense barrel—short in length and unencumbered by cooling rings and other things common on weapons of the period, such as the Thompson, Suomi M31 and M37/9, and Beretta M38. Certainly, the barrel is perfectly adequate for an SMG designed for 200 meters or less.

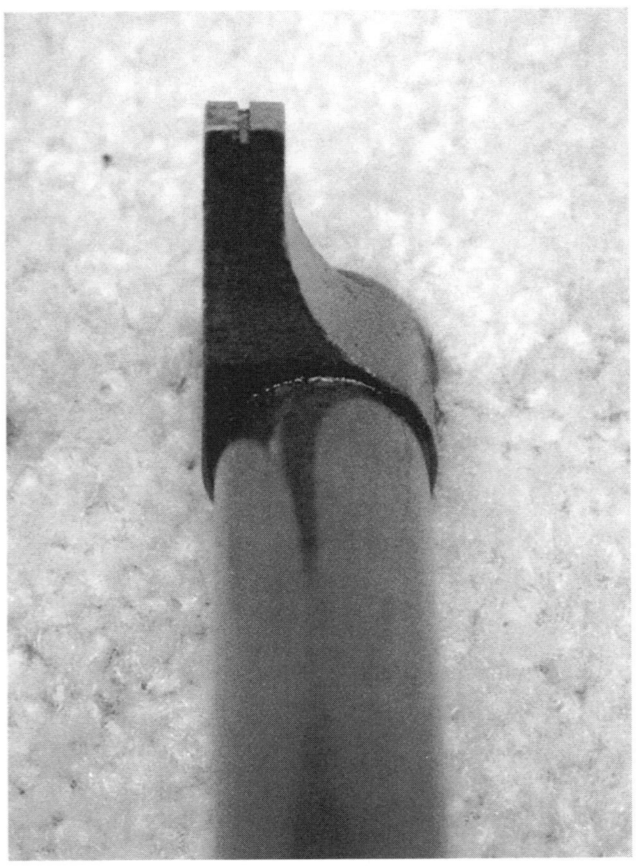

The MAS 38 has an extremely clever front sight. Note that it is very wide to allow for quick pickup and alignment in poor light, yet the slot in the center allows fine alignment on the target for good accuracy, much like on the Model 07/15 sights. This is a great idea.

This top view shows the clever fold-down sights. Here, the 200-meter leaf is raised, while the 100-meter leaf is in the down position.

The weapon no doubt took a lot more time to make than later wartime stamped creations because it uses a lot of machining and wood that must be carefully hollowed out to permit the recoil tube to be installed. Still, that issue is one for the suppliers to concern themselves with, not the users.

Overall, the MAS 38 seems to be a very handy, remarkably solid little SMG with a lot of very good points going for it. However, no number of strengths could overcome the cartridge for which it was chambered. The French service cartridge of the time, the 7.65 French Long, simply was not up to the task. It is rather like designing a very fine automobile with a carefully tuned chassis and elegant body design and then installing a vastly underpowered engine. No matter how mechanically interesting or lovely, such a vehicle will never be a good race or even town car. The keys here are having the power plant and then getting that power properly delivered. If it is pretty, so much the better. So it is with SMGs, and the MAS 38 fails to achieve the first goal of a proper SMG: having the properly provided engine in the first place.

MAT 49

The MAT 49 was the standard French SMG in the hard campaigns of Indochina and Algeria. Although it is likely that the weapon was obsolete from the time it came on line, it did represent a rugged piece of equipment that was cheap to produce.

The French, of course, entered World War II with the MAS 38 SMG, which, as we just discussed, is a light and handy weapon with a caliber so small that it is not very useful. Had some specialty ammunition, such as incendiary or armor piercing, been produced, the situation might have been different. Additionally, there were so few MAS 38s available to face the Germans that in 1940 the French had to turn to the United States to order Thompsons. By the time the Thompsons were available, Germans were sitting in Paris cafes. The MAS 38 was used by police forces and saw some use in the immediate postwar situation, but it was obvious to everyone that the MAS 38 was not the answer to the needs of the French army.

The MAT 49 offers a few of those very

The magazine has been removed and the magazine well cover folded to prevent dirt from getting into the MAS 38. The 200-meter sight is in the up position.

French soldiers carry MAT 49 9x19mm SMGs during the Indochina wars, 1946–1954.

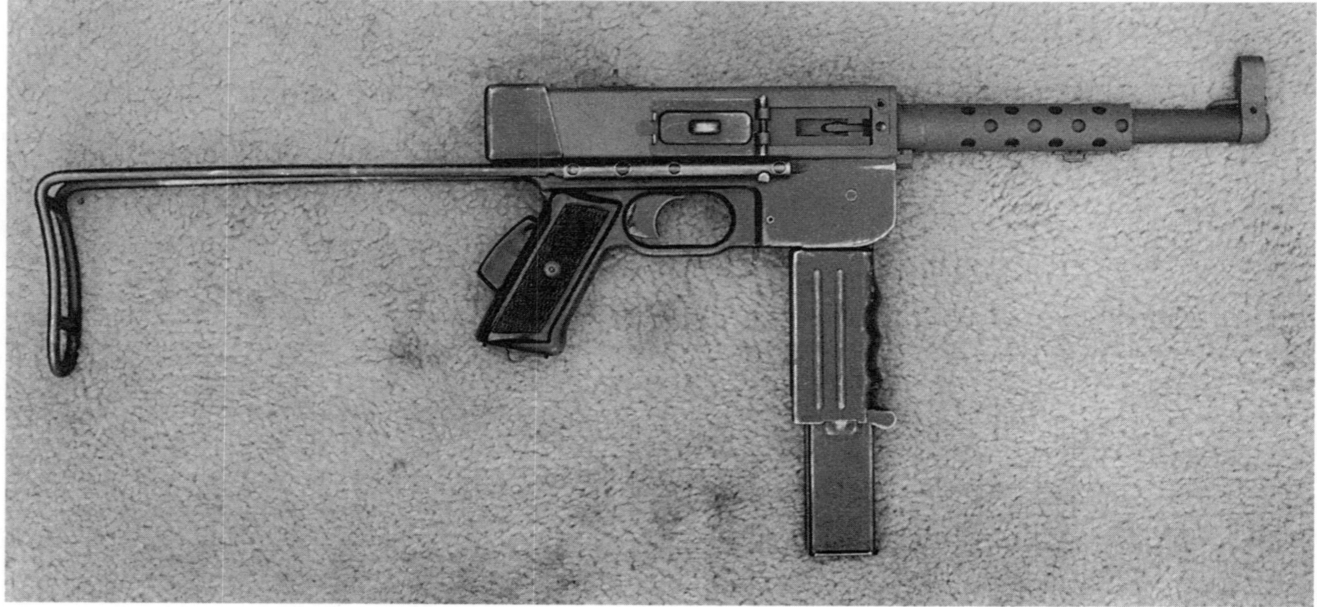

The MAT 49 SMG with stock extended.

"French" design features that make its weapons different from those found elsewhere. For example, although most countries had abandoned the bicycle at the time, it was still an important part of the French army, and the magazine housing on the MAT 49 was designed to fold up to allow convenient storage while a soldier was riding a bicycle. The barrel is covered by a short ventilating jacket, which is long enough to protect against burns but not so long as to increase the weapon's weight excessively. The stock telescopes much like that found on the M3/M3A1 SMG, and although this does not make for a good shooting platform, it does provide a convenient short package for carrying on a bike, in a vehicle, or on an airplane. Extended, it is fairly stable, and, of course, the 9x19mm cartridge keeps recoil light so that the shooter's cheek doesn't get bruised.

The pistol grip is nicely angled, and the grips allow the weapon to fill the palm well, unlike the grip on weapons such as the M3/M3A1. A grip safety is incorporated, which is helpful because it guards against the typical problem found with open-bolt SMGs (such as the MAT 49), where dropping the weapon back enables momentum to pull the bolt to the rear, thereby firing the weapon. The ejection port is big to allow the brass to get out easily yet has a folding dust cover that can be pushed into place to guard against foreign matter getting inside. Pulling the bolt to the rear automatically removes the dust cover.

The front sight is well protected by a sturdy hood and is a good blade shape, although it is better if painted a light color. The rear sight offers two positions, and, although a mere notch, it is well protected against damage. Still, notch rear sights are not nearly as effective as a well-placed peep sight.

Fieldstripping is rapid and easy, thereby encouraging field maintenance. The parts are basically big and sturdy. The weapon opens up easily, so the barrel can be cleaned from the rear

One of the distinctively French design features of the MAT 49: the magazine housing folds up flat under the barrel to facilitate the soldier's carrying his weapon while riding a bicycle. Here, the latch that holds the housing in place is being pushed to allow the housing to swing into position.

The dust cover on the MAT 49 pops open when the bolt goes forward and the weapon is fired. This allows the weapon to be carried with the dust cover in place, unlike on the M3 and M3A1 SMG, where the dust cover also acts as a safety.

with hot water—always a useful feature on SMGs that use corrosive ammunition frequently, as was the case with French units until the last decade or so.

Because of the rifles the French army had at the time—the MAS 36 bolt rifle, the 10-shot MAS 44/9, and later the M49/56—the French used the SMG in many roles that would have been filled by a rifle in other armies. Excellent tracer ammunition was designed for use with the MAT 49, and, of course, the ball ammunition was loaded "hot" and had a bullet with a thick jacket, allowing excellent penetration. Although not up to rifle power, obviously, the MAT 49 could still be used instead of a rifle in many situations. The MAT 49 was no lighter than a rifle, but it was shorter, of course.

The cyclic rate on the MAT 49 is low enough that it is no trick to fire single shots, even though a selector is not present on the weapon. The weapon does not mount quickly, however, because of wire stock, so reaction time is slowed. The weapon is heavy between the hands and feels somewhat dead.

The front sight is too dark and should be painted white for better contrast.

Lack of a safety, other than a grip safety, means that the shooter must either carry the weapon with the bolt open ready to fire—always a dangerous undertaking—or cock it when ready to fire. Fortunately, the bolt handle is on the left side, which allows the shooter to keep his hand in the firing position. Even so, having to cock a weapon before firing slows up reaction time substantially. I did not get a chance to try the MAT 49 on my standard clay pigeon course, but I could tell I would have been disappointed with the results.

The rugged, simple parts on the MAT 49 make fieldstripping fast and easy.

Germany

BERGMANN M1918

The Bergmann M1918 was not technically the first submachine gun issued, but it was the first one really used by infantrymen in a way that is still common today. As such, the Bergmann M1918 set the pattern for SMG use that still holds true even today, except that SMGs have gotten lighter, are made out of stampings, and are frequently more compact. The typical characteristics are a short barrel, an open-bolt firing mechanism, a pistol caliber, a high magazine capacity, and a marginal safety.

The cyclic rates for the guns that followed the M1918 often were not as good as that of the Bergmann, which fires about 450 RPM, depending on ammunition type. As a consequence, even though the Bergmann lacks a selector, single shots and short bursts of two shots are easy to fire.

Sights on the M1918 are typical of the period and need to be painted white on the front sight top to allow more rapid pickup. The rear sight will soon turn into a blur and is difficult to use. It would be much better if it were widened a bit and deepened.

The safety on the M1918 consists of merely pulling the bolt to the rear and turning the handle into the locking slot. Unfortunately, not only is it slow to disengage and subject to slipping out of cold or wet hands, it also will jump out of the slot if

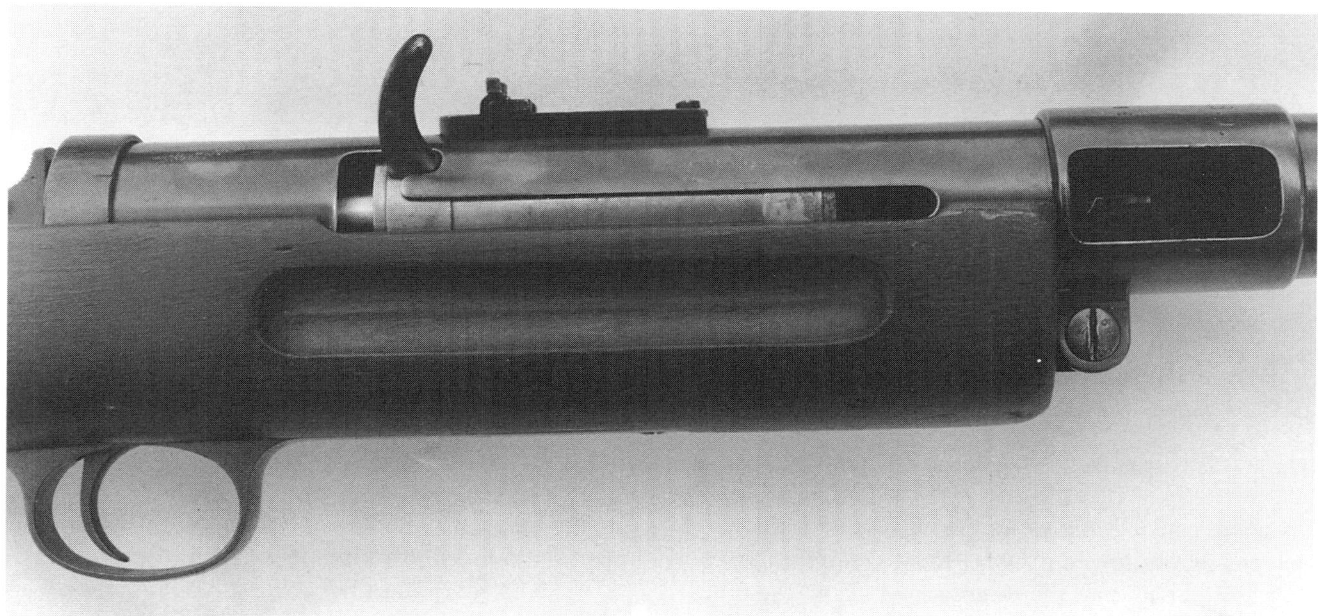

The bolt on the Bergmann M1918 is in the safety notch in this photo. It is a marginal safety system at best.

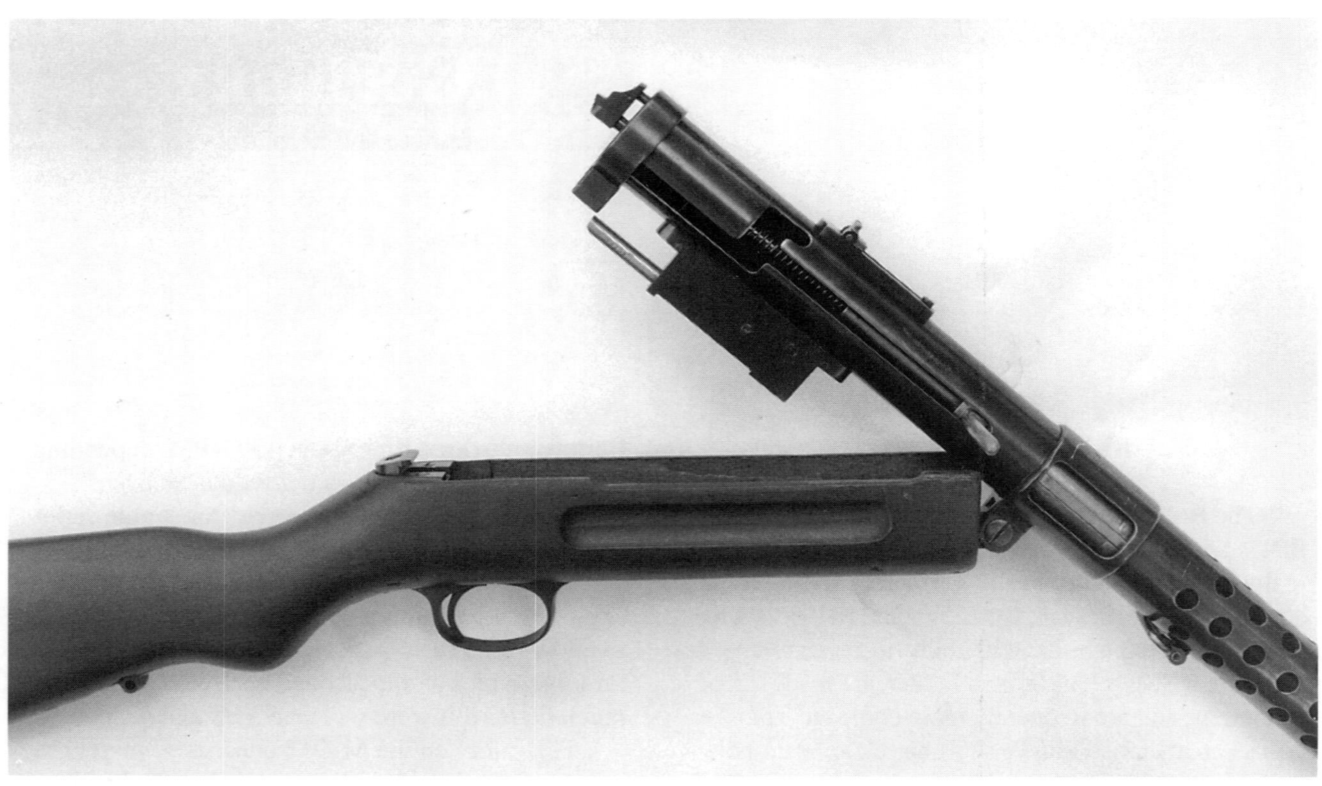

An M1918 with the action open.

The M1918 Bergmann SMG equipped with Luger snail-drum magazine.

dropped, causing inadvertent firing. As with many designs that followed the M1918, if you have the bolt closed and drop the weapon on its butt, the bolt will come back far enough to rack and fire one shot at least. If you carry the M1918 in the field, you should take care to hold the bolt in the forward position to avoid this kind of accident.

The barrel is short but covered with a rather massive cooling sleeve. Although it can be used as a handguard, it really has too much metal in it and

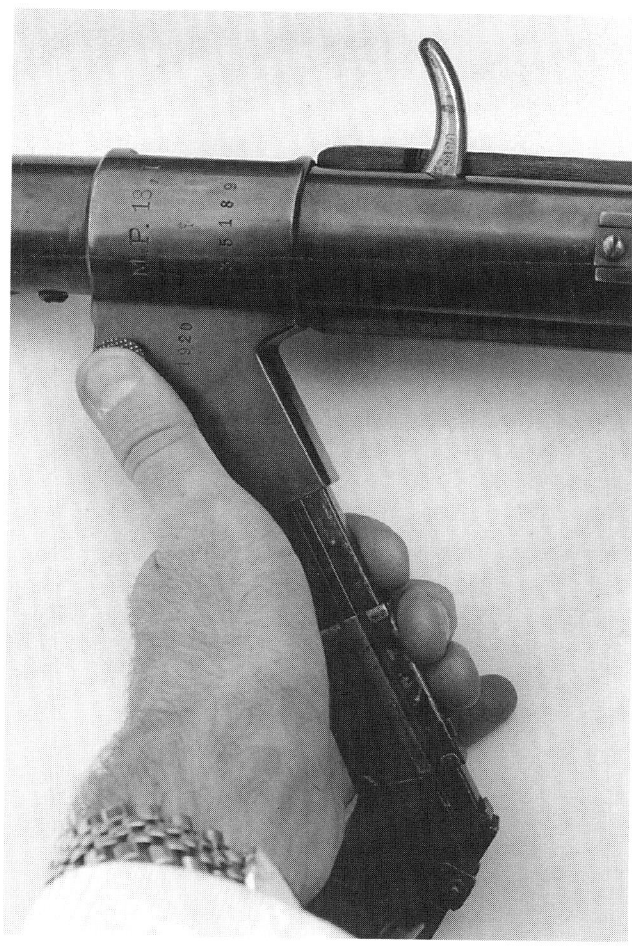

Removing the Luger snail-drum magazine from the M1918 SMG.

adds weight to the weapon. Although such weight on the forward half will allow the shooter to get good control on long bursts and is thus helpful to the "recreational machine gunner," this extra weight is just that much less food and ammo that the infantryman can carry and is thus undesirable. It also makes for extra machining that should be avoided in the rush of wartime production.

The original M1918 SMG used the snail-drum Luger magazines, which, of course, meant that truncated bullets had to be used because regular round-nose ammunition would not feed through the drums. Additionally, such drums are time consuming to load and expensive to make. They also place the rounds farther out on the weapon than is desirable, adversely altering the balance of the weapon. In the postwar era, the M1918 SMG was modified to accept standard box magazines, and this was much better.

The M1918 feels like a good, sturdy, long-lasting weapon. It does have a few drawbacks to it (such as weight and slam-firing bolt-design defects), but once modified to a standard box design, it has all the features necessary to make an effective SMG with very few that are superfluous to the job. This is quite a compliment to those original German designers back in 1918.

MP 28

The MP 28 is basically a slight refinement of the Bergmann M1918, which as we just discussed was developed and briefly used during World War I. The Bergmann made quite a splash in the field but, of course, using the Luger snail-drum magazine greatly limited the ability to field the weapon. The MP 28 was designed to use simple, double-column, box-type magazines. Developed at a time when SMGs were uncommon and the only real competition was the Thompson M1921, the MP 28 was widely sold around the world. To countries that wanted something other than a .45 ACP weapon, the MP 28 was the answer.

The MP 28 was made with high-quality machining. It included a heavy, ventilated barrel shroud that no doubt was time consuming and expensive to make. Additionally, as with all such shrouds, it made it very difficult to maintain the weapon. Mud and debris penetrated the many holes in the shroud, making it very difficult to clean it properly.

The front sight is a typical European pyramid style, and the rear sight is a small notch that blurs quickly upon firing the weapon. Widening the rear sight and painting the front one in a contrasting color will make the weapon easier and faster to use in the field.

The MP 28 suffers from the same type of safety system found on the earlier Bergmann. Such safeties are always slow to disengage, slightly dangerous to engage if one's hands are slippery, and offers no safety to avoid problems with inertia causing an accidental discharge if the weapon is dropped. The only good thing you can say about the MP 28 is that they are simple to

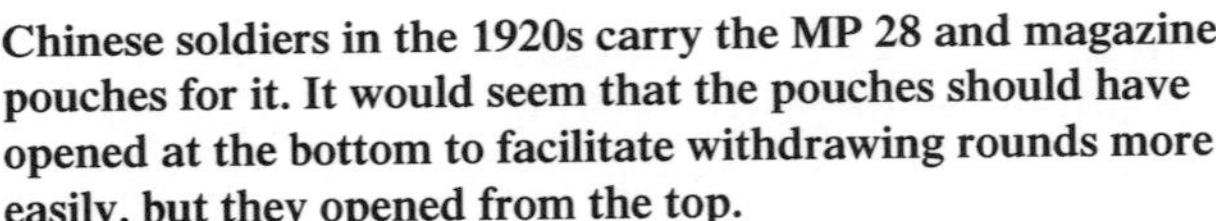

Chinese soldiers in the 1920s carry the MP 28 and magazine pouches for it. It would seem that the pouches should have opened at the bottom to facilitate withdrawing rounds more easily, but they opened from the top.

The MP 28 was designed to replace the earlier Bergmann. One of its most obvious refinements was the simple double-column, stick magazine that replaced the snail-drum magazine found on its predecessor.

design and make for the home hobbyist.

The stock is a traditional wood, fixed stock with a solid buttplate. As such, it makes for a very stable platform for shooting and is obviously very durable over a long period. All this results in the weapon's weighing more than many rifle-caliber carbines produced during the period, but I suppose its rapid fire made up for the excessive weight to a great extent at ranges of under 200 yards.

As with most SMGs produced, the MP 28 fires from the open-bolt position. The heavy bolt provides the only locking mechanism for the weapon, and the resulting heavy-shifting weight makes sighted fire difficult without sufficient practice. At close range, this does not make much of a real difference, but at greater ranges, this causes much misalignment and misses. However, because the weapon is generally used at close range, it is not a major problem. Of course, when you use the MP 28 more as a carbine and less as a pistol or shotgun, this becomes more critical.

The weapon can be quickly stripped for cleaning, and the tolerances are such that it would appear that sand and mud should have minimum effect, other than caking up the barrel shroud. Easy cleaning is especially important, in my opinion, for any weapon used when corrosive ammunition was the norm. However, the finish supplied is a standard blue, actually much better than many commercial rifles finished in the 1990s and, as such, will quickly disappear under rough service conditions. That, of course, leaves the metal unprotected and shiny. Such was the method in the late 1920s when the MP 28 was made, however. Although not rugged by any means, perhaps it both encouraged pride of ownership and forced the soldier who was issued it to maintain it well because the slightest delay or hesitation would be promptly noted by his superiors.

The MP 28 uses a side-mounted magazine, and the release button is not very well protected. As such, it can be inadvertently hit, thus releasing the magazine at the wrong time. Taking side-mounted magazines through doorways is difficult, but such magazines do allow a lower prone. They also result in less fight against gravity, increasing feeding reliability somewhat. Although these magazines appear awkward, the more you use them, the less awkward they actually feel in operation. In my opinion, however, the top mounted solution is better, because it gets gravity to help you even more and it avoids the problems associated with the prone position and with going through doorways. Weapons with top-mounted magazines are difficult for left-handed shooters, but those with side-mounted magazines are likewise somewhat ill balanced.

The cocking handle on the MP 28 is smooth and can easily slip from the palm, especially if hands are wet or cold. On a positive note, it can be withdrawn by either hand equally well.

Overall, the MP 28 does not represent a great advance over the MP 18, but then the MP 18, except for its magazine system, was actually quite good at its intended role. It was not designed to be a long-range precision rifle nor a machine gun. Rather, the MP 18 was a short-range weapon designed to augment the traditional bolt-action rifles found in armies of the day.

The MP 28 uses a much superior magazine system, and although it was heavy, it did fill its role in many armies in the 1920s and 1930s when the SMG was just coming into service. It was expensive to produce, which could be viewed as a flaw, but this is not a matter of concern except as to how it impacts the number of weapons that could be fielded. The soldier, as well as the reader, should only be concerned about how the weapon rates as a weapon. Viewed in this fashion, the MP 28 comes out quite nicely.

MAUSER SCHNELLFEUER (M712)

During the 1920s, various Spanish manufacturers copied the Mauser Broomhandle or M96 pistol. Although the weapons were physically alike, frequently these knock-off manufacturers cheapened the design somewhat. They also tended to use softer steel in the various small home-built sights common in Spain at the time. However, some Spanish pistols were well made of good material and had superior design features, such as a rate reducer that was missing on their German counterparts.

Many of these weapons were sold to China, where the League of Nations had imposed an arms embargo on rifles and machine guns in hopes of keeping the various factions from fighting (or the country from unifying and thereby remaining unable to resist the various "unequal treaties" imposed on it by European powers, depending on your viewpoint). As a consequence, pistols—especially pistols with buttstocks that allowed them to serve double duty as lightweight semiautomatic carbines—were popular because they were not subject to the embargo. The Mauser Broomhandle had been popular in the Orient before World War I, and cut off from their traditional supplies in Germany, the Chinese looked to the Spanish manufacturers to supply the look-alike alternative.

The Spanish manufacturers, however, went Mauser one or two better and offered a detachable-magazine model (which is far superior to the clip-loaded model because it no longer had to be emptied before it could be reloaded and it held more ammunition—typically 20-shot magazines were available, whereas, except for rare examples, the Mauser Broomhandle held only 10 rounds). Then some clever Spaniard got the idea to allow the weapon to fire both semiautomatic and in bursts. The buttstocked pistol had thus crossed over the line to a lightweight SMG. Please recall that at this time SMGs were rare: basically only the Bergmann M1918, Thompson M1921, and perhaps the MP 28 existed. All were heavy and fired from an open bolt. The M1918 was available in very limited numbers from ex-war stocks, and the Thompson was expensive. The MP 28 was available but subject to the embargo. The Spanish Broomhandle selective pistol was light, fired from a closed bolt for better accuracy, was considered well designed, and—most critically—could be sold in China.

Soon business was thriving, and Mauser realized that its traditional market had been invaded successfully. Mauser modified its pistol in 1930 with a couple of designs and sold them worldwide. I would imagine that many people reading this book had their first experience with a machine pistol using a wartime "bring-back" Mauser Schnellfeuer M712. Although they were never officially adopted by a German military formation, apparently a lot of them were taken into military or paramilitary units from factory stocks awaiting shipment to China in 1939; commonly seen examples today have Chinese characters on them and are weapons captured by U.S. soldiers in Europe. Because they were lightweight and short, could be easily stashed in a "war bag," looked like a conventional pistol to the ill educated, and were exotic, these Chinese Mausers made ideal bring-back weapons for American GIs.

Also encountered occasionally are Mauser M712s that were imported by Stoeger prior to World War II, in both in a semiautomatic-only version (known in its catalog as the 712) and the standard selective-fire version. These pistols were also wildly popular in China, and thanks to the recent flood of weapons of Chinese origin into the United States we now have many available. They were also copied in China both in semiautomatic only and selective fire. As a result of the demand for the weapon among U.S. shooters, a special run of semiautomatic-only lowers was made in China and mated to Mauser Schnellfeuer upper receivers, rechambering the no doubt shot-out barrels to 9mm and resulting in a rather nice piece of kit.

As does the standard M96, the M712 has the typical European pyramid front sight that needs to be painted a contrasting color to improve pickup and an adjustable rear sight that is too narrow for my eyes. Widening it helps, however. The sights are adjustable to very long range, but actually the weapon can be used out to 500 meters with some efficiency on semiautomatic with the butt affixed. Therefore, despite statements by some, the M712 is not totally silly.

At first glance, the Mauser Broomhandle design appears rather awkward, but actual testing on the cinema range established that it is a very fast, handy weapon. The safety was easy to disengage quickly, the long barrel was quickly picked up in the lower field of vision, it had great indexing ability, and repeat shots were quick. On the cinema range, the

Right-side view of a Chinese "box cannon" Mauser pistol with detachable magazine chambered for 9x19mm.

Mauser pistols with detachable magazines are rare but very useful for people who need to carry light loads and yet still be able to deliver accurate fire (e.g., smugglers, explorers, military combatants, law enforcement personnel). Although the pistol without stock can be shot accurately with a Weaver stance under normal conditions, the stock does help less well-trained shooters or even well-trained shooters who are weak, cold, or frightened.

detachable-magazine version was even better than its fixed-magazine cousin because it could be reloaded more quickly, and, more important, it permitted tactical reload, something not possible with the stripper-clip-loaded Mauser pistol. The magazine release button was easily used, and although I suppose some type of fence around it to avoid inadvertent dumping would be nice, in actual testing, it was not any more prone to dumping than a Colt Government Model release.

The stock fits nicely, and it can be attached and detached quickly. The stock, if fitted properly, provides a very firm shooting platform. If wobbles exist, a little hammering on the lug to spread it will usually solve the problem. The holster stock doubles as a container for the pistol and makes for a handy outfit for someone burdened with other objects, such as mortar base plates, tripods, or contraband cargo.

The cyclic rate on the German weapon is higher than is desirable, but then the weapon should always be used in a semiautomatic mode, except at very close range. As with the Glock 18, it should be carried in full-auto mode because a quick emergency at short range is best handled with burst fire. Additionally, if longer ranges exist, there will be time to flip the selector, and it can be converted into a handy semiautomatic carbine. Viewed in this fashion, it is more effective than many open-bolt SMGs and obviously lighter. Bursts should be reserved for 5 yards and under, in my judgment, but at that range the machine pistol, in properly trained hands, becomes the deadliest hand-held weapon available.

I rather like Mauser Broomhandle-style pistols. They are surprisingly fast, handy combat weapons, although they lack some target shooting features. Of course, they are not designed for the target range, but rather the battlefield, and in that place the selective-fire detachable magazine version is the best of the family. The Chinese warlord who armed his troops with them in the 1930s was supplying his troops with weapons that, in good hands, were far better than the weapons supplied to the armies of Europe or the United States at the same time. Even today, the Mauser remains a very fine and effective battlefield weapon within the limitations of its cartridge.

BERGMANN MP 35

When most people who are not firearms enthusiasts think of German submachine guns, they tend to think of the MP 40. Essentially, that was merely a very common SMG; there were many others that were not used as often but were much better. The MP 35 is one of those weapons. It actually is a much better SMG than the MP 40, but it was so expensive to make that few orders for it were received. Additionally, it was perhaps a little old-fashioned and did not have the dashing image of the folding-stock SMG spitting death at the hands of a German parachutist.

In the United States, the MP 35 is fairly rare, I believe. Most were sold to the SS, and I imagine that they were mostly lost on the Eastern front. The example I tested was formerly the property of a biker gang member who no longer had a need for it, thereby providing me and some other law enforcement types with an opportunity to test it. I was only able to put perhaps 500 rounds through it, so I may have missed some of its good or bad points. However, permit me to at least share my impressions with you, in the event you have not tested one yourself.

The Bergmann MP 35 is a rather typical first-generation SMG. It was made with some care out of machined parts and has a fixed, solid-wood stock. In fact, the only apparent serious weak point seems to be the stock. Because of the angle of the pistol grip, the stocks occasionally break there. Obviously, the stock should have a strap running through it to strengthen it, as do the Japanese service rifles. Failing that, I suppose a person could pin or screw the stock together or wrap a wet piece of hide on it and allow it to dry. The Native Americans did that when they broke a rifle stock, and many of their repairs are as good now as they were 125 years ago.

Bergmann MP 35s are rare in the United States, but the author was fortunate enough to be able to shoot about 500 rounds through an MP35 like this one.

The Bergmann MP 35 uses a very nice, easily loaded, and reliable two-position box magazine. It feeds from the right side rather than underneath. This allows you to assume a lower prone position and helps ensure feeding by allowing gravity to help rather than retard your actions, at least to a degree.

The front sight is a stout European pyramid that can be adjusted to get the correct windage. I find it somewhat coarse and dark. Painting at least the tip would prove helpful. The rear sight is a tangent with "V" notch graduated to 1,000 meters. That is, of course, silly for a 9x19mm SMG, but certainly the weapon is accurate to 300 yards. Using Czech steel-core, 1949-dated ammo, I had no difficulty hitting a 10 x 14-inch metal plate at 300 yards when firing on semiautomatic. Having the tangent that permitted elevating the point of

Pulling the handle forward on the Bergmann MP 35 cocks it to fire, but the bolt stays to the rear since it is an open-bolt design.

The magazine housing on the MP 35 is located on the side.

impact was nice. This is not a light SMG—10.4 pounds loaded—so recoil is nil, and controllability on full auto was quite good. Rated at 650 RPM, it seemed slower to me, and I did not have any trouble firing short 3-shot bursts.

The bolt handle is located on the right side. Pulling it to the rear cocks the bolt, but it does not reciprocate with the bolt. It also is a closed unit that helps to keep dirt out of the system. The weapon has a safety lever on the left side. It is difficult to move positions rapidly, so it's not likely that many soldiers used it, preferring instead to cock the weapon when ready to fire. I think the latter method would be faster, and also the bolt being down on an empty chamber prior to actual use would tend to keep the weapon cleaner.

The trigger system is selective by trigger squeeze. In this, it is much like the Steyr AUG. Pull it back partway and it will fire semiautomatic; pull it completely to the rear and you get full auto. Obviously, as with all other SMGs, the MP 35 should be used as a semiautomatic, low-recoil carbine except in the oddest of emergencies. I wonder how frequently bursts got fired during World War II when an excited soldier pulled too hard on his weapon, triggering off a reckless burst rather than a planned single shot? I am not completely sold on such dual-position triggers and think either a separate selector should exist or dual triggers, as on the Beretta M1938, should be used. The weapon is held in the front hand by the wooden forearm. The magazine should not be touched. Because of the side location of the magazine, the weapon when fully loaded feels slightly ill balanced, unlike on a Sten gun, where the hand wraps around the magazine housing and balances the weapon better. The pistol grip is at a fine angle, and the stock feels comfortable and is very solid, as is the entire SMG.

Sling swivels are provided but must be carefully wrapped to avoid noise during night operations. The weapon can be easily stripped to remove the barrel to allow full and complete cleaning with hot water, always important when shooting corrosive ammo, without having to pour water into the entire mechanism.

Although somewhat heavy, the Bergmann MP 35 is a very well made, highly accurate, and controllable SMG. It appears to be very reliable and is quite easy to use. The day of the 10-pound SMG may have been over before the MP 35 was even made, although the designers may not have realized it, but certainly the MP 35, along with the Suomi gun in all its variations, can be viewed as the height of first-generation SMGs.

MP 40

The German MP 40 was actually the most common version of the SMG series that started out with the MP 38, then went by degrees to the MP 38/40, and finally was refined into the MP 40. The MP 41, which is occasionally encountered, was merely an MP 40 with a solid one-piece wood stock. When this series was first introduced, the weapons appeared to be a revolutionary breakthrough. The SMGs of the day (mainly the Suomi, the Thompson, and the MP 28) all used machined parts and had wood stocks. True, the Thompson SMG stock could be removed, but if removed, it was likely to get lost. The other SMGs were all heavy and expensive to produce.

The MP 38, 38/40, and 40 were much cheaper to produce because stampings were used extensively. At the time Germany had the stamping capabilities to allow them to make the weapon, while in the United States such technological know-how was apparently missing from the factories. The MP 38, 38/40, and 40 also were also compact because they had a folding stock. This made them even more convenient to the growing number of administrative soldiers who worked in crowded areas and yet who might need something to fight with if it came to that. Couple these facts with the image of the German paratrooper armed with an MP 38 floating down from the sky onto the British countryside, as they

The folding stock on the MP 40 makes it compact, but the struts hit the shooter's cheek and the lock will loosen over time and cause the stock to wobble.

had done in Belgium, Holland, Crete, and elsewhere, and you had many people who liked the MP 40. Today they may be in very limited use in Norway and some Third World back-country revolutions and rebellions, but at one time they were common and well respected.

The first thing you notice when picking up an MP 40 is that the weapon feels alive in your hands, unlike many SMGs that just lie there—just so much metal. With its good balance and lightness in comparison with other guns of the period, the MP 40 is very nice to handle.

The weapon fires from an open bolt, and while it has a bolt lock to lock the bolt forward on an empty chamber to avoid inertial firing, it has no safety except for a notch in the receiver. The lack of a safety is not really too disturbing, however, because it is faster to simply put the bolt home on an empty chamber than pull it to the rear to ready it for firing. Using a safety would not achieve any real savings in time or money, and it might lead to a false sense of security. Firing from an open-bolt position does tend to cause the weapon to jump forward after the trigger is pulled, as a heavy bolt shifts forward under spring pressure, but the MP 40 is no worse than any other open-bolt gun in that regard. Accuracy with the MP 40 is about the same as with any other similar weapon. Thus, the quality of the design or the cost of manufacture is not a key element in accuracy: the roughly made Sten MK II is as accurate as the more sophisticated and expensive MP 40.

The MP 40 has a folding stock, which the author finds unreliable in combat.

The front sight on the MP 40 is nicely protected by a hood that shields the front sight blade. As with all such sights, I find them rather dark, and especially when you consider that you are typically shooting dark targets, I prefer to put a dab of white paint on them. The rear sight is a two-position leaf with a "U"-shaped notch. They seem to be correct for 100 and 200 meters and can be adjusted by the hammer-and-punch method. Although the rear sight is adequate for single shots, when you fire a burst, the rear sight is soon lost in recoil and becomes worthless as a means of maintaining the correct elevation and windage. I prefer a peep sight. The cocking handle, although located on the right side, projects far enough out that it can be reached with either hand with relative ease. As noted earlier, the safety consists of a simple notch in the receiver. As a faster alternative, I would simply ignore it and cock the weapon when a shot was anticipated.

The MP 40 has a folding stock, and many people were terribly impressed by it during World War II. Although I will admit that such units make it easier to carry the weapons in cramped spaces, none of them is very good when the shooting starts—and shooting, not storage, is what an SMG is really about. To open or collapse the stock on the MP 40, you depress the button at the end of the receiver and then unfold or fold the stock. The metal struts are not comfortable on the cheekbone when shooting and were undoubtedly hot in Africa and cold in Russia. But this isn't their worst fault. As the weapons are folded time and time again, the single locking point becomes worn and the stocks begin to wobble. I have seen the locking points so worn that they cause the stocks to wobble an inch or more. True, most don't wobble this badly, but still any wobble is not good for combat work. A fixed wood stock is much better than folding stocks.

The pistol grip is nicely shaped, and the panels are comfortable, although apparently they are prone to breakage because I have seen numerous chipped and broken MP 40 grips. The cyclic rate is low enough (generally about 550 RPM using standard military-grade ball ammunition) that single shots by trigger control can be fired easily. No selector is present. The MP 40 makes a dandy carbine if so fired, although if bursts are limited to three shots (easily done, given the cyclic rate), they can be effectively delivered out to 75 yards. On semiautomatic (by trigger control, of course), chest-sized targets can be hit easily at 200 yards, and once the proper holdover is discovered a 50-percent success rate is common at 300 yards.

Many people tend to shoot SMGs by holding the magazines, which will ultimately result in malfunctions. The MP 40 has a plastic piece on the lower receiver that apparently was designed to be the proper holding location. I find that such a location cramps my arms and puts too much of the weapon's weight out beyond my arms. I prefer to hold farther out around the magazine housing. Just take care not to bump the magazine release or get a finger in the ejection port because it will tie up the weapon or hurt your hand (maybe both) if the cases hit your hand and bounce back into the weapon.

The magazine release uses a button rather than a centrally located lever. Although such releases are really designed for right-handed shooters, they are not impossible to master for lefties.

The MP 40 has been out of production since 1945, but some receivers have been manufactured in the United States in recent years so they can be married to the rest of the MP 40 parts taken out of the imported guns. This is so that "transferable" SMGs can be made to comply with eccentric U.S. law on the subject of SMGs. Despite the fact that MP 40s were last made a half century ago and surviving examples have suffered all sorts of abuse at the hands of any number of ill-trained individuals, most MP 40s you encounter, no matter how beat up on the outside, will continue to function without missing a beat. If you do encounter problems, replacing the magazine or changing ammunition to something stronger to give better recoil impulse (thereby avoiding the runaway gun problem) will solve the problem nine out of ten times. Although the MP 40 is not nearly the SMG many people think, it certainly is acceptable, and it is historically important.

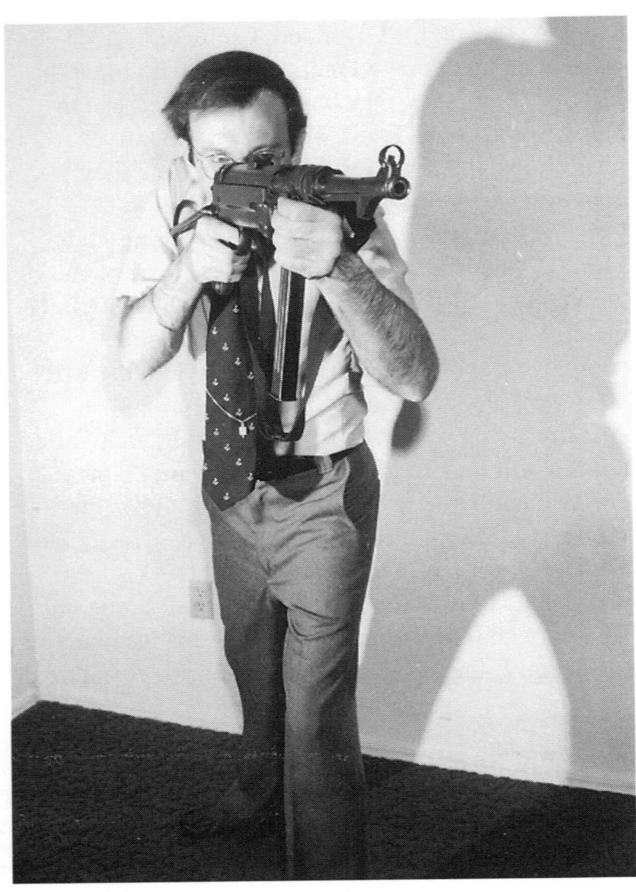

The author first tested the MP 40 in 1976, using a weapon confiscated from a biker gang member.

WALTHER MPL/K

In the mid-1950s when West Germany reorganized its military and police forces, officials were confronted with a situation where a lot of former Allied military weapons were used. It appears that the Germans thought their old World War II weapons were better than what the Allies had given them (frequently true) and further that a modern nation like Germany should not be using World War II cast-offs. Consequently, a lot of research went into designing new weapons to meet the demands of

Top: Walther MPK. Bottom: Walther MPL.

the German military and police forces.

One of those weapons developed was the Walther MPL/K series of SMGs. The only difference between the two models was the length of the barrel: the K model was shorter than the L model. The Walther SMG was designed to use modern stamping techniques to keep costs and production time down and also to produce a short overall length. Except for small orders to the German army, the users in Germany were the border police and similar police units. Abroad, the most noted user was the South African navy. Neither organization is exactly at the cutting edge of weapon use or techniques, but their choice was adequate, if not great, for the tasks they demanded of an SMG.

The MPL/K has a number of drawbacks for practical use and a few good points. As the good points are fewer, let's tackle them first. The barrel can be quickly removed, as well as other major parts, to allow for quick cleaning. The bolt cocker is easy to use and does not reciprocate with the bolt when firing, as it does on many SMGs, which I always find distracting. The pistol grip is nicely shaped and does have a flip-type safety at hand, and it can be used by right- or left-handed shooters. The safety selector system shows the typical German approach of safe, full auto, and then a long stretch to semiautomatic. Flipping it to semiautomatic requires that you adjust the grip in your hand unless you have really long thumbs. Unfortunately, it is only suitable for use by a right-handed person. Cyclic rate is low enough that single shots can be fired without difficulty, although the rate is higher than I prefer. The trigger guard is big enough for gloved fingers but not mittens, and it should be capable of folding out of the way to allow true hard winter use. The sights are well protected against damages and offer both a peep and open sight at the same time. The rear is a peep unit, but the top of the peep has a wide-open slot for an open sight to be used in conjunction with the front sight. The

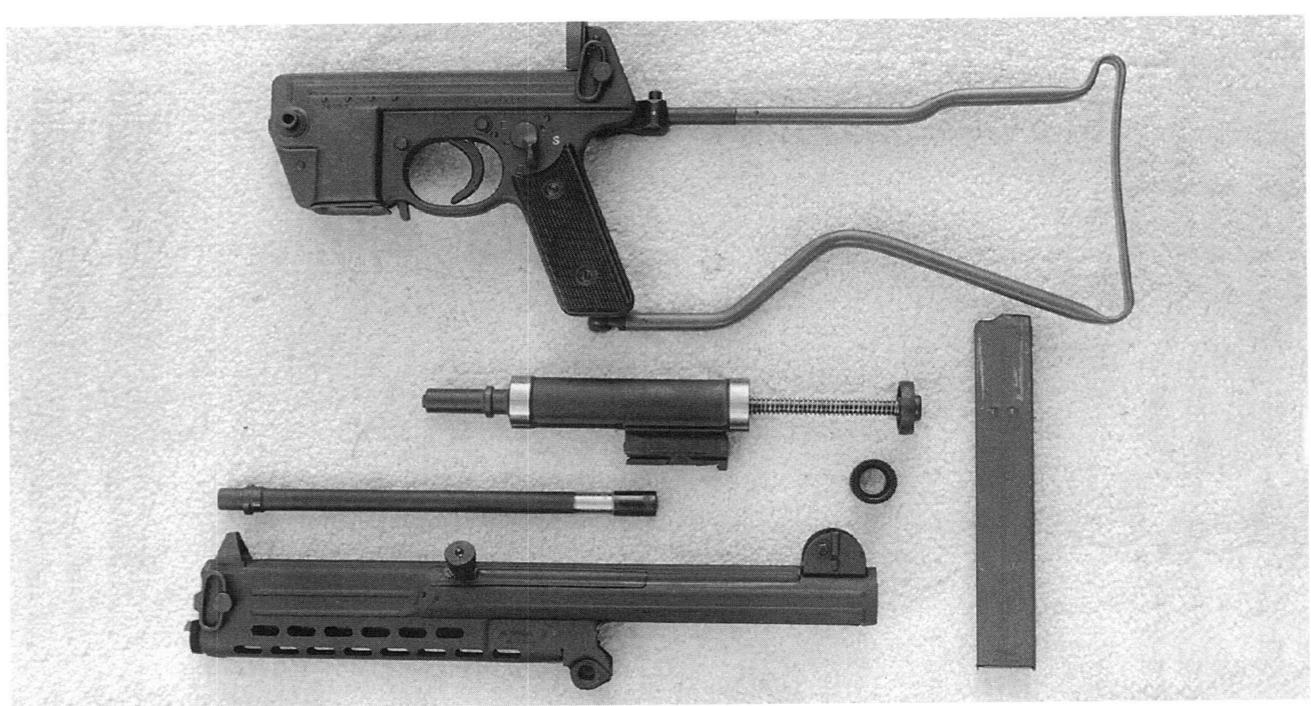

The Walther MPL field-stripped.

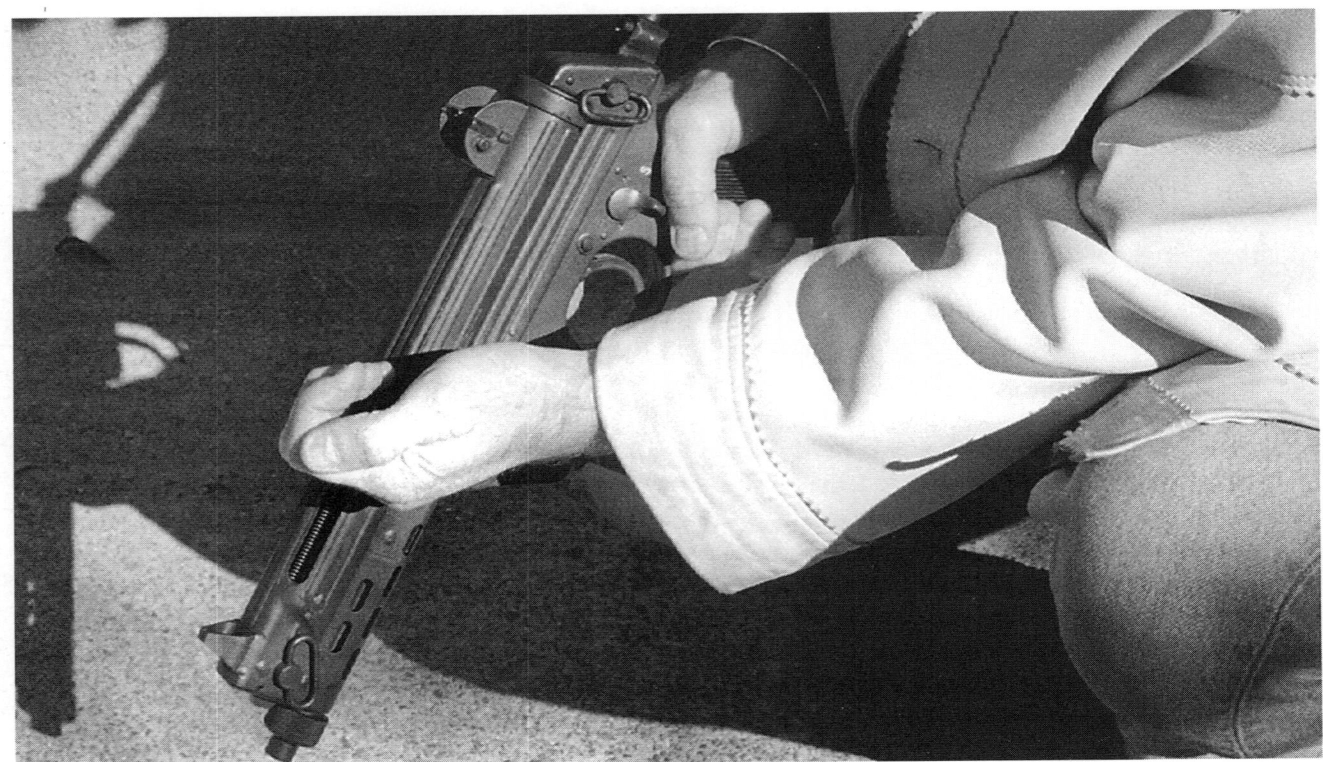

When cocking the bolt on the Walther MPK (as seen here) or MPL, the cocking knob does not follow the bolt when actually shooting the weapon, as it does on many SMGs.

The safety on the Walther MPL/K can be used from either side.

standard front sight is a regular post, but the top of the circle of metal surrounding the post is itself a sight blade. It is very open and wide and, coupled with the open rear, is designed for rough work at night or when you are operating at very close range and are effectively looking over the top of your sights. This is an interesting concept and not otherwise seen.

Having run out of good points, let's explore the drawback to the design. Being made out of metal stamping, the MPL/K is supposed to be cheaper and faster to make. But as a user of the weapons, I frankly do not care about either point. I only care about how they actually work and whether they are handy to operate. Such all-metal guns suffer from weather-related problems. In cold weather, they are hard to use since the metal is cold in your hands and against your cheek when aimed. In hot weather, it is, if anything, worse. Carry your MPL/K slung over your shoulder or around your neck all day in either really cold or hot weather and then try to hold it in your hand and you will quickly see what I mean.

Because the magazine housing is in front of the pistol grip, it is not as short in overall length as might be the case. The grip frame is also metal and difficult to hold. The magazine releases on some of the examples tested were stiff and difficult to operate, but not on others. The amount of wear determines this, I suppose. None were protected against accidental dumping. The magazine housing is not beveled, but rather is a straight-in type housing, so that it is time-consuming to insert magazines into the weapon. Although it is not like threading a needle, it is much harder to do than loading an Uzi or MP5, where the magazine housing is sufficiently wider than the actual magazine to allow off-side insertions to go into position.

The Walther MPK folded. The two latches on the folding stock give it stability, but the metal design of this stock makes it inadvisable as a combat weapon.

The author shooting a Walther MPK 9mm SMG.

The stock folds and has two latches for stability, but its metal construction makes it cold or hot to the touch. More critically, collapsing it is difficult, and I found it quite easy to pinch my fingers in the latch area if not careful when operating it. Metal strut bar stocks are also hard on the cheek, even in a caliber as light as 9x19mm. When the weapon is fired on full auto, the stock continually pounds the cheek. Such distraction, if not painful, is not particularly good for performance.

Sling swivels tend to rattle on the metal receiver frame and need to be taped to avoid this noise. With a sling installed, swivels also are positioned so that the sling will sometimes interfere with your mounting of the weapon.

The Walther MPL/K represents an interesting design made with stampings, but it is actually no more clever in that regard than the Madsen M50/53 series—other than the fact that it looks very German in comparison with the Scandinavian Madsen. The Walther MPL/K offers very few, if any, improvements over such World War II designs as the MP 40 or Sten. It does not reflect any real practical knowledge being applied to the problems such designs encountered a decade before the Walther MPL/K appeared. Rarely does a manufacturer succeed with an SMG that was obsolete in many regards before the first one was even issued, and so it was with the Walther MPL/K. There are a number of good reasons that the Walther MPL/K is only rarely encountered.

HECKLER & KOCH MP5

This is one of the most commonly encountered SMGs in police and special response military units, but not in standard line military units. The points that make it a fine police SMG make it less desirable as a military SMG. Actually, its unsuitability as a combat weapon is rather surprising given the worldwide acceptance of the H&K G3 design when chambered for 7.62x51mm NATO.

The H&K MP5 is used by specialist troops who can be expected to engage in hostage rescue operations, raids, and other actions where pinpoint accuracy is needed, low penetration is desirable, and short duration missions are the norm. The MP5 has sights very similar to those found on the G3 model, except the rear sight is not adjustable for distances up to 400 meters. Instead, it is sighted for the same range, but turning the sight allows the peep to get bigger or smaller, depending on the conditions the shooter anticipates and his preference. Obviously, the bigger peep opening is faster to work with, especially in poor light, but generally results in large groups; the smaller peep yields smaller groups but is slower to get into operation. Since most times you need to shoot faster at closer ranges, I prefer to leave it on the larger opening and change it if extreme precision is called for.

The MP5 is used by special police and military units that require extreme accuracy and low penetration in operations.

The MP5 is unusual in that it fires from a closed bolt. It is this feature that endears it to many. Instead of having a heavy bolt slam forward each time, jarring the weapon and destroying accuracy, it operates more like a traditional semiautomatic rifle. This feature permits much easier shooting, and

This MP5 has a button on the selector that must be depressed before the selector can be flipped to full-auto position, thereby encouraging the shooter to stay on semiautomatic fire. Not all MP5s are so equipped.

when you are trying to hit a hostage taker in the head at 25 yards while he is surrounded by innocents, this feature is much appreciated. The MP5 should, like all other SMGs, be used as a semiautomatic short-barreled carbine, reserving full-auto fire for extremely close-range targets where the consequences of a stray round are not critical. The MP5 also offers a suppressed version that is especially handy at night or on other occasions when a small amount of background noise will obscure the remaining report to the extent that the shooter will be able to fire the suppressed MP5 without alerting all others present.

The MP5 has two buttstocks: the sliding stock and the folding stock. The sliding stock is uncomfortable to use because it has metal struts that hit the cheekbone, which is especially annoying when firing the weapon in the full-auto mode. The fixed stock is much better, and although some complain that it is short, when you wear battle dress or body armor, it takes up enough space that the stock will fit an average-sized man without difficulty. Stick with the fixed stock on any SMG unless you have some essential reason to pick a slider or folder.

The safety/selector on the MP5 is too short to be comfortably flipped with the thumb. You must shift the weapon in your hand to work the selector. Because it fires from a closed bolt, I suggest you use the safety and carry it loaded with a round in the chamber, as with a conventional rifle—unlike the advice I would give to someone with an open-bolt gun. Simply train yourself to shift the weapon to disconnect the safety or weld an extension on it. The safety is also the selector lever, as on the G3, but fortunately the first stop after off is semiautomatic fire, and I suggest you stop there unless you really need to fire a large number of rounds very rapidly in a general direction. Fast semiautomatic is much more accurate generally. The safety/selector is not very convenient for a left-handed person, but fortunately the magazine release is centrally located.

The author with pepper-popper shot with the MP5 at 50 feet off-hand fired in the 2-shot-burst mode. The first round hit at aimed point on the lower portion of the plate, and the next round hit about 6 to 8 inches up.

On the range, the MP5 can be shot with equal ease from either shoulder once the safety/selector lever is properly released.

Different types of trigger housings are available. The standard provides for safe, semiautomatic, and full auto. Newer versions use pictures of bullets to do the same thing. There are some new ones coming out now that offer 3- or 5-shot bursts in addition to the semiautomatic and full auto. Avoid them because the cyclic rate on the MP5 is low enough that anyone with a little training and some manual skill can shoot similar groups, and you avoid the mechanical complications that come with such units.

Pistol grips now also come in two shapes: the older version that I like and the new one that looks more modern but does not feel any better in the hand. Forearms also come in two types: the skinny version and the tropical version, which is fatter and allows you to fire more rounds without burning your hand. Frankly, I do not anticipate firing any MP5 in combat enough to get it so hot that I cannot hold it, and I prefer the feel of the slimmer unit. I will admit, however, that in training courses I have fired them long enough on hot days that I could not hold the forearm. About seven 30-round magazines on a 90-degree day will do it.

The trigger pull on the MP5 is as bad as that found on a G3, but since all other SMGs have worse pulls, the MP5 feels good. It is just the opposite with rifles, where everything else is better than the G3 trigger. As with the G3, the weapon is designed so you could load it, put a round in the chamber, lock the safety off, throw it out of a helicopter at 300 feet onto a steel deck, and it will not fire. This is a nice feature, considering a common problem with SMGs: dropping them can cause the bolt to ride back, pick up a cartridge, chamber it, and fire it.

Various muzzle units are available, but except for the blank device useful for training, I really do not see any reason to buy anything. The recoil is so low in a 5 1/2 pound MP5 that I do not believe a muzzle brake is necessary.

The MP5 is light, well balanced, handy, and reasonably accurate. Cleaning it is often difficult because of the small nooks and crannies in the receiver, something that makes it much more involved to maintain than, say, an Uzi. However, it does serve its intended purpose well: to provide low-penetration, short-range, reasonably precise fire over a limited period both as to actual shooting and duration of time spent in operations. I prefer the H&K 53 or even an M1A1 carbine with the barrel shortened to 12 inches for my own use, but I will admit that the MP5 is a very fine if somewhat overengineered SMG.

HECKLER & KOCH VP70

Heckler & Koch has developed some of the most advanced fabrication methods found in post-World War II Europe as far as small arms are concerned. I do not think H&K weapons are very "user friendly," but it is clear that many of its designs are clever. When H&K released the VP70 in the 1970s, it was considered highly unusual; most people thought the day of the machine pistol, as opposed to the SMG, was over. The fact that H&K thought it worthwhile to develop and market such a weapon caused many people to rethink the issue, wondering if something had been overlooked.

In 1979 I invited H&K representatives to Columbia, Missouri, to put on a weapon demonstration for a variety of local law enforcement agencies that I ran training programs for and that I thought needed better equipment than the 5-shot pump shotguns, M94 Winchesters, and .38 revolvers they were using. Also I wanted to try out H&K's weapons. I had an opportunity to wring out the VP70 quite thoroughly that day, and on subsequent occasions, I have been fortunate enough to get one from time to time to try. Even though I do not claim to be an expert with the VP70, I have put perhaps 3,000 rounds through several of them. I like the weapon, and if I could buy one that I could own legally, I would definitely do so. Alas, the restrictive laws in the United States prohibit that.

The VP70 without its stock is the same as the VP70Z pistol. It looks quite clunky, but when you put it in your hand, you find that it is really quite comfortable. It is lightweight and has a good grip, the sights are very good when tested on the cinema range, and the magazine capacity is high enough to allow a burst-fire weapon to make sense. The trigger pull is consistent, although heavy, which certainly could prove helpful in avoiding accidental discharges. The magazine release is centrally mounted, which is slower than the method I usually prefer for handguns, but I must say that, given the magazine capacity involved, it likely is not a critical issue and does allow left-handed people to use the weapon more easily.

The author with an H&K VP70 with stock attached. He found it an excellent weapon and would purchase one if federal regulations did not prohibit it.

The VP70 does not shoot bursts until you clip on the stock. Then it can either fire single shots or 3-shot bursts. The bursts are fired at the extremely high rate of 2,200 RPM. I admit that I did not have access to a PACT timer when shooting the VP70 with a stock so I cannot verify it, but it does fire so fast that all three shots are gone before I can even begin thinking about stopping the first. I can fire

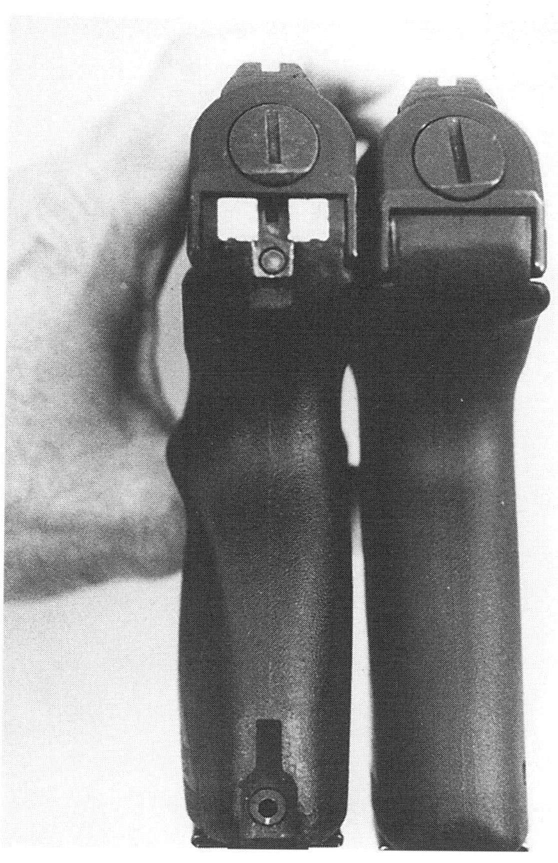

Comparison of the rear view of the machine pistol VP70 (left) and semiautomatic version VP70Z (right).

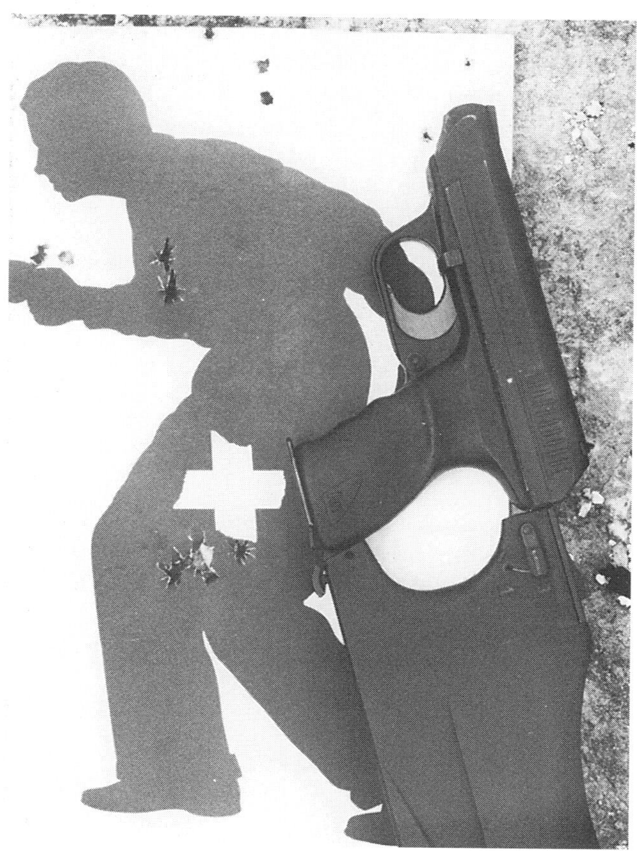

This target illustrates a 3-shot burst shot by the author with the H&K VP70. The first round hit centered, the next round was up 6 inches, and the last round was up an additional 4 inches. The rate of fire with the loads used was 1,950 RPM. The target was at 5 yards.

single shots from a micro-Uzi that fires at a tested 1,500 RPM, so the VP70 must be higher. I have quick fingers and quick reflexes. When you pull the trigger on the VP70 set on burst, you have a long trigger pull, much like a staple gun, and then when the weapon finally fires, it just seems to come alive as the entire burst is fired down range. The stock is well designed and allows you to keep the weapon high on the shoulder, which adds control. Jack Cannon of Glaser Safety Slug fame told me once of hitting a cat with a three-round burst of Safety Slugs when he was using a VP70, and that the cat seemed to explode. I believe it. I have always wanted to see if I could jam something in the burst mechanism and get the weapon to fire bursts without the stock but have never had access to one with someone who both owned the weapon and had an experimental bent. My P35 Browning machine pistol is, I believe, along with the Glock 18, among the most effective entry weapons made. I imagine the VP70 would be as good.

Besides giving you a third point to stabilize the weapon, the VP70 stock contains the burst-selecting mechanism. Fired with the stock on semiautomatic, it is not difficult to hit man-sized targets at 200 yards. The best thing about stocked handguns generally is that they give you additional stability when you are tired. When equally fit and relaxed, a trained shooter can do as well with the Weaver stance as he can do with a stocked pistol. But when that same shooter is tired or hungry, the stock helps. On the VP70, the stock also acts as a holster, as it does on the Mauser, Astra, Browning, and others.

I think such stocked pistols—especially if the shooter is trained to keep them on semiautomatic unless a very close range situation presents itself—

are quite useful for some elements of the military unit. As a helicopter pilot, I would rather have a VP70 than a simple revolver. The stocked machine pistol is not the tactical equal of the standard SMG, but it can be useful. Given a choice between carrying an H&K MP5PDW (an H&K MP5 K with a stock) or a VP70, I would choose the VP70. It would be lighter and easier to handle, faster to get into action, and if the shooter was trained right, just as effective if not more so.

Great Britain

LANCHESTER

By the time the British finally decided to stop the Germans and declared war in 1939, the German soldier had already made a great name for himself with his MP 38 SMG. There were many other SMGs in use by the German forces, but it was the MP 38 (and later MP 38/40 and MP 40) that came to symbolize the efficiency and firepower of the German soldier.

When British officers had originally encountered the SMG, they rejected it out of hand, declaring that their military had no use for such "gangster guns." This has always surprised me given their activities in postwar Ireland and other hot spots around the world, not to mention the experiences they must have had in World War I trench warfare. I recall reading what Captain Tracy, who ran a combat pistol shooting school in France during World War I, had to say about this—that he preferred the Colt Government Model .45 but wanted it to fire bursts. My only explanation for the British attitude toward SMGs was that the real warriors had returned to civilian life as machinists, elephant hunters, lawyers, or plantation managers and left the military to be run by less intelligent but more traditional people.

Certainly, the Germans and the Italians had no such prejudices and fielded large numbers of SMGs (or at least what appeared to be large numbers at the time). When the British finally realized that the SMG was going to be a very important weapon, they were stuck. Obviously, they could not get them from Germany or Italy. Finland had the excellent Suomi, but the Finland was far away, had little production to spare, and was at least nominally allied with the Germans. That left the United States, and Britain purchased every Thompson SMG it could get. Unfortunately, the weapons were expensive (at $200 per copy in 1939), on the other side of the Atlantic Ocean (which was infested by German U-boats), and frankly not the best SMG

The Lanchester SMG is a British version of the German MP 28.

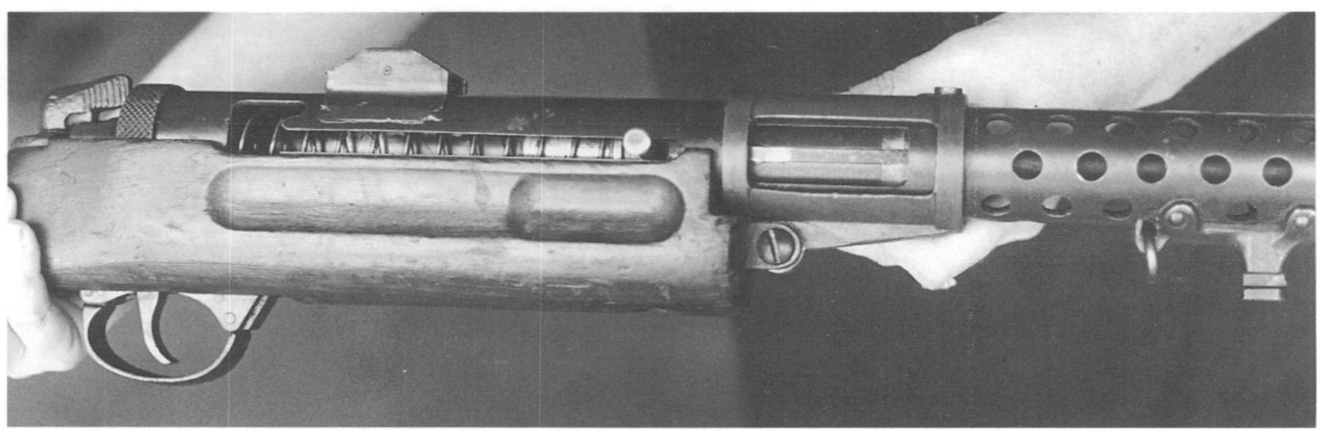

Right-side view of Lanchester SMG. Note the bayonet lug and simple bolt-turning safety notch.

around. (See the Thompson section beginning on page 166 for a more complete evaluation.)

The British took the MP 28 of the Germans and attempted to reproduce it but apparently did not understand what was really involved: the MP 28 was expensive to make, consisting basically of an involved machining project with a fixed wood stock. By April 1941, the Sterling Engineering Company was ready to go into production. The company made about 100,000 examples of its version of the MP 28, the Lanchester, but because of the advent of the Sten gun, they were earmarked for the British navy. To this day, there are many Lanchesters about, and most are generally in good shape due to lack of real use since they were shipboard weapons, not infantry guns. I well remember when the Lanchester was a very popular deactivated war trophy (DEWAT) selling for $39.95. I rather wish I had purchased one now.

The first thing one notices when handling this weapon is the massive nature of it. Not that it is so big, but that it is built so solidly. It is a heavy weapon: more than 9 1/2 pounds unloaded. It may have been built in wartime, but Sterling Engineering cut the stocks out of solid wood, carefully shaped the finger grooves, made the stock look as much like an Enfield rifle butt as possible, and then fitted a brass buttplate to it. That all adds up to a heavy weapon but also one that is quite stable. It is one of friend John Ross' favorite "recreational machine guns."

The Lanchester uses the typical bolt handle safety mechanism, where you pull the bolt to the rear and twist it to engage the safety. That method is certainly cheap and simple, but I doubt anyone really carries an SMG that way. It is faster to keep the bolt closed and rack the weapon when ready to fire. The bolt has no lock on it, and while I have never tried it myself, I imagine that dropping a Lanchester from chest height would cause the weapon to fire a round by bolt inertia. The weapon does have a selector, allowing you to fire semiautomatic as well as full auto. Later models omitted this, and many Lanchesters had this feature removed when they were refurbished. The cyclic rate is low enough at 600 RPM to permit any trained individual to fire single shots by trigger manipulation, but it is a mystery why the selector would be removed. It clearly shows me that

The magazine housing area of the Lanchester.

somebody did not understand how the SMG was to be used tactically.

The sights are a protected blade front with tangent "U"-notch rear. Adjustable out to 600 yards, they serve as examples of fuzzy thinking. I can handle 300-yard shooting with an SMG, but 600 yards with an open-bolt SMG? If that time comes, the shooter who can hit at that distance will know enough to adjust his elevation by holdover. "U"-notches are always difficult for my eyes to use, and after the first shot in a burst they seem like a blur. A dab of white paint on the front sights does help rapid alignment, I have found.

The barrel jacket is quite massive and holds the lug that accepts the long Enfield bayonet. Again, this shows fuzzy thinking. I can accept such thinking in 1941, but why Sterling Engineering persisted with it in 1943 is beyond me. The Lanchester's weakest point from the standpoint of shooting is its magazine. It uses a single-column-feed 50-round magazine and in some examples, depending on fitting, will accept Sten magazines. Single-column-feed magazines are simply not the best way to go for SMGs. Only the fact that they are side-mounted (and hence semi-gravity-assisted) allows the Lanchester, or the Sten for that matter, to work as well as it does. If you start getting malfunctions, pitch the magazine and insert a new one. Chances are you have solved your problem.

I find the Lanchester to be somewhat ill balanced, with so much weight to the front, as well as a loaded 50-shot magazine pulling it to the side. The forearm is short and tends to cramp my left hand back toward my right, giving me a slightly unnatural grip. It is certainly nowhere near as good as the Suomi, which was designed and made at the same time as the MP 28, from which the Lanchester developed. The Brits would have done better to copy the Suomi, but perhaps it was beyond their ability at that time and under the circumstances. The Lanchester is not light and handy, nor does it feel "alive" in my hands. There are many other SMGs I prefer, although I agree with John Ross' assessment that "it's a fine recreational SMG." I view them from the infantryman's vantage point, I fear, and thus do not appreciate that point.

STEN GUN

At the Enfield arsenal, it was obvious that something better in the way of SMGs was needed: something that could be made cheaply, did not require extensive machining, and could be made in many small shops to minimize the risk of German air raids disrupting production as well as to permit the expertise of Enfield to be concentrated on Bren gun production. The Sten gun was born in 1941. A lucky fluke caused it to be made in 9x19mm: the capture in the desert of vast stocks of 9x19mm ammunition from the Italians. No telling what caliber the British would have gone to had that event not occurred at that moment.

The Sten gun was created during World War II in 9x19mm because the British had captured a large quantity of ammunition in that caliber from the Italians.

The first Sten was the MK I. It had a wooden forearm, a downward projection stud for grasping with the nonshooting hand, and a flash hider on the barrel. Although allegedly 100,000 were made, they must be very rare: I have never shot one. Next came the MK II Sten. This is what most of us are familiar with when we think of Sten guns. In series production in Canada, they got down to a little more than $10 in costs: this compared with the $200 Thompson. The Sten MK II uses a simple tube for the receiver, yet, interestingly enough for what many people perceive as a mere bullet-hose, it offers semiautomatic fire.

Perhaps the first thing people always note about the Sten is that the magazine projects from the side. Although it appears to be awkward at first, a little use with it will quickly establish that it is really quite charming. It allows you to get a very low prone position, something not feasible with normal long magazine submachine guns, and because of gravity, it improves the feeding reliability since the springs do not have to push 30 cartridges directly up into the weapon, but rather shove them to the side. That is fortunate indeed since the major weakness of the Sten has always been its single-column-feed magazine. Basically, if you have a malfunction in a Sten, it is the magazine. Once a magazine stops working perfectly, pitch it—they are not worth repairing. Test all magazines before you carry them; one malfunction and they go to the discard pile.

The Sten magazine housing is also quite interesting in that it can be rotated down, sealing the weapon from dirt. Many people do not carry their weapons that way, but since the action on the Mark II Sten magazine housing is otherwise open to all sorts of debris, that is the proper carry mode. The Sten barrel comes out quickly for cleaning or replacement, always a helpful feature for ensuring good maintenance. The rest of the parts on the weapon are large and solid, so there are few that are likely to be lost or broken. Sometimes the springs in the trigger mechanism will break, but if it happens, merely pulling out the remains, making a hook with your pliers, and reattaching will suffice until something better is available.

The sights on the Sten are a fixed peep and a front pyramid sight in a slot, which may be drifted for windage with a hammer. I find it quite big for good work at long range, say 200 yards, and too dark, but at close range, it does pick up quickly, especially with a slight dab of white paint on the tip. I doubt that many people bother to target their Stens, but I am always very concerned where my bullets hit so I know whether it is me or the gun at fault. Therefore, I always shoot my weapons on paper, even it if is only a discarded C-ration box thrown out in the muddy field.

The Sten safety is very elemental. Pull the bolt back to the notch, rotate, and put into the safety notch. Take it out by pulling to the rear and rotating downward. I doubt that anybody actually carries his Sten in combat with the weapon on safe. It takes more time to pull it off safe than to pull the bolt to the rearward cocked position, and the noise involved is only marginally lower, if at all. At the same time, the safety was elementary; the designers understood that the Sten gun was meant to be fired in fast semiautomatic for best results, not in bursts, and included a selective-trigger assembly. It makes a dandy little low-recoil carbine and must have been appreciated by the British Tommy, who otherwise would have had a long No. 1 MK III Enfield rifle or No. 4, which was a newer design but just as long.

Stocks on Sten guns come in many patterns, including the simple tube and the wire frame. Of the two, I prefer the wire frame assembly, but it makes little difference. Although the Sten will not fire with the stock removed, the stock can be quickly removed, thereby shortening the weapon for transport. No doubt this feature was greatly appreciated in occupied Europe where thousands of Sten guns were air-dropped to arm resistance groups.

The cyclic rate on the Sten, depending on ammunition, runs about 550 RPM, which is quite dandy. Single shots can be easily fired even with the selector in the full-auto position, and controllability is quite good. The weapon is light for a World War II design SMG, less than 7 pounds, which is always welcome.

After the MK II was developed, the suppressed version, the MK II (S), was created for use by raiding organizations. Until the last 10 years or so as suppressor technology got better, the MK II (S) was still a viable piece of equipment.

Right-side view of the Sten MK II with the bolt to the rear and in the safety notch.

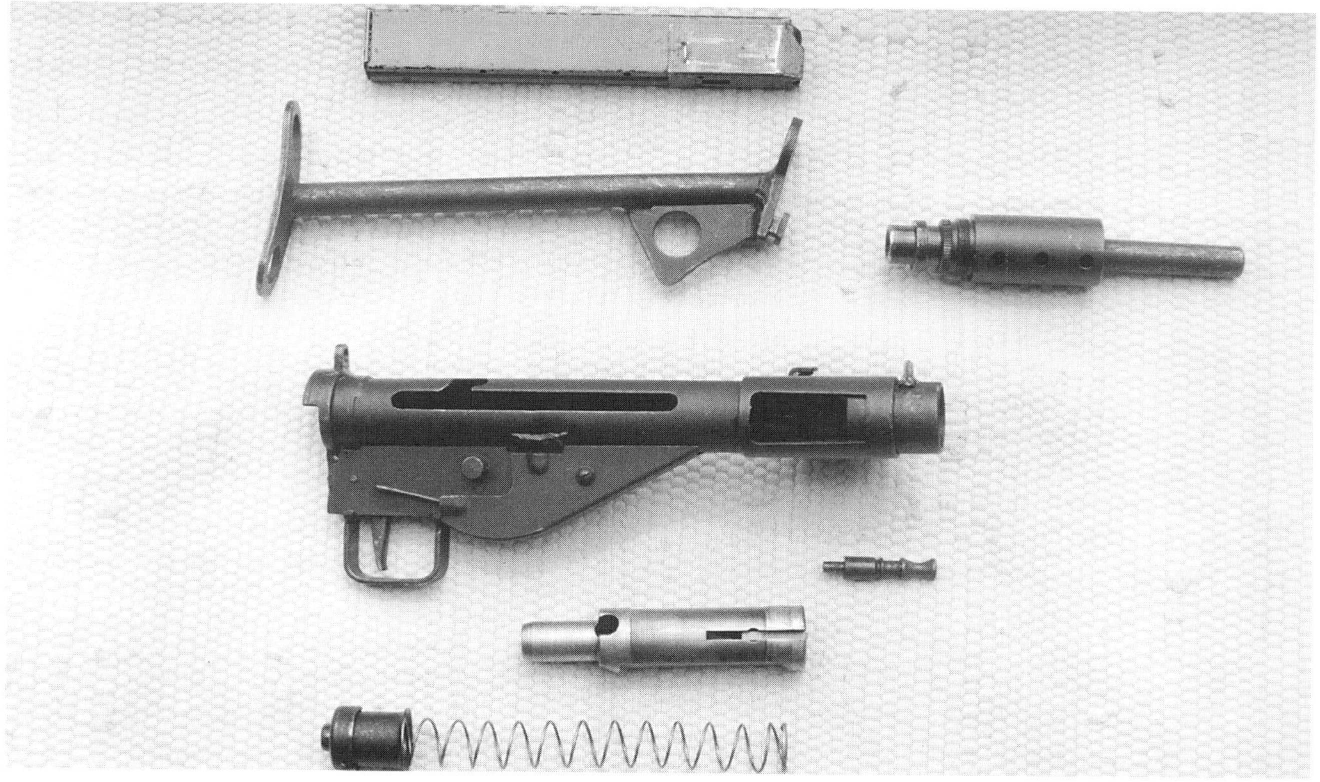

Sten MK II disassembled for cleaning.

The forward pistol grip on early Sten MK V 9x19mm SMGs frequently broke and was later removed. The magazine housing is swung down here to act as a dust cover.

The demand for SMGs was high among British forces during the war, and the MK III was developed to make an even cheaper, simpler weapon. It used a pressed-steel tube that is welded together, thereby avoiding the honing problem frequently encountered with the MK II Sten. The honing problem was created because the interior of the Sten tube was not totaly smooth. This, combined with bolts that varied in size due to manufacturing tolerances, often led to get bolt hang-ups. Just such a thing happened to Canadian troops who before going to Dieppe in 1942 turned in their Thompson SMGs for newly issued Stens, which then proceeded to hang up. The MK III looks a little less crude to some eyes but is harder to make at home, hence the MK II remains the preferred home hobbyist SMG.

Later still, in an attempt to upgrade the Sten, the MK IV and V were introduced. Originally available only to elite airborne units, the MK V became the standard postwar British SMG until replaced by the Sterling. The old MK II and III, which had served so well in war, were quickly taken out of service and replaced with the fancier but no better MK V—much like the noncareer soldiers who did so well in war but were not peacetime soldiers.

The MK V had a bayonet lug on the front, some

The portion of the housing that covers the trigger system is missing on this Sten MK V. The safety on the Sten is slow and not especially efficient; it consists of a locking bolt in the slot in the tube. A good jar can cause the bolt to jump out. Interesting enough, the Sten allows semiautomatic fire via the selector switch, which, given the low cyclic rate and the wartime conditions, you would think would be missing from the design.

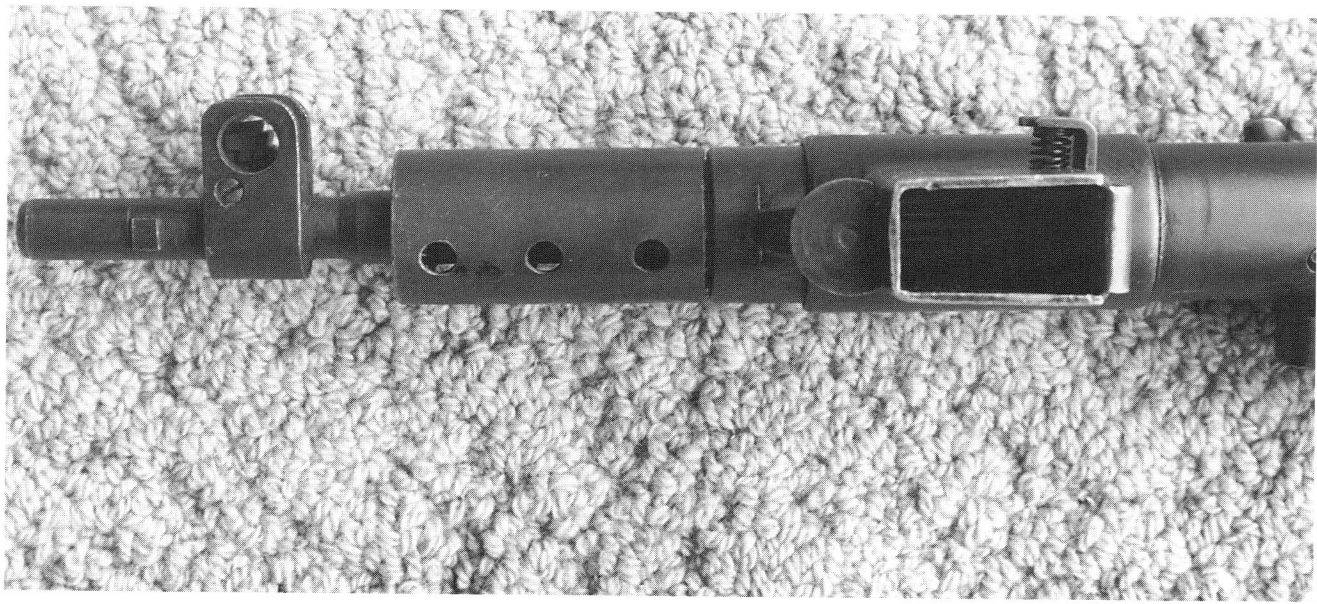

The MK V has a well-protected front sight and will accept a bayonet. The magazine housing turns to the bottom of the tube to prevent dirt from getting into the action when the weapon is not loaded. The shooter's grip should be placed around the magazine housing, not on the magazine itself because it will cause malfunctions.

Top: Sten MK II. Bottom: Sten MK III.

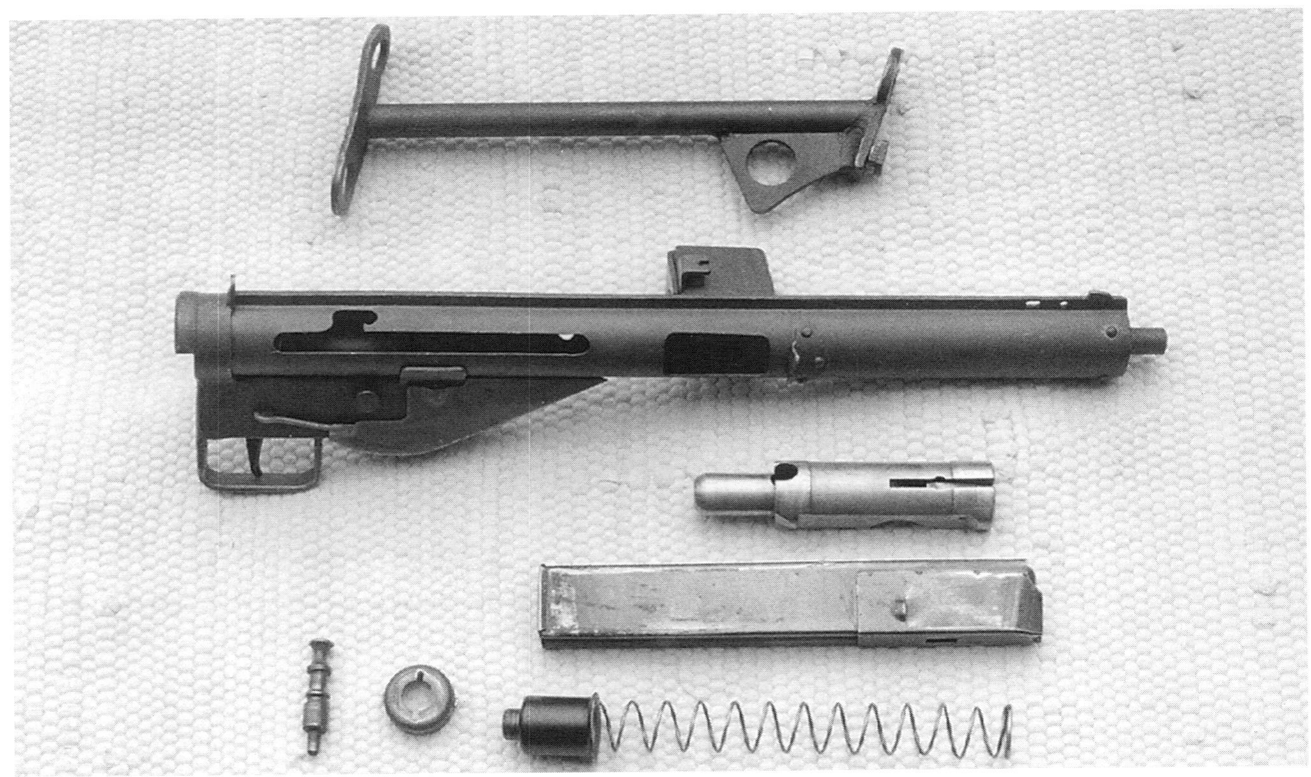

Sten MK III broken down for cleaning.

had pistol grips on the front (until they broke so frequently they were removed), and in the rear a Thompson-like grip was installed as well as a quite solid rifle-style butt. The MK V was no doubt easier to shoot because of the comfortable grip and stock but was not really any better than the MK II, though heavier and more expensive to make. A silenced version, the MK VI, was also made.

The Sten served the Allies well. These are fine SMGs and to this day soldier on in many areas of the world. Even now, more than 50 years after they were made, the parts are frequently made into new guns, perhaps to wrest liberty once again from an oppressor?

STEN MK III

The Sten MK III was, if anything, simpler to make (at least for a factory, if not the home builder using a parts kit) than the earlier MK II. Unlike the MK II, the MK III used a lightweight sheet of steel that was wrapped around a cylinder and then spot-welded on top to hold it together. At the front, the barrel was pinned in place, which, of course, made it impossible to simply unscrew the barrel for either cleaning ease or concealment, but the tube also made a good handguard to hold the weapon. Interestingly enough, putting three fast magazines through the weapon on a mid-90s Midwestern day was enough to get it too hot to hold. The slight sheet metal lip riveted to the side by the ejection port prevented a hand from getting into the port to either be injured or tie up the weapon—a nice design feature.

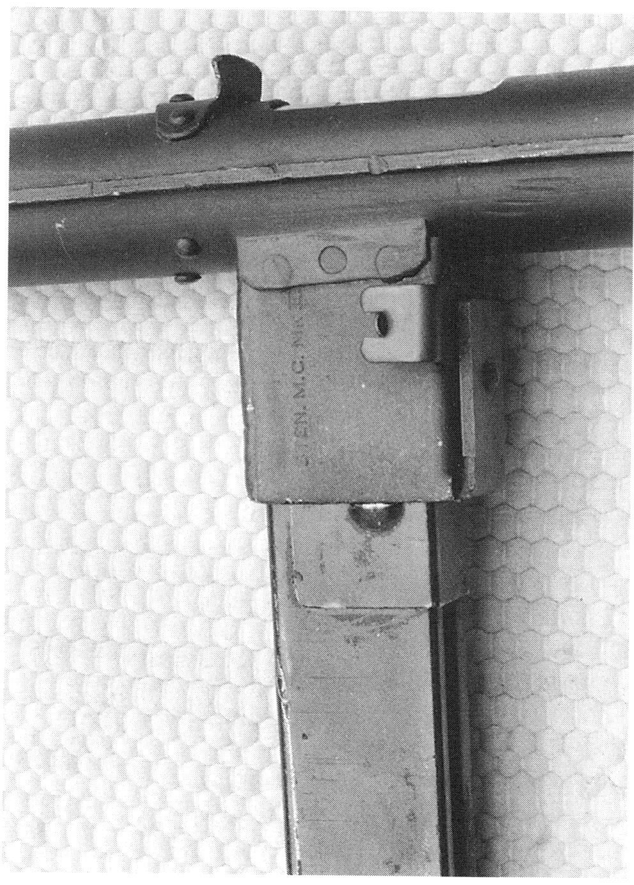

The magazine release and guard on the right of the receiver shown here prevent the shooter's nonfiring hand from slipping into the ejection port, thereby tying up the weapon.

The MK III has a fixed peep rear and a front blade type sight that was too dark and too short to allow quick pickup. It seemed to be sighted in acceptably for short-range work, but I doubt it would have been good for fine work beyond 150 yards. However, since the Sten (whichever model) is really only a 75-yard gun, I suppose it is adequate.

The cyclic rate on the MK III is the same as the MK II and quite controllable. The push-button selector switch is quite handy, although naturally the bolt safety system is slow. If the gun is carried with the bolt closed, you need to push the handle in to avoid inertia slam if the weapon is dropped or you jump over a ditch or down from a truck. However, doing that makes it substantially slower to draw the bolt to the rear to fire the weapon. The magazine release on the MK III is the same as that found on the MK II, but you cannot swing the magazine housing on the MK III around to act as a dust cover as you can with the MK II. Both models will accept the two variations of buttstocks: the T-type and the loop type. Both buttstocks have good and bad points but fortunately lock up tightly and provide a fairly stable platform. Still, the wood stock found on the MK V or MK VI is really better for shooting purposes.

Besides the convenient cyclic rate, one of the best things about all Stens, but especially with the MK III, is that it is quite lightweight for an open-bolt SMG and feels very lively in the hands, unlike many such weapons that are heavy and feel dead. As a consequence, you can quickly get on target, shift point of aim promptly, and, because of the cyclic rate, keep your rounds on target.

This group photo of British soldiers taken in the mid-1950s during the Malayan "Emergency Days" shows a variety of weapons. Left to right: Sterling SMG, Bren LMG, Sterling SMG, and Remington M870 shotgun.

Unfortunately, the safety is slow and awkward to use, and the sights are very marginal for placing rounds at anything beyond shotgun ranges. That said, the Sten remains a benchmark in the field. If a weapon designer cannot make a weapon that is cheaper, works as well, and is as handy, he might as well go on to another project because his weapon will not make it in the marketplace. Not too many SMGs have been developed since 1945 that are substantially better than the MK III.

STERLING L2A1 AND SUPPRESSED STERLING

During the last year of World War II, the Sterling Engineering Company developed a new SMG called the Patchett. This represented quite an improvement over the Sten MK V, not to mention the Lanchester. The Patchett was not adopted, of course, because the war was soon over, and the military had plenty of SMGs by that time. In fact, Sten production was so successful that they were sent into occupied Europe in large volume.

The Sten in all its variations proved to be a very fine SMG for wartime, but it did have some definite limitations. It was not overly long, but it did not offer a folding stock. This meant that it could not be fired until the stock was fixed. This was important because the weapon was frequently broken down to hide under clothing in occupied areas. The weapon had a very rudimentary safety, and, more critically for many, it looked "crude." The Patchett solved all of these problems.

The British did not actually adopt the Patchett (now renamed the Sterling but known as the L2A1 in British military terms), until the Korean War had ended, but by the time of the Mau-Mau crisis in Kenya in 1954, the Sterling was replacing the Sten. In fact, the Sterling Company made a very interesting variation called the "Planter's Gun," which was a semiautomatic-only version of the Sterling SMG. It still fired from an open bolt and

The author found this MK VI "police style" carbine equipped with 8 1/2-inch barrel preferable to the open-bolt model.

The rear sight on this L24A1 is in the "night" position. The theory is that the multiple small holes help the eye gather light when using the peep sight in dark conditions. That is an interesting idea, but I am not certain it works.

was identical in all terms to the Sterling except that it lacked the ability to fire bursts. It is not the same gun as was later sold in the United States as a semiautomatic carbine.

The Sterling uses a heavy-gauge metal tube as a receiver. The forward portion of it is cut with numerous holes to lighten it and allow the barrel to cool more quickly.

The front sight on the Sterling is merely a black sheet-metal post protected by two wings. It would take quite a blow to knock the Sterling sights out of adjustment. The rear sight is a two-position peep unit that is likewise well protected by wings. It is calibrated for 100 and 200 meters. Apparently Patchett realized that SMGs were not being shot at 800 yards, so the tangent sight of the Lanchester was not needed. But on the other hand, the SMGs were used at ranges in excess of 100 yards, so the one-position sight found on the Sten was too limiting.

The bolt handle is angled slightly upward, which allows you to cock the weapon with either hand. Unlike the Sten, the Sterling has an actual safety, which is located quite conveniently in the grip. The grip also is well shaped and angled in a pleasing, comfortable fashion. The safety falls quickly under your right thumb and allows you to choose whether to fire in a semiautomatic mode or in bursts.

The stock folds under the weapon. It takes a little while to get used to the method for collapsing or extending it, but after a half-dozen tries, you will figure out how to do it without pinching your fingers. Once extended, the stock is quite solid, but the steel struts do cut into your cheeks, especially when you fire bursts. The ventilated tube acts as the forearm where the shooter grabs, except on the silenced version that has a wood forearm.

The "star" feature on the Sterling is its magazine. As with the Sten, the magazine is fitted from the left side. There is a large, convenient button to push to release the magazine, and it is much easier to withdraw the Sterling's magazine than it is on the Sten gun. Sterling used the Beretta M38 as its model and adopted its double-column magazine. To increase reliability, it uses rollers and is curved

A little-known (or appreciated) fact about *all* Sterling SMGs is that they use Sten magazines and function perfectly with them. A Sten magazine is being used in this photograph.

because 9x19mm ammunition, which is not straight-walled, works best in magazines that curve. The horizontally mounted magazine, the grooved bolt to allow mud to fall out when its bearer is on the move, and the general care that goes into the Sterling have made it one of the most reliable SMGs in the world.

The cyclic rate is about 550 RPM, which allows good control. Single shots can be fired even when the selector is in the full-auto mode. It is also smooth, which is more critical. The Suomi fires at 900 RPM, and it is smooth. The Sterling is more controllable than many slower-firing SMGs that are not so smooth. Although the Sterling is nice, the question that must always be asked is, does it do anything better than a $10 Sten MK II? Clearly, it is more nicely finished than a Sten of any variation. It looks quite professional, and the finish applied is long wearing. After comparing the Sterling and Sten at length, I must conclude that, except for the far superior magazine, the Sterling really has no better features or performance than the humble Sten. That, of course, is not a poor reflection on the Sterling, but rather an indication of my esteem for the Sten.

Besides the normal Sterling, a suppressed version is also available. The military version does not have a wooden forearm like the civilian sales model. Similar models are found all over the world in elite units because it is a very fine suppressed SMG. It fires from an open bolt, unlike some suppressed designs, but the bolt seems to be cushioned so that bolt noise is minimized.

During the war in the Falklands, British SAS troopers found that they could shoot the suppressed Sterling within 10 meters of an enemy position, and because of the the constant wind the Argentines could not hear the shots being fired. During the Rhodesian war a friend used his suppressed Sterling to kill enemy sentries when as a Selous Scout he was tasked with blowing up a bridge. When he was less than 100 yards away he fired at a soldier and

This suppressed Sterling is a former military model without the wooden handguard.

The author fires the military-version Sterling L24A1. Note the lack of earmuffs, the case exiting the weapon, and the minimal recoil climb.

killed him, and yet the other soldiers on the bridge did not even realize a shot had been fired.

Testing suppressors is always difficult without a lot of fancy equipment, and even then you end up with figures that do not mean much to anyone. When I tested the suppressed Sterling, I found that it rated slightly higher in noise than clicking an acoustical tile staple gun, something most of us are familiar with since we all use them to put up targets. I was easily able to shoot it indoors on a small range without any earmuffs and with no harm to my ears. Enough said!

Israel

UZI

One of the most familiar of the post-World War II SMGs is the Uzi. Some people claim that the Uzi was the first SMG to use a bolt that surrounds the barrel, thus allowing a longer than normal barrel yet still retaining a short overall length, but this is incorrect. That feature appeared on Czech SMGs available in the immediate postwar era. Even though the Uzi was not the first with this design feature, it was the first widely available in the West. The Iron Curtain had closed off Czechoslovakia from the West.

Two members of an Israeli commando unit armed with Uzis prepare a demolition charge.

Faced with hostile neighbors and familiar with 9x19mm SMGs, the Israelis developed the Uzi. Original Uzi SMGs used a detachable wood stock, which was very handy. Soon the demand for a shorter weapon led to the introduction of a folding stock, which collapses into a nice, small package. It is both easy to collapse and extend, but because it is made of metal, it is not as convenient as the wood stock for shooting purposes. The metal struts hit the cheek, and even with the low recoil of a 9x19mm cartridge, a long repeated burst tends to leave the cheek tender.

The rear of the stock has a fixed swivel on it, and the front has a moving swivel. This allows you to carry the weapon in a variety of positions, but as with most such swivels, it should be taped to avoid its striking the weapon's metal surface, resulting in a clearly identifiable noise at night.

The bolt handle is large and easy to grasp, even with cold, slippery hands. The Uzi uses a ratchet system that, coupled with a grip safety, avoids slam-firing if the bolt slips out of your hand or the weapon is dropped.

The front sight is a cylindrical post that is adjustable for elevation. It is well protected by wings on either side. The rear sight is a peep and is likewise protected. The weapon sights can be adjusted to match the shooter, always a nice feature. No night sights are provided, which is odd since the Israelis were always big on operating at night. Aftermarket front sights that glow in the dark are available.

This Uzi 9mm SMG has a wooden stock and the shorter "Secret Service" length barrel.

This Uzi has a folding stock and the shorter "Secret Service" barrel, which yields the same overall length as a Mini-Uzi while still retaining the low cyclic rate of the standard unit.

The folding stock on the Uzi is somewhat complicated but does offer stability and compactness.

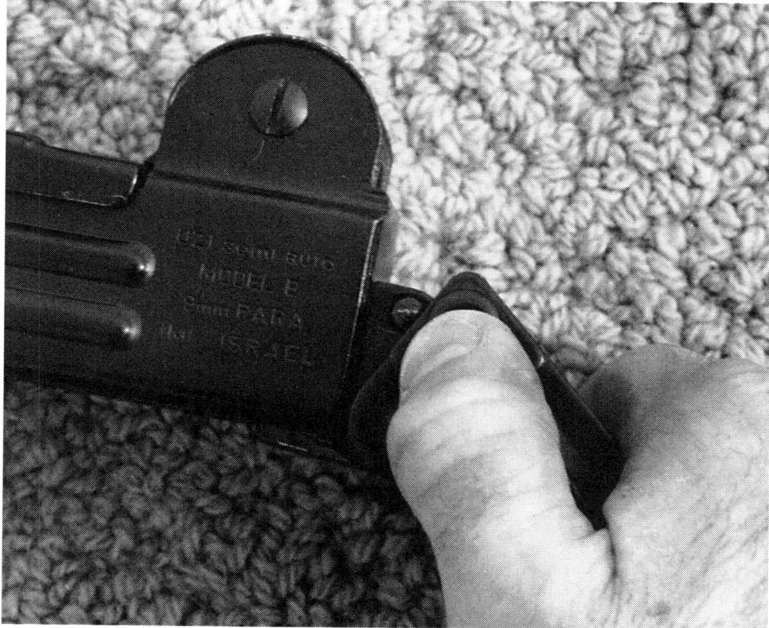

This detail of the collapsing stock on the Uzi shows that it is a carbine modified to an SMG with registered open bolt.

The pistol grip is nicely shaped, although a little thicker than really desirable and just a little too straight. If it were slightly thinner and had a steeper angle, the shooter would not have to cock his hand at such an angle. The grip safety helps the shooter avoid dropping the weapon and having it fire by inertia. Such accidents with open-bolt guns have occurred since the first SMG was developed. Years ago aboard *Air Force One*, a Secret Service agent was putting a loaded Uzi away in a rack, and it slipped out of his hands. The grip safety had been taped in the off position, and when he dropped the Uzi, it slam-fired and struck a glancing blow off another agent's skull! *Do not tape your grip safety*. Because of the grip's shape and angle, it is quite easy to not fully depress the safety, in which case a pull of the trigger results in a click, not a bang. Incorporating a better angle to the grip would help alleviate this problem. The magazine release is located on the left side of the grip and is fairly easy to release when loading if you are shooting from the right shoulder. It is not as fast to use left-handed, but it is still quite good. The pistol grip also contains the safety selector level. Once it is broken in properly, you can flip the weapon from safe to fire easily and rapidly. Spend a little time breaking a new Uzi in by firing a few thousand rounds through it.

The trigger guard often is a little sharp on the edges, but a few quick strokes with a file will solve that problem. The front grip on the Uzi is comfortable. Made of high-impact plastic, it will keep you from burning your fingers, and it seems very strong. I have never seen one broken, as is common with M16A1 handguards.

The barrel on a standard Uzi is 10 1/4 inches long, which allows you to get the maximum possible velocity from the cartridge and helps keep muzzle blast down. The Mini-Uzi uses a shorter barrel to reduce overall length, and the Micro-Uzi is even shorter.

The barrel on the Uzi can be easily removed for cleaning by unscrewing the barrel nut. This makes cleaning a breeze, always nice if you shoot as much corrosive ammunition as I do. The rest of the Uzi also disassembles for easy cleaning. The parts are big and sturdy, resulting in a very rugged weapon.

The author fired these rounds at a 50-foot target with an Uzi SMG equipped with the Secret-Service length barrel.

At the Secret Service school, Uzi SMGs used in training are known to take more than 250,000 rounds through them without breaking down.

The cyclic rate of the Uzi is typically reported at between 550 and 650 RPM, depending on the ammunition used. The Mini-Uzi has a higher cyclic rate. A better solution in my judgment is to chop the barrel to 8 3/4 inches like the Secret Service does on its Uzi SMGs. Then you get a weapon the same overall length as the Mini-Uzi, yet you still retain the lower, more easily controllable cyclic rate of the standard model.

I think the Uzi makes a dandy carbine within its cartridge limitation, especially with the wood stock. You can fire on semiautomatic or full auto effectively because it uses advanced primer ignition rather than simply blowback. This means the cartridge actually has fired before the bolt slams home, jarring your aim otherwise. I never had any problems hitting chest-sized targets at 200 yards with my Uzi in semiautomatic. Although I like the Star Z-70 better than the Uzi because of its tougher finish, faster safety, and pistol grip angle, you can never go far wrong by selecting an Uzi.

MICRO-UZI

Uzi SMGs are now like Goldilocks' bears in the children's story—they come in three different sizes: the standard model, with fixed wood or folding stock; the Mini-Uzi; and now the smaller Micro-Uzi. Obviously, this last model was designed to compete with such things as the MAC 11 .380 SMG and the Czech M61, as well as Yugoslav versions of the same weapons. Most other micro-SMGs (for lack of a better word) come in .380 (9x18mm) or 7.65mm caliber, hence from the start, the Micro-Uzi has an advantage over them. Being a full 9x19mm weapon, it has greater power and avoids the complication of having another caliber in the inventory. Additionally, if you already have Uzi SMGs, you may use the existing magazines—which is a nice feature.

The main problem with all of these very small SMGs is that the high cyclic rate makes them very difficult to handle. Whereas the standard Uzi SMG will run at about 550 RPM (at which a trained shooter can fire single shots easily), the Micro-Uzi with the same ammunition runs about 1,800 RPM. In a course I recently ran that involved training officers from the British SAS and former members of the Rhodesian Selous Scouts, I found that it took quite a bit of practice to get bursts down to three shots with the Micro-Uzi. In fact, I alone was able to get off single shots, and I could not do it all the time. I usually got two or three shots, but if my attention wandered at all, I was up to five shots, as were most of the people in the course. If we were getting such results on a course, you can figure that we would be getting twice that number in the field. Hardly sufficient!

The Micro-Uzi comes in two different models: open bolt and closed bolt. The open-bolt model was originally supposed to have a heavy bolt available for it to slow the weapon, but I have never seen one and assume that it was only a prototype item. Both the closed-bolt and open-bolt models fire at the

Top: Micro-Uzi.
Bottom: Standard Uzi fitted with "Secret Service" length barrel.

As collapsing stocks go, the one on the Micro-Uzi is better than most.

same rate, but, naturally, the first shot fired from the closed-bolt version is most likely to hit the target because the jarring of the open bolt is avoided.

However, in my judgment, the issue is somewhat moot if the Micro-Uzi is used correctly as a short semiautomatic weapon. Put the selector on semiautomatic and fire rapidly and you get better results than in the burst-fire mode. In an actual test I conducted at 5 yards with 3-shot bursts, the first round hit point of impact, the second about 4 inches higher and 2 inches to the left, and the third about 3 inches higher and 1 inch farther left. By starting at the belly-button area, however, I ensured that all were on target. At 1,800 RPM (30 per second) all rounds went out in one roar, and I was unable to distinguish individual reports. With a 5-shot burst, the results were similar in that they all were on target, but the last round was only 2 inches below the top of the shoulder, so clearly a longer burst (as might well occur in a real-world field experience) would have resulted in the remainder of the burst being off target. With a 5-shot burst, I could distinguish individual reports, interestingly enough. Trained ears?

When I fired the same course on semiautomatic as fast as I could so the rate of fire was running about 300 RPM, I put all three shots into a 2-inch circle and repeated the results with five shots. Although some may argue that the impact of 30 rounds hitting per second is greater than five rounds hitting per second, or that spreading the rounds around the target means more area of the body damaged and thus greater stopping effect, I do not really believe such arguments are anything other than feeble attempts to justify excessive dispersion.

As a small, easily controllable semiautomatic carbine, however, the Micro-Uzi shines. It is short in overall length; is heavy enough to result in minimum recoil, thereby allowing rapid second and subsequent shots; offers a high capacity; and, due to the collapsing shoulder stock, provides a very firm shooting platform. It is only slightly larger than a Colt Government Model, yet once in hand is easily a better offensive weapon. I found that it fit perfectly

The sights on the Micro-Uzi are excellent, although peep sights would be even better, in the author's opinion. Because the Micro-Uzi was originally designed as a pistol rather than an SMG, it has open sights.

into the small locking box I have in my vehicle that is set up for large-frame self-loaders. With my Micro-Uzi in it, I believe I have a far superior weapon to a standard semiautomatic pistol should I need a firearm, but it is still small enough to be contained in the same box. I could not put my standard Uzi in a box between my seats, but I can with my Micro-Uzi.

As with the standard Uzi, the controls fall easily to hand. The selector can be pushed off with the right shooting hand fairly readily, especially if broken in carefully. For a left-handed shooter, it is not so easy. The magazine release is handy and, of course, the "hands-find-hands" theory behind the location of the magazine on the Uzi is evident.

As with the standard Uzi, the grip is somewhat wide and broad, because of the double-column magazine, so people with small hands may have problems. It is somewhat a stretch with my size 9s. The Micro-Uzi uses the grip safety system of the standard model and has proven to be a problem in some situations when the shooter fails to depress it properly. As the Secret Service found out, the grip safety should not be taped off because if the weapon is dropped it prevents the bolt from coming back to produce a slam-fire. However, that is really only a problem with open-bolt firearms. A slam-fire cannot occur on closed-bolt weapons, so permanently disabling the grip safety might make sense. As an attorney, I realize that many people recommend that no safety system ever be disabled because of civil liability concerns, and I also believe than a person can train himself (or herself) to depress the safety properly. But if a problem persists, I think I would rather face a lawsuit than an attacker if I have to worry about the possibility of a malfunctioning weapon. Because of the straight angle of the Uzi grip, this grip safety sometimes presents a problem, especially with hasty presentations.

The magazine release is located exactly as on the standard Uzi and is of good size, so magazine withdrawal is fast. I suggest downloading magazines by one round because the Micro-Uzi fires from a closed bolt. A completely loaded magazine is difficult to insert because the top cartridge is pushing against the bottom of the bolt and very little space remains in the magazine. Removing one round makes insertion much easier.

I found the Micro-Uzi stock much easier to deploy than the one on the standard Uzi. It is the same stock used on the Mini-Uzi, so it is obviously a positive development based on user feedback. To deploy the stock, merely pull it back by the buttplate; it locks firmly into place. To collapse, firmly strike the buttplate with your open hand, and it will jump out of the locking position; then close it the rest of the way. There are no buttons or levers to push and no fingers to catch in the action. The stock has a single strut and is rounded, so it actually feels better than the standard collapsing stock. Of course, no collapsing stock is as good as a wood stock for shooting, but for the limited shooting you will probably do with a Micro-Uzi and the light recoil of the 9x19mm cartridge, it is more than sufficient.

Unlike the standard or Mini-Uzi, the Micro-Uzi uses open sights rather than peep sights. This is probably because the Micro-Uzi was descended

Note the aggressive stance taken by the author as he fires the Micro-Uzi at clay bird targets thrown from the rear.

from a pistol rather than an SMG. Fortunately, the sights are readily adjustable, offer a nice white dot on the front and back, and are more than adequate to the task if you accept that this is a 75- to 100-meter weapon, unlike the standard model that is a 250-meter weapon. Frankly, I would prefer a good peep coupled with the front sight fitted, which—with its white dot and square, flat-top appearance—is better than the cylindrical front sight fitted to standard Uzi SMGs. But I can accept the rear open sight. I did find, however, that you had to be careful not to confuse the cocking handle with the rear sight because the cocking handle projects upward much more than the rear sight. Practice is the only solution there, I believe, although perhaps painting the sight wings a more obvious color might help avoid confusion.

All in all, I was rather taken with the Micro-Uzi. When you first encounter it, you may think the weapon has no practical use since it fires so rapidly that control is a problem, and it is too heavy and big to be worn on the belt. Yet the Micro-Uzi fills a niche; it allows you to carry a powerful, easily controlled, semiautomatic carbine, yet it is little bigger than a conventional pistol. For a car gun or briefcase weapon, the Micro-Uzi has a lot to recommend it. It should not be confused with a typical SMG as used in the military context or the machine pistol carried by the entry man on a raid team because it is not suitable for either of those tasks. But in its own special sphere, it is superior to the MAC 11, VZ 61, and PM 63, which are its competitors.

GALIL SAR

The differences between the SAR (short automatic rifle) version of the Galil and the standard model are its fiberglass handguard, its 13 1/2-inch barrel, and its flash hider. One of the drawbacks of the standard Galil is that it feels heavy as a result of its fully machined receiver (as opposed to a stamped receiver) and the small hole in the barrel. The shorter 13 1/2-inch barrel shifts the point of balance rearward to an area closer to between the hands and makes for a much more lively weapon. As a consequence, presentation is improved. The Galil SAR, of course, has the same sights and safety system as the standard version. Although representing a substantial improvement over the safety fitted to an AK-47 (from which the Galil is derived), it is not as good as the safety used on the semiautomatic variant of the Galil. On selective-fire weapons, you push forward to put the safety on and pull it to the rear to flip it first to full auto and then fully to the rear for semiautomatic. That system is awkward, backward, and slow.

Although the Galil SAR has only a 13 1/2-inch barrel, I did not notice much in the way of muzzle flash when shooting M193 ammunition. This was a distinct improvement over the situation with the 8-inch barrel found on an H&K 53 SMG in the same chambering. Still, when using the SAR at night you should anticipate a much greater muzzle flash than that with an 18-inch rifle. The handguards are much nicer to handle on the SAR variant than the boxy

The Galil SAR 5.56x45mm SMG.

Firing the Galil SAR in a 3-shot burst at an 8 x 24-inch plate, the author only hit on the first shot. The other rounds were off the plate. Firing in fast semiautomatic, his results were better.

wooden forearm found on standard infantry rifles. The Galil SAR also lacks the bipod commonly encountered with the infantry rifle. This should be viewed as an improvement, however, because such bipods have little legitimate use and merely rattle, add weight, and encourage prone shooting.

The SAR was fitted with the standard folding stock of the Galil, which is sturdy and quickly unfolds, although it is often difficult to collapse. However, unless compactness is critical, I prefer the solid wood stock because it makes a much better firing platform. In fact, in my opinion, a semiautomatic variant with the standard wood stock and 13 1/2-inch barrel would make a dandy little carbine.

Of course, with any automatic weapon the proof is in the shooting. How will it actually work on the range? Although the cyclic rate was fast, I could get off single shots with the SAR set on full auto without difficulty. Firing 2-shot bursts at 25 yards, I found that my first shot would hit the target, but the next shot would be over it, although windage was identical. Later when I tested it off-hand at 15 yards on 8 x 24-inch plates using 2- or 3-shot bursts, I discovered that the first shot hit where aimed, some 6 inches below the centrally painted dot, but no subsequent shots hit the target at all. Effectively, this meant that shots two and three were totally wasted or, worse in a police scenario, a hazard to the general population.

Firing fast semiautomatic, I found it no trick at all to fire two or three quick shots and keep them on the target. Obviously, the shots were fired more slowly than if fired on full automatic, but the hits were better. Firepower, however, is about bullets hitting people, not merely noise being made. When you compare this performance of no hits with subsequent shots fired on full auto with the performance of an Owen SMG fired on the same day under identical circumstances where 28 out of 30 rounds in one continuous burst hit the target, you quickly realize that for hand-held, full-automatic fire, the Galil SAR's performance is substantially below that of a pistol-powered SMG.

As a full-automatic firing platform, the Galil SAR does not offer much to recommend it. However, with the shorter barrel, and if you added a solid wood stock and use it as a semiautomatic (with the semi-style safety), you would have a much better weapon than the SAR I tested.

Italy

BERETTA M38/42

The M38/42 was the last in a line of wartime SMGs manufactured by the Beretta company for the Axis forces. Earlier examples of the series (such as the M38) had a longer barrel, an involved barrel jacket, and better machining than the M38/42; the M38/42 had all the features of the earlier models yet was easier to make, something that was critical as wartime supplies became restricted and available labor and machine time evaporated. Even so, the M38/42 would be considered too involved to be made today.

Perhaps the most important thing about any self-loading machine gun is its magazine, and the Beretta M38 series has one of the best magazines ever made to fire 9mm ammunition. Because of the M38's fine magazine, excellent workmanship, and

A German soldier armed with a Beretta M38 SMG covers a soldier filming the action.

The Beretta M42 is an outstanding SMG even now, 50 years after the last Beretta of this series was turned out for the German armies in Italy. Note the good dust cover over the bolt.

good design, reliability is very high. All models are sturdy and use a full-sized wood stock, so they present firm shooting platforms, unlike on some folding-stock models. The safety is located on the left side of the receiver and is rather worthless. Of course, I usually ignore safeties on open-bolt SMGs, so it really makes no difference to me. Still, a more convenient location that would not require the shooter to break his shooting grip, or alternatively his nonshooting grip, to work the safety system would be appreciated.

The M38/42 is selective fire, but unlike most selective-fire weapons it uses two separate triggers rather than a selector switch. By using the dual-trigger system, the shooter can quickly decide what system to use and then rapidly shift between them as tactical needs arise.

Sights are an open "U"-notch rear with an unprotected blade front. When I tested this weapon on a typical SMG skill drill, I found it difficult to get the blade down into the notch fast enough to equal my time on the same course with an H&K MP5. I think if the sight was painted white and the rear notch widened a bit, my eye would pick it up and align it with the notch more rapidly. Given the short range involved, what might be lost in fine alignment would be more than made up in speed.

The Model 42 SMG has a dust cover over the ejection port, which causes the bolt to kick it open upon firing. The shooter can cock his weapon and then close the cover. As the weapon is fired, the bolt will knock the spring-loaded cover open. Whenever a pause in the action merits it, the cover can be closed. Given the wear and tear on equipment and the lack of well-trained, experienced troops, this little trick might be interesting to consider if the M38 Beretta SMG series is unfamiliar to the shooter.

The sling swivels are well positioned to permit a proper carry strap to be installed. The weight and size of the weapon make a nice package. Off-hand or kneeling work is easy to accomplish because the M38/42 is well balanced, resulting in a very handy weapon. The tested M38/42 had an integrally designed muzzle compensator that was part of the barrel. Similar devices were found in barrels of earlier models as well. Because these compensators were part of the design and cut into the barrels at the factory, I was unable to test an SMG without a compensator, but it looks like it might work—although the recoil of a 9x19mm cartridge when fired in a 9- to 10-pound SMG certainly is not much. Its cyclic rate is slow enough that single shots could be easily triggered even if you pull the full-auto trigger.

The weapon is a solid, well-made example and can certainly be used effectively at 200 yards or more, depending on the ammunition and the person shooting. The ability to switch between semiautomatic and full-auto fire by merely shifting your trigger finger without having to worry about hitting some switch or button someplace is a benefit. It may not be up to the level of convenience found in some postwar examples, and I found the safety to be marginal because of its location, but it is an excellent weapon and a memorial to the good

Removing the magazine from the Beretta M42 requires that you depress the small lever hidden in the wood stock. This is quite slow, especially when the shooter is wearing mittens.

The selective-fire system on the Beretta M38/42 features two triggers. The rear trigger allows full-auto fire, while the front trigger is for semiautomatic fire. The safety on this Beretta M42 is in the off position. Note also the two-position flip-style rear sight.

To cock the Beretta PM12, pull the bolt handle to the rear and the handle will then go back into position. The bolt remains to the rear in this open-bolt SMG. Note the well-protected front sight in this photo.

qualities of the designers even now, a half century after the last Beretta M38/42 was turned out for the German armies in Italy.

BERETTA PM12

Beretta came out of World War II with what may well be argued is one of the top SMGs manufactured: the M38 and its variants, the M38/42 and M42. Even after the war, the design was produced for a wide variety of users. Of course, much of the design's merit is attributable to the fine, double-column-feed magazine, but the weapon was also well made of good materials.

Although the weapon continued to be made in the 1950s, it was obvious to the people at Beretta that the day of the fully machined, wood-stocked SMG was over. People wanted more compact weapons, and making them at an affordable price required that they not need much in the way of machining. As a consequence, the PM12 was born.

The PM12 is rather conventional in many ways and represents nothing new in the way of SMG design. The weapon fires from an open bolt and uses the same magazine design as its predecessors. It does use a tube-type receiver, and the bolt is obviously a lot less work to make than the ones on earlier SMGs. Of course, cyclic rate depends on ammunition, but the PM12's seems equal to that of other conventional blow-back, open-bolt SMGs.

The weapon has a number of good design features. First, the barrel can be easily removed for cleaning. Although this is less important in this day of noncorrosive primers, it is still nice to be able to simply run a cleaning rod directly down a barrel and not have to worry about solvents getting into the weapon's action.

Earlier Beretta designs had the cocking handle on the right side, but on the PM12 the bolt handle is located on the left so the nonshooting hand (assuming a right-handed shooter) could draw the bolt to the rear without the shooter's having to break

The rear stock latch on the PM12 is easy to use. Simply push the button to collapse it.

his grip. Many SMG accidents occur when the weapon is used by a moron or is dropped and the bolt comes back far enough to pick up a round and chamber it but not far enough to catch the sear. The PM12 has a grip safety that must be depressed before the bolt will move. This feature also exists on such SMGs as the Uzi, and it is always a good idea on such designs. The safety on the PM12 can be operated rapidly if used by a right-handed shooter. The levers are big enough to be turned rapidly.

The grip panels, both forward and rear, are plastic and thus do not transmit heat or cold. Although the trigger guard is not as big as would be desirable for use with mittens, it is not impossibly small.

The stock folds and collapses readily. Even though there was only mounting on one point, the examples tested seemed sturdy. I am not recommending using the PM12 to butt-stroke someone or dropping it to the ground and allowing it to take the weight of the fall, but for typical tasks it seems sturdy enough.

Sights are fixed and well protected by wings on some models of the PM12. The rear sight is adjustable, a feature I always like, although I concede that a lot of soldiers will play with them, adversely affecting impact. Of course, people who play with their sights are also the type who never use them anyway, so I do not suppose any real loss is incurred. For those who know how adjustable sights work and who appreciate them, better results are often possible.

The finish on the PM12 is quite good, although on many of the police SMGs that I have seen it seems a lot brighter than expected for a military weapon. Some models appear to have a painted finish, whereas the models I have observed being carried by Italian police officers invariably had a conventional blue finish. Even though they often were worn from the handling they received, the finish seemed to hold up on parts that were not subject to constant rubbing. Interestingly enough, in Rome the police always seemed to carry their Berettas with the stock extended, thereby forfeiting the benefit of a folding-stock SMG while suffering the drawbacks of using a strut-type stock. The PM12 does have a fixed wood stock available, much like that seen on the Uzi SMG, and it certainly produces a more solid, easier-to-use shooting platform on either weapon.

Of course, the major benefit of the PM12 comes from its short overall length. Because it uses a telescoping bolt/barrel system, the barrel can be quite long in comparison with the overall length of the weapon, yet the bolt weight can be high to keep the cyclic rate down. Additionally, it distributes some of the weight out beyond the firing chamber to further reduce muzzle rise. To have a similar-sized barrel/bolt combination absent this telescopic bolt system, a much longer weapon would be needed. Because the goal of postwar SMG designs is to have a weapon that is shorter and lighter than a conventional rifle, approaches a conventional handgun, and still retains the firing accuracy of various prewar designs, this telescoping bolt design offers a number of solutions while not causing any new problems.

The PM12 with stock extended.

The PM12 Beretta SMG is a conventional postwar weapon in the same league as the Uzi and Sterling. It represents a handier design than the French MAT49 and is easier to use than the Ingram M10. Whether the PM12 does anything that its predecessors didn't is unclear, but it certainly can do anything its predecessors did—and is lighter to boot.

BERETTA M12(S) 9x19mm

The M12(S) SMG is a variation of the standard M12 and basically differs only in the safety/selector system. Unlike the push-through system on the M12, the flipper/lever system on the M12(S) is more conventional. The selector/safety system is easy to use and quick for a right-handed shooter but is slower for a left-handed shooter. Additionally, it would be more difficult to use with cold or wet hands. I prefer the push-button mechanism found on the earlier model. It is one of those things that seems odd and slow until you use it, and then you discover how really fast and convenient such push-through safety/selector systems really are in operation.

However, despite this, the M12(S) has all the other good qualities of a Beretta SMG. The quality of the finish and manufacture is obviously high on this well-made weapon. The front and rear sights are both well protected by sturdy ears that also allow a lot of light to fall on them, unlike the hooded sights on the H&K series. The rear is a two-position peep to adjust for distance. Although the rear blurs upon firing full auto, it does offer a good sight picture to get started, and I much prefer peep rear sights on SMGs to open-notch sights. The front sight is a square-faced blade and needs to be painted white or some contrasting color to allow rapid pickup; the black sight is slow to pick up except in especially bright light.

The M12 and M12(S) are typical open-bolt designs. They do use a telescopic bolt system, however, which pemits the barrel of the weapon to be longer than otherwise would be the case with the same overall length. Additionally, the bolt overhangs the barrel at firing, which both protects the shooter

The PM12 is a conventional SMG with a folding stock.

When gripping the Beretta PM12, care must be taken to depress the grip safety fully.

in the event of a cartridge mishap and puts weight forward at firing, thereby keeping recoil down somewhat. I did not have a Pact timer with me the day I shot the M12(S), but I did have my Star Z-70 SMG. Tests with my Star Z-70 showed it to run about 525 RPM, and the Beretta was a little faster. I would estimate 550 RPM, but, of course, this will vary with individual guns, the conditions of the weapon, and ammunition. However, it is clear that the Beretta M12(S) is not a fast firer. It was quite controllable in my firing tests. No doubt the forward hand grip of the design helped to control it a great deal; I find weapons with vertical foregrips typically easier to control than ones with horizontal grips. Of course, such vertical grips tend to break off when you go prone rapidly and do result in a higher prone firing position, which is the reason they are frequently omitted from designs.

The rear grip contains a grip safety on the front that must be fully depressed before the weapon can be cocked or fired. The shooter must remember to depress it firmly with the finger or the weapon will be inoperable. Whether to choose a rear-mounted grip safety, as on the Uzi, or a forward-mounted one, as on the Beretta, is a matter of taste. Both can cause malfunctions if not firmly depressed, so care must be taken to do so. They do prevent SMGs from racking a round and firing it if dropped, so they do have a place, I suppose. I note, however, that the Star Z-70 avoids slam-firing, and it seems not to be a problem if the shooters are not terribly fumble-fingered and simply remember to put the safety on when jumping about.

The magazine release is a flipper style, which is easily used by either hand and thus preferable to button types for left-handed shooters. Additionally, the flipper style seems to hold the magazines in position more firmly. The magazine holes, when used with button types, can wear over time, allowing the magazine to drop down and cause malfunctions. With flipper release types, this wear problem is not as critical. Of course, this is not really a serious problem except with range guns subject to many times the normal wear.

The M12 and M12(S) typically are deployed with folding stocks, although a wooden stock is available and better for shooting, just as it is on most other folding-stock SMGs. Still the Beretta stock is easily released once the technique is mastered and quite firm, at least in new weapons. As the stock gets older, I could see wobbling developing, because it is locked at only one point. The buttplate also folds, and it must be released by a button to open it. Because of the dark finish and bare metal, the stock strut gets hot in the summer and can burn the face. In winter, it is cold and can similarly burn the face. I know that in late spring the weapons in Rome got hot to the touch even though they were being merely carried over the shoulder by the police officers. In a desert environment or in the Arctic, this defect may make it impossible to use the weapon comfortably. If I owned one of these weapons, I'd wrap the stock strut in rubberized tape, but the factory could solve the problem more efficiently by encasing the tube in plastic.

Even with the defects noted, the Beretta M12 and M12(S) are both nice designs overall. I find them to be more comfortable to use than the Uzi SMGs. But after testing, evaluation, and reflection on the matter, I must say that I prefer the Star Z-63 because of its safety/selector location, its lighter weight, its sturdier stock, and the fact that it has no forward grip, which is likely to break when the shooter goes prone. Still, the Beretta M12/M12(S) is a fine weapon, and no one would do poorly using it.

BERETTA M93

The Beretta M93 machine pistol is built along traditional pistol lines, unlike some of the current breed, such as the H&K VP70 and the Glock. The M93 includes an interesting collapsing, detachable metal strut stock and 3-shot burst device. When you first look at an M93, you think it is merely a wood-gripped M92 modified to fire 3-shot bursts. However, that is not the case—the M93 is substantially different.

First, the M93 is a single-action pistol. The trigger guard is larger than is common for single-action pistols, but that is because of the need to put the thumb through it when using the front-mounted foregrip. Second, the safety is a side-mounted unit, not on the slide. Therefore, the safety is much like that found on the M1911 Colt. The weapon does not fire burst, but rather semiautomatic or 3-shot bursts—because of the design, however, a button must be pushed before the selector can be depressed

The foregrip on this Beretta 93R is lowered, and the selector is in the 3-shot-burst position.

to the 3-shot-burst mode. This is no doubt to prevent flipping the safety off and firing bursts when only single shots are actually desired.

The sights are similar to those found on the M92 and are quick to pick up. The tested example did not have a tritium element, but I do not see any reason why it could not be so equipped. The stock is a collapsing, single, metal strut unit. When affixed, it is rigid and the stock nicely shaped to hit the shoulder, but the weapon cannot be carried with the stock affixed. Further, unlike most machine pistols with stocks (such as the Mauser, Stechkin, or Star), the M92 pistol cannot be carried in the stock. Thus the shooter needs two separate containers for the stock and pistol. I recently saw a custom holster to carry the M93 set up exactly in that fashion, but I still find it rather awkward. Fortunately, the Beretta M93 can be used in burst fire without a stock, unlike the H&K VP70, whose stock is an integral part of the weapon system.

The barrel on the M93 is longer than that found on the M92 and is ported. The slots are designed to hold the weapon down, but they actually do nothing more than increase noise and muzzle flash. I think the M93 would be better if a standard M92 barrel was fitted.

An interesting element of the M93 is the foregrip, which is attached to the weapon's trigger guard. When folded down it locks against the trigger guard. By putting his hand on it and pressing down, the shooter pulls down on the foregrip, resulting in greater control over the weapon. Although the foregrip is clever, it makes the weapon much bulkier for carrying concealed. The same thing (or nearly so) could be established by making the trigger guard larger and stronger to permit the thumb to be hooked through it and then having the shooter pull down with his nonshooting hand in a fist with the thumbs surrounding the trigger guard.

Probably the worst aspect of the M93 is not really noted until it is picked up. All double-column 9mm pistols (except the Browning BDM and Glock) are fat because of their double-column magazine. The M93 Beretta is fatter than even the M92, which

Label from the box that contained a Beretta M93R machine pistol.

is far from slender. This excessive size results from all of the M92-type problems, as well as a set of wood grips that are thicker than plastic and the ratchet system found on the selector that gives the weapon its 3-shot-burst capacity. This makes the M93 grip bulky and uncomfortable. It rather feels like a thick, square 2 x 4 in your hand, thereby reducing your ability to use the weapon instinctively. The 3-shot-burst system should be removed, and thin, strong fiberglass or other materials used for the grips. If that had been done, at least the weapon would feel no worse than an M92.

Many people condemn machine pistols as worthless because they find them difficult to control. Generally, this is more an admission of the shooter's failure to train with the weapon and use the proper techniques than it is a failure of the weapon. Frequently, manufacturers try to cure the problem technologically by changing the rate of fire. They lower it through rate reduction, such as found on the Spanish Royal, or increases, as on the VP70, so that all rounds are fired and out of the weapon before the recoil starts to affect the spread. Neither approach provides the proper solution; for that, you need training. With proper training, it is possible to keep all the shots fired on a man-target at 5 yards. Naturally, the proper stance must be used, and the shooter must be practiced enough to get used to the recoil of the weapon. However, once mastered, the machine pistol becomes the single most deadly close-range weapon available to the soldier, police officer, or civilian seeking a defensive weapon. Its limitations must be accepted—it is not a machine gun or even an SMG. But in its unique role as a

The author holds an M93 Beretta machine pistol with its stock affixed.

close-range, defensive/ offensive weapon, nothing even comes close.

The M93 Beretta may not be the best example of the breed because of the stock and foregrip problems detailed earlier and the fact that the grip is far too fat to be comfortable, but it is reliable and incorporates sound materials and design. I would throw away the foregrip and stock, shorten the barrel to standard M92 length, and slenderize the grips if I carried the M93 on my hip.

BENELLI SUPER 90

In testing weapons for my books over a long period now, I have discovered that the weapons produced by various countries often reflect peculiar national attributes. Sometimes these tendencies result in very good weapons with some eccentricities (such as French weapons that are always accurate and svelte but unfortunately chambered for odd cartridges). Other times you get lesser weapons (such as the Japanese Type 26 revolver) that combine a number of features that serve to illustrate that the country involved has very little in the way of practical handgunning experience. Too often this amalgam of national traits results in a weapon with a lot of poor features. The Benelli Super 90 is an example of this type.

A look at the fine over/under and double shotguns produced in Italy quickly establishes that the Italians know how to build well-balanced, lively shotguns. Germans often build very good autoloading weapons. A person might logically conclude, therefore, that the Benelli autoloading shotgun, marketed through Heckler & Koch at the time the test example was imported, would be a good piece of equipment. Such a conclusion would be wrong.

The Super 90 does cycle quickly, but any autoloading shotgun will fire faster than a shooter can pull it down out of recoil to fire a second aimed

The author firing the Benelli Super 90 12-gauge shotgun with tactical 12-gauge buckshot loads. The weapon has a quick response time because of its fast cycling, light recoil, and tactical loads. In this photo, the case has just cleared the weapon and already is on the target ready for the next shot.

Loading the Benelli Super 90 is more complex than on a typical autoloader. This and the size of the cocking handle are real drawbacks. The shooter loads the ammunition tube and then pushes the button to return the round to the gate, as seen here.

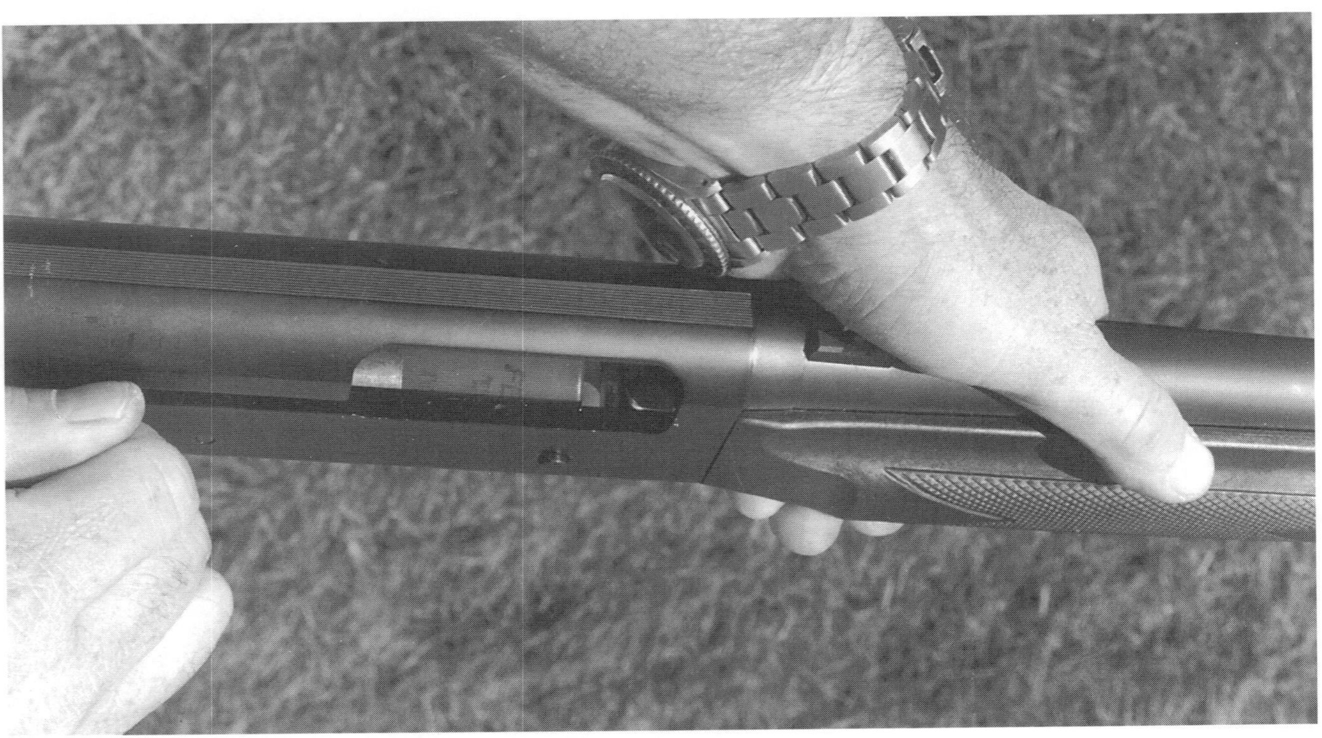

After returning the round to the safe, then you may chamber the round by pulling back on the cocking handle. This process is far too complex, in the author's judgment.

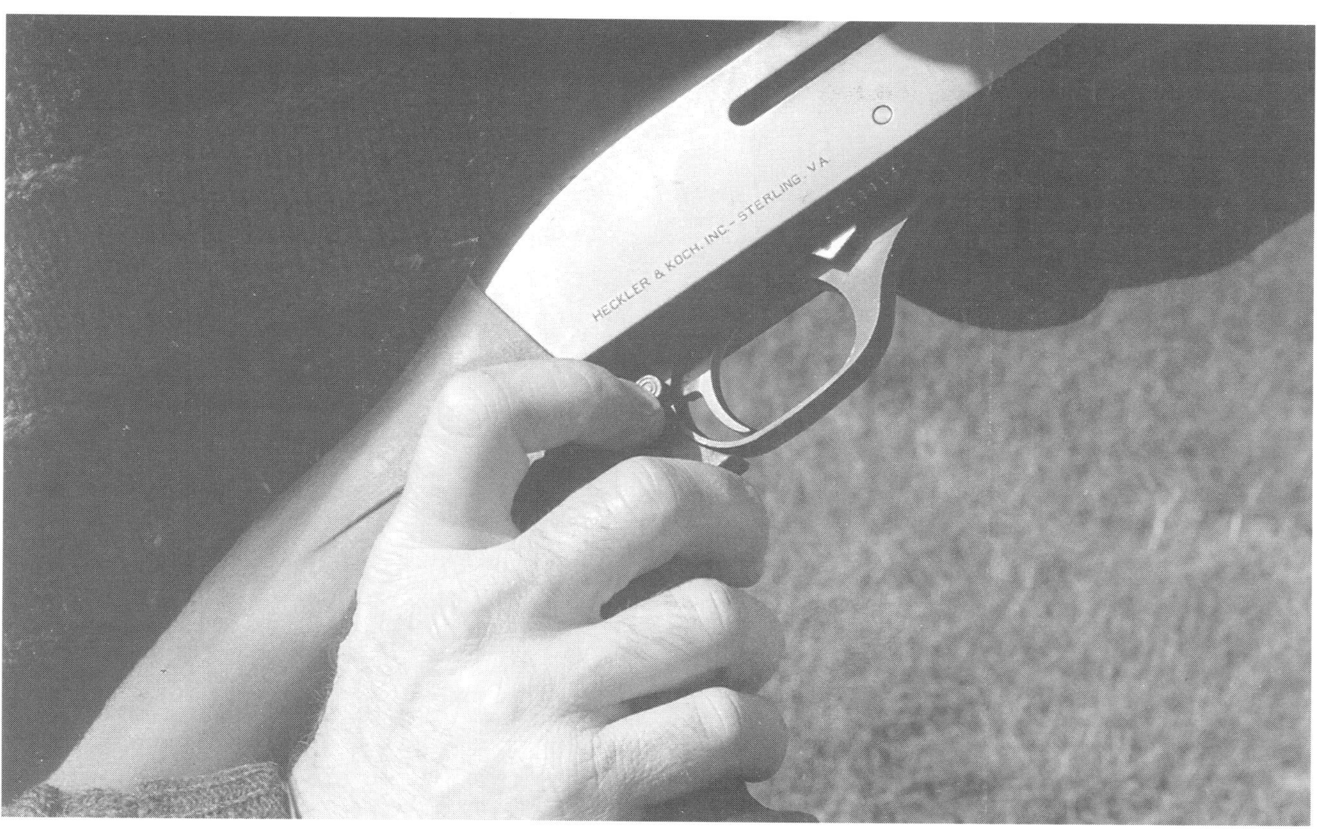

The author is disconnecting the safety on the Benelli Super 90 autoloading shotgun.

shot. Recoil is also mild when contrasted with that on older autoloading designs. But once we get past these two attributes, it is downhill from there.

The trigger guard on this "shotgun designed to be a combat weapon" is no bigger than that found on a typical trap gun. Why designers of a combat shotgun cannot seem to realize that the trigger guard should be larger to accommodate a heavily gloved (or, better, mittened) hand is beyond me.

The safety button is small and slow to disengage. It is also at the rear of the trigger, which I find slower than a forward trigger location.

The bolt handle is small and weak looking. I have eventually had to kick open every autoloader at some time with my boot, and I do not believe the Benelli's bolt handle is sturdy enough to survive a vigorous kick even from my size-9 boots, much less from bigger guys. Only a great regard for the property of my friend Leroy Thompson prevented me from trying to kick the shotgun open to test its sturdiness.

The weapon uses a magazine tube for spare ammunition, when obviously any purpose-built combat shotgun should be using a box magazine of the readily detachable type.

All of these things would be bad enough, but it gets worse. Showing a love for mechanism over practical use, the designers incorporated a slow, two-step chambering system. To chamber a round, you must put a round in the magazine tube and then pull the bolt back until it locks into position. At this point, the bolt is rearward. Next, you must move your hand to the button located on the receiver, hit it, and allow the bolt to run forward. This is certainly slower than on a Remington autoloader, where you vigorously pull the bolt to the rear and let it run forward under the spring pressure.

The sights are too small on the rear and consist of only a slot in the rear blade, offering no adjustments except by hammering on them. Of course, no elevation adjustment exists at all. The front sight is good-sized but lacks protection wings, which you would logically think a combat shotgun would have.

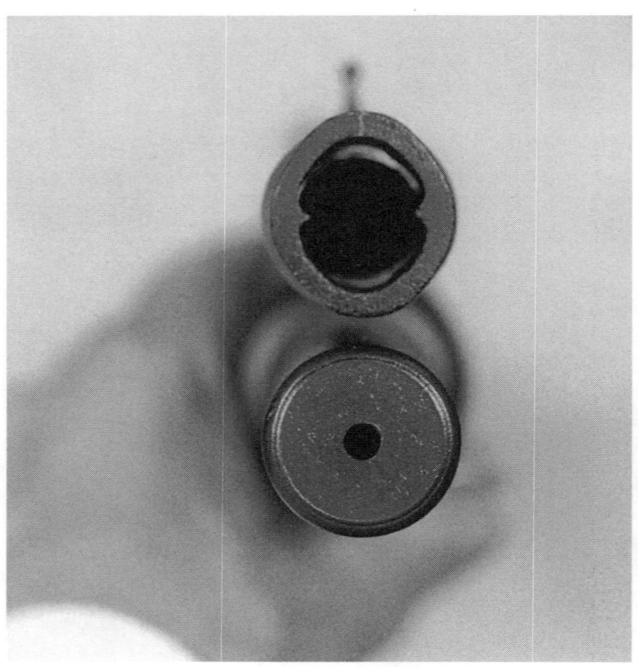

A front view of the muzzle device designed to spread shot on man-shaped targets.

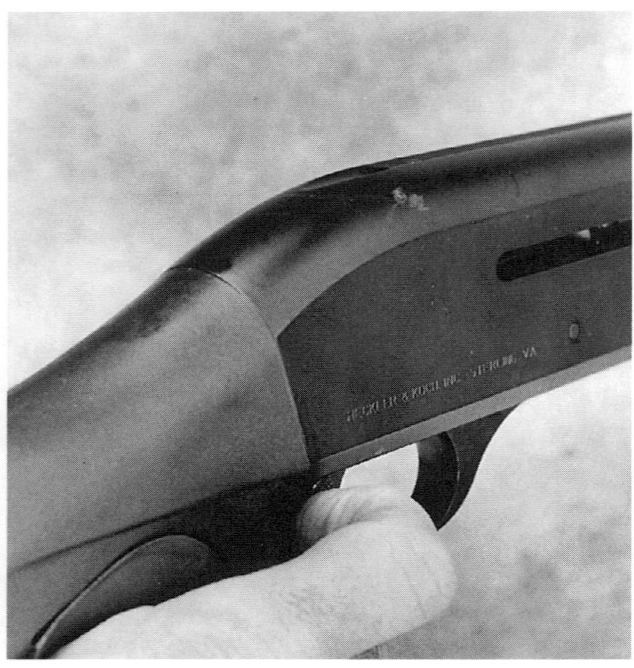

Disengaging the safety on the Benelli Super 90 is awkward and slow because it is located at the rear of the trigger guard rather than at the front.

Trigger pull is rather typical of all autoloading shotguns: full of creep, slack, and overtravel.

Last, for a shotgun marketed for police or military operations, it has a couple of serious shortcomings: it cannot be stripped rapidly, and the finish is available only in matte blue, which is not very rust-resistant. It would be far better to have as an option some of the finishes applied to combat handguns today, as are typically found on Glocks, Berettas, and Smith & Wessons, not to mention H&Ks.

The Super 90 is rather disappointing as a combat shotgun: it merely represents a sporter with a few cosmetic changes to make it look "mean" and perhaps be slightly more useful in nonsporting applications. A person would do much better to get one of the new AK-style combat shotguns if he were looking for a serious combat shotgun.

Japan

TYPE 100 (M1944) 8mm

Many people wonder why the Japanese were not quicker off the mark in developing SMGs since these weapons would seem so useful in jungle warfare. A few points of clarification are needed here.

First, the Japanese did experiment with SMGs; they purchased some German or Swiss pattern M1928 Bergmanns and also likely encountered a variety of patterns in the hands of Chinese forces in the 1930s. Of course, the generally poor performance of the Chinese forces may have caused the Japanese military to conclude that SMGs were not worth developing.

Second, remember that the SMG was not popular even among the Allies until the war was seriously under way. The British Sten did not go into production until 1941; the prewar Thompson shouldered the burden for the Allies until then and even later.

Next, I am not totally convinced that the SMG is, in fact, the ideal jungle weapon. It tends to fire from an open bolt, has limited range, is heavy, and suffers from very limited penetration. Lack of penetration can be a serious drawback when operating in an area with heavy, dense brush and fallen trees.

Last, the Japanese had some excellent LMGs, such as the Type 96 and Type 99. Both of them could provide a serious base of fire and had much greater penetration in the jungle than any SMG.

All of the above points do tend to explain the lack of development of the SMG in Japan, although SMGs were developed and fielded in some

The Type 100 Nambu 8mm SMG suffers because of the caliber of ammunition it was designed for.

The rear sight on the Type 100 offers both a peep and notch for night work but is unprotected from damage and does not allow for adjustment.

The front sight on the Type 100 is also poorly protected from damage.

quantities. One of the most common of uncommon guns is the M1944 Type 100 evaluated here. It is as well made as any Sten, and, although it exhibits a lack of fine finish or polishing, it certainly is as well finished as many European SMGs produced in later years.

The Type 100 has a nice fixed peep sight that is not protected from damage. It would take a serious blow to knock it out of alignment, but if it were to be dropped from shoulder height onto a hard surface (such as a truck bed), the sight could very easily be bent out of proper alignment. Of course, fixed sights rarely fire to the point of impact anyway, and generally they need to be adjusted by the pliers or vice method. Besides the peep, the rear sight has a small notch at the top to allow quick alignment in poor light, I suppose. I would stick with the peep and paint the front sight white if it were my SMG, especially if I were operating in the jungle. The front sight is pyramid shaped, unprotected, and dark; it too needs to be painted white to allow quick pickup in a jungle environment.

The Type 100 has an interesting vector-type compensator on the muzzle. I did not get a chance to fire it without the compensator, and although it looks like it should work, I am not convinced that the 8mm Nambu cartridge has enough muzzle velocity to really make a difference. I suppose it does no harm, however, except to take valuable machine time.

The Type 100 can be taken down quickly, and the barrel can be quickly removed for cleaning. Both features are useful in any military weapon and especially one that is likely to be used in a jungle environment. It certainly is easier to access and clean than a Thompson. The safety, which is located in the trigger guard, is convenient and quick to remove.

Although the Type 100 fires from an open bolt, which limits fine accuracy because of the bolt's jarring, it is a fairly lightweight weapon that is nicely balanced. Of course, the 8mm Nambu caliber is a drawback, but I suppose the Japanese did not want to introduce yet another caliber into supply channels. At that time, the Japanese military already had four rifle cartridges alone!

The Type 100 was a rather interesting development, even though it was already obsolete by the time it appeared. It had some good features that other militaries would have been wise to include in their designs. I do not believe the Japanese lost a lot by not fielding large quantities of SMGs, and thus I do not believe the Japanese were as foolish in this regard as is commonly supposed.

Soviet Union

PPSh-41

This is one of the most common SMGs used during World War II. It is estimated that the Soviets made more than 5 million of them. In fact, the Soviet Union used SMGs much more extensively than any other country. Whole units in the Soviet army were issued SMGs. In many ways, it was an ideal weapon for them because it was cheap to make and easy to maintain for troops who had little experience with firearms. Further, the SMG's lack of fine accuracy was not nearly the drawback that it would seem to be because the Soviet armies weren't well trained in accuracy to begin with. An SMG cannot be used as a sniper rifle: you must close with the enemy to inflict damage on him, and that type of high-volume, short-range weapon fosters an aggressive spirit among troops.

The example I tested, a late-war model, had a good two-position peep rear sight that was well protected by wings. Earlier examples had open sights with tangent leaf sights calibrated to ranges well in excess of what the weapon would ever be used at. By the end of the war, it was obvious that 200 meters was all you needed to worry about as far as sights on an SMG were concerned. The front sight is a good-sized

Soviet troops equipped with PPSh-41 on the move. Photo from the Imperial War Museum.

Soviet soldiers during World War II with the PPSh-41 7.62mm SMG. The shooter in the foreground is holding the drum incorrectly; such a hold induced malfunctions. The shooter to his immediate right is holding the drum correctly.

pin or shaft protected by a sturdy cover.

The safety/selector system is quite handy, being in the trigger guard. A person could flip it off without breaking the shooting grip. I am never totally at ease with safeties on open-bolt SMGs, but certainly putting a safety on as you run forward is not a bad idea. It is easier to flip it off on a PPSh-41 SMG than it is to turn the bolt out of the safety notch, as you must do on an MP40, Sten gun, or similar weapons.

Although a very simple design, the PPSh-41 has a selective-fire capability, which, given its rate of fire, is a very good feature. In this way, the Soviet soldier could use his PPSh-41 as a semiautomatic weapon and reserve full-auto fire for situations in which it would be truly effective.

The magazine release is small and not a simple push-and-dump type, which I prefer, but it is easier and quicker to operate than the magazine release on the Suomi M31 or M37/9 SMG. I imagine it would be troublesome if the shooter were wearing mittens. Similarly, the trigger guard is small for mittened use. It always surprises me that designers do not take this type of cold weather use into consideration—especially when their troops fight in arctic conditions for much of the year.

Drums of 71-round capacity are typically seen with these weapons, but they must be carefully matched to the weapon to ensure reliable feeding. Additionally, the drums will rattle on night patrol. Thirty-five-round magazines also fit the weapon and are my choice for patrolling because they make the weapon more comfortable, less noisy, and lighter. However, if I rode into battle atop a T-34 battle tank, as many Soviet troops did during the war, I would pick the drum simply to give me a longer period of fire between magazine changes. Of course, I would back it up with a belt full of spare magazines.

The cyclic rate of the weapon is fairly fast, so you must use care to avoid excessive bursts. However, because you can keep it on semiautomatic and use it that way for the most part, it is not a major issue. The wood stock and weight give the whole

This is a Chinese version of the PPSh-41.

weapon a nice solid feel, and the fact that the weight is between the hands keeps the balance from feeling heavy or awkward.

One of the most interesting things about 7.62mm Soviet SMGs was the wide variety of ammunition available for them. Beside standard ball, they had AP, tracer, and incendiary rounds loaded for them. I would imagine that a drum full of incendiary rounds laced with a tracer round every three rounds or so would be just the ticket in a PPSh-41 for a night patrol.

One last nice feature of the weapon is its simple maintenance. Merely pulling the cap at the end of the receiver allows you to tip the entire receiver forward. The bolt is easily removed, and the barrel, which is chrome-plated to avoid corrosion, is accessible from the rear for easy cleaning. Because it does not use a gas system, the bore can be wiped out and the weapon put back into action rapidly.

Besides the Soviet Union, other communist countries produced the PPSh-41; the Chinese copies are the most common ones in the United States because of veterans bringing them back from the Korean and Vietnam Wars. Although the can be seen as a symbol of communist expansionism, one should not be blinded to the good qualities of a tool because of its use or misuse by the person who wields it. We must admit the PPSh-41 is really as good as anything made in the United States, Britain, or Germany during the same time period.

PPS-43

The PPS-43 SMG has an interesting story. It was developed in 1942 at the height of the siege of Leningrad (St. Petersburg) by the Germans, when the Soviets had very limited supplies and machinery available. Stories abound of factory prototypes being immediately taken to the front and used to shoot at Germans. That is real field testing in the most critical testing mode possible. After some slight changes, the design was standardized and more than a million were rushed out during the war. The PPS-43 was not as widely used as the PPSh-

The grip on this PPS-43 is correct. Because of the sturdy housing on this SMG, the grip does not touch the actual magazine, which would cause malfunctions. Yet the grip keeps the shooter's hand off the chamber area, which gets hot because of the all-metal construction and high intensity of the 7.62mm cartridge.

41, but countless war photos of soldiers armed with the PPS-43 are still seen. Later, the Chinese made the weapon and gave it away all around the world. Similar weapons with different back stocks were also made in Poland, and these examples are often still encountered in Africa.

Unlike the PPSh-41, the PPS-43 is made entirely of metal, except for the grip panels. The stock is a folding design patterned after the German MP38 series. Naturally, the struts hit your cheekbones, which adversely affects your shooting, and the metal is cold in the winter and hot in the summer. Wear will result in the stock's wobbling—as it does on the MP38 series—and is also not good for accuracy. To make matters worst, the stock release is not easy to operate: the button must be depressed to either open or close it, and then the stock must be moved while the button is depressed until it swings clear. Folding-stock SMGs are all the rage among designers, but it has always seemed to me that a good shooting platform is more important for most infantry fights than compactness. No one should attempt to shoot an SMG with the stock collapsed if there is time to open it because accuracy will suffer. Only if compactness is absolutely essential should a folding stock be adopted. They make sense for tank crews and perhaps for airborne forces, but not for standard ground forces.

Unlike the PPSh-41, the PPS-43 does not use a drum magazine, but rather a 35-round magazine. The magazine is well made with sturdy sides and seems able to withstand a lot of abuse. The inability to accept a 71-round drum has never seemed a real drawback to me—the drums always make too much noise for my taste. Only if you are a "tank rider" does such a drum make sense. In that context, the ability to fire a long time without reloading would be wonderful, but for other applications I believe

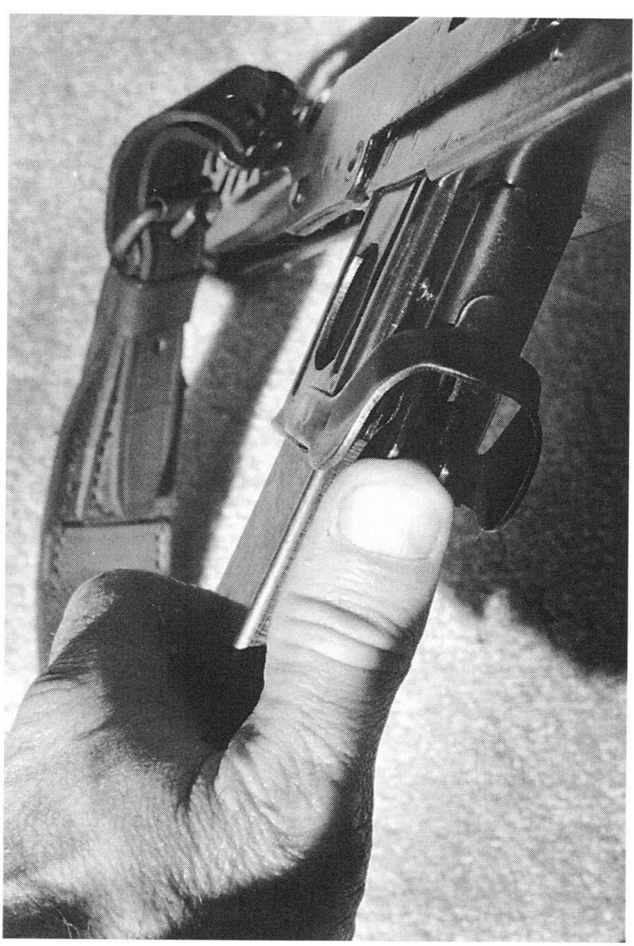

The magazine release on the PPS-43 SMG is well protected and is fast to use even in cold weather with mittened hands.

that standard double-column magazines are better.

The trigger guard is a good size, and the safety has always reminded me of the one on an M1 Garand. It is fast to operate, can be used with either hand with gross motor skills, and can be felt in the dark—always good qualities in an SMG. I must say, however, that open-bolt gun safety systems are not my favorite, but at least the PPS-43 design is quick to use and does not require the shooter to abandon his firing grip to disengage it.

The PPS-43 lacks a forward handgrip and does get quite hot when more than two or so magazines are fired through it rapidly. Perhaps Soviet soldiers always wore mittens, but holding it by the magazines is obviously improper technique and will lead to malfunctions. If you hold it in the area in front of the magazine, you must watch that your hand is not struck by the bolt handle, and your hand will get burned if a number of magazines are fired quickly. I would imagine the feature would be appreciated in the wintertime, however; I have occasionally been happy to be able to warm my cold hands on heated rifle barrels. The problem is that the barrels always seem to get so hot that your hands burn; they never simply get warm enough to be comfortable.

The PPS-43 has a rather crude muzzle brake, which may or may not work. I have never shot one without it, but it certainly makes the weapon loud.

The front sight is a simple cylindrical post well protected by wings, as is the rear sight. I would prefer to paint the front sight to brighten it up and make it quicker to see. I suppose my usual white paint would not work so well on the Soviet fronts, but it needs something because the gray/black post simply disappears as it gets dark. Perhaps orange?

Cyclic rate is higher than I would prefer, but this is, I believe, mainly a result of a lightweight bolt and high-intensity cartridge. While firing fully automatic only, it is possible to get off single shots with a little practice, so the lack of a selector is not critical. In an actual encounter, those single shots are likely to be 2-shot bursts, but, even so, that is not terrible for actual work.

The bolt handle has a smooth finish, and a wet or cold hand can easily slip off it. If you do not get the bolt far enough back to pick up the sear, it is possible to chamber and fire a round accidentally. The bolt handle should be knurled for better purchase, although no doubt this would have increased production time. On the other hand, it seems to be sturdy to permit the shooter to kick the weapon open with a boot in the event of a stuck case. I always like this ability to kick the bolt open; it has been my experience that on all self-loading shoulder weapons sooner or later you get a stuck case and need to clear it by force. A ramrod is a poor substitute for dislodging because it isn't as effective or fast. Perhaps I use too much cheap surplus ammunition, although I do not imagine Soviet soldiers using wartime ammunition in the mud or snow/ice of the Soviet front had a lot better luck than I do in this regard.

The finish on all wartime Soviet SMGs is quite rough, but, interestingly enough, the bores were

Removing the safety from a PPS-43 is easy to do, even with mittens on.

This side view illustrates the bolt-closed safety on, which locks the bolt in place to avoid firing by inertia. Note the metal blocking bolt handle's rearward movement.

The author carries the PPS-43 muzzle forward. His hand fits into the area in front of the trigger guard and behind the magazine housing, effectively holding the bolt to the rear safely while he is moving, an excellent design feature of the PPS-43.

The PPS-43 has an excellent ejection port and two-position rear sight. The sight is set for 100 and 200 meters and has sturdy wings to protect it.

chromed. Although rough on the outside, Soviet SMGs are very reliable and dependable pieces of equipment that were made in large volume and contributed greatly to the Soviet victory. The PPS-43 is every bit as good as the finest Thompson (except for getting too hot to hold sometimes), and when you consider the circumstances under which it was designed, made, and then fielded, it is amazing.

The finger position shown here for the PPS-43 permits the shooter to fire single shots readily on burst-fire only. Lowering the position allows more control over the trigger, permitting the shooter to fire single shots easily even on such high-rate-of-fire SMGs as the PPS-43. Apparently, depth of engagement of the sear notch is more readily felt.

The standard finger position on the PPS-43 that allows bursts to be fired.

STECHKIN

In the 1950s, the Soviet Union developed the Stechkin machine pistol. This was rather odd, because many thought the day of the buttstock-detachable machine pistol was over. Yet apparently the Soviets made the weapon in some numbers. However, it also appears that most were kept inside the Soviet Union, with only limited numbers being given away abroad. With the destruction of the "evil empire" in the late 1980s, however, the weapons were taken out of the Russian inventory and sold for hard currency abroad. It was just such a weapon that fell into my hands to test for this volume. The weapon was manufactured in the mid-1950s, at the height of the Cold War, and its previous owner had likely been a Soviet KGB or other specialized soldier.

This illustration from a Soviet military manual shows the Stechkin machine pistol being used with the buttstock attached. In reality, a much more aggressive stance should be used for maximum control.

The Stechkin is, in many ways, a weapon of the 1930s with a few enhancements. First, it is a 20-shot, double-column pistol. Today, with the advent of various high-capacity pistols, we might not realize it initially, but the Stechkin was a radical development in its day. It was a high-capacity, double-action autoloader. With the exception of the P35, there were no other double-column, high-capacity pistols at the time. As such, it was ahead of the various Star pistol designs common in the 1930s.

The availability of the double-action trigger meant also that it was faster to get into operation than a Star for some types of troops (those with less skilled with weapons), and the double-column magazine meant that the shooting could go on longer than with a Star unless an extended magazine was used. Such extension magazines are awkward and cannot be easily carried in the weapon or on the belt without snaring on every object passed.

The sights on the Stechkin consist of an adjustable rear sight and a fixed European pyramid front that is narrower than I like and too dark. The front sight can be improved greatly by painting it white, but I can imagine a Soviet soldier might prefer a different color, given the prevalence of snow. But some contrasting color is needed. The rear sight has a "U"-shaped notch that I always find slow to use (I prefer a square notch), but it does offer a four-position setting: 25, 50, 100, and 200 meters. It is rugged and not likely to be pushed up or down accidentally, as can happen with the leaf rear sights used on Star or Mauser pistols. It is also a small, handy sight not prone to snagging. The 200-meter maximum setting is also a realistic range for the weapon; hitting man-sized targets at such range is quite easy with this weapon. For those who say that the power level of the 9mm Makarov cartridge is inconsequential at those ranges, I say let them prove their position by standing down range at 300 yards while I shoot at them with a weapon chambered for the cartridge. No takers? Certainly, the Stechkin is not a rifle, but it is also not a BB gun.

The Stechkin machine pistol is a weapon of the 1930s with a few improvements added.

Each magazine pouch holds two spare magazines (for a total of four per load), and the magazine is of the double-column type. It is cut away to allow dirt to fall clear, as were early "military style" Smith & Wesson M39 magazines.

Top: Standard selective-fire Stechkin pistol.
Bottom: Semiautomatic-only version. The changes in hammer mechanism to provide full-auto fire are obvious.

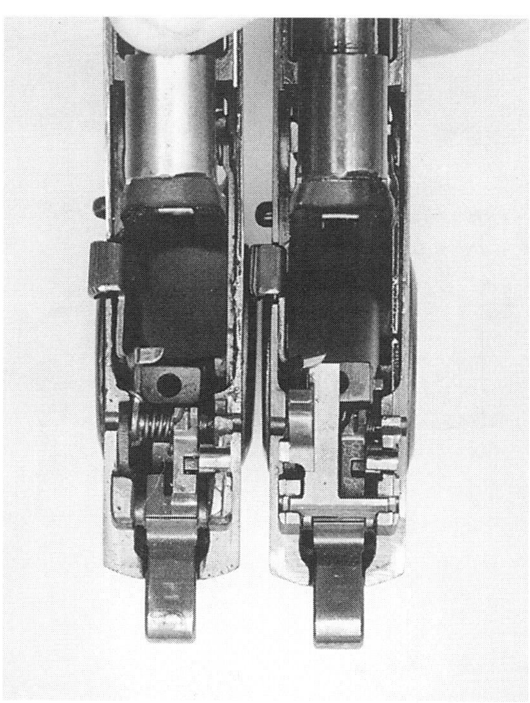

Right: Full-auto version of Stechkin machine pistol.
Left: Semiautomatic-only version.

The Stechkin operates much like an overgrown Walther PP pistol and is easily stripped for cleaning. The magazine release is easy to operate and is not likely to be bumped accidentally. A weapon that has a longer barrel than a Makarov but shoots the same cartridge will have slightly greater velocity and power. I do not think such slight gains get you up to 9x19mm level, but a person hit at 75 yards with a 9x19mm and at 50 yards with a 9x18mm Makarov fired out of a Stechkin is unlikely to know the difference because the velocities of the cartridges are roughly the same at those distances.

The Stechkin has a slot on the back of the grip to fit the buttstock in, much like on a P35 pistol, and, as with the latter, if the stock lug is well fitted to the catch, a firm, solid stock results. Someone firing from the stocked position usually gets no better accuracy than does a fresh expert shooter firing from a Weaver stance. But such pistols come into their own when the shooter is less well skilled or when the shooter is tired, cold, hungry, or otherwise not up to his best work. When those situations arise, my tests show that results are better by a 50-percent margin or more with the stocked handgun.

The selector is a combination safety/selector system and not particularly fast to put into operation. However, it should be carried in the full-auto mode because it is much

Underside view of the Stechkin machine pistol slide showing how the selector functions.

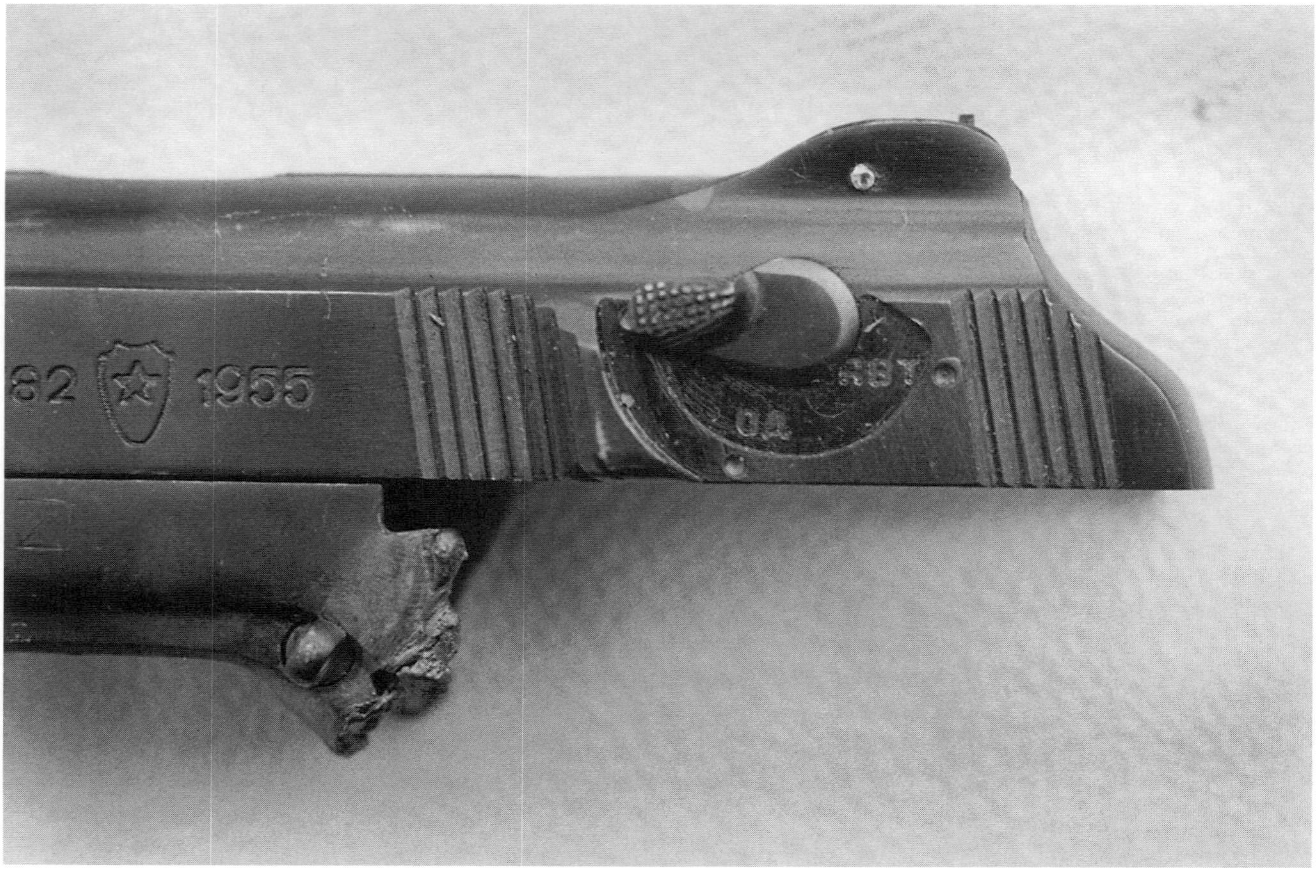

Left-side view of Stechkin slide showing how the selector/safety functions. The safety position is on the left; center is semiautomatic; right is full auto.

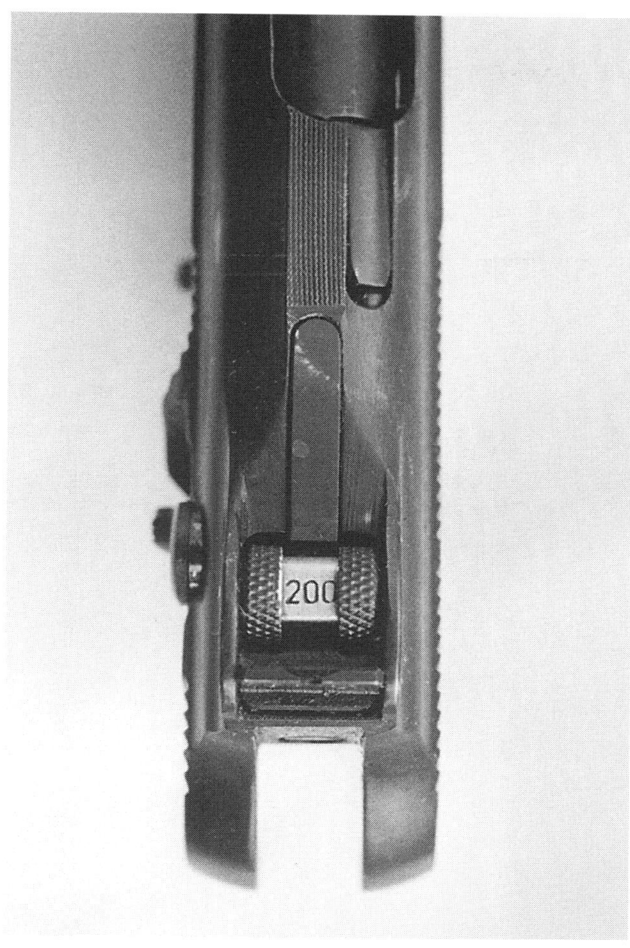

The 200-meter setting on the four-position rear sight.

more effective at close range in that mode. If you need the more precise accuracy that semiautomatic gives, you are likely to have the time to change the safety/selector lever because distances that require extreme accuracy usually provide you with additional time to respond to the threat.

Unlike the H&K VP70, but like other such machine pistols as the Beretta and Star, the Stechkin can be fired on full auto without its stock in place. Its weight and the power of the cartridges result in lower recoil and greater control than with its 9x19mm big brother.

I was rather taken with the Stechkin, but I admit that I like machine pistols. The only feature that truly can be questioned is the caliber (and even this is a marginal issue, as my earlier comments made clear). Recently, however, a variety of better ammunition has been developed that gives greater velocity and better penetration and if loaded in your Stechkin goes a long way toward erasing the criticisms aimed at the weapon. If we compare the Stechkin of the 1950s with the Beretta M93 of the 1980s, an honest appraisal would favor the Stechkin. The stock is easier to use and carry, plus it gives a better, shorter platform. It holds more ammunition than the Beretta, unless you go to an extended magazine. The Stechkin sights are adjustable to permit engaging targets out to 200 meters by direct aiming, whereas with the Beretta you must aim over at such ranges. The Beretta does offer a 3-shot burst mechanism, but the cyclic rate on the Stechkin is low enough that a well-trained person can keep bursts short. The felt recoil on the Stechkin is lower than on the Beretta. Last, and perhaps most critical, the Beretta feels like a 2 x 4 in your hand while the Stechkin feels alive.

All in all, the Stechkin is a very impressive piece of kit. It is a shame that it is so rare in the United States that few people will get an opportunity to try one out.

Spain

STAR MD

The Star MD is a modification of the standard Star military-model pistol that resembles a Colt Government Model in many aspects but is modified to fire bursts. Typically, the weapons are fitted with a hollowed-out buttstock similar to those used on Broomhandle Mauser pistols. With such stocks, they are quite effective; as noted elsewhere, a pistol with a stock attached may not be any more inherently accurate but it is easier to get good results when you are cold, tired, or scared than with a standard handgun even in well-trained hands.

The Star MD is a 9x23mm pistol (it also shoots .38 ACP, naturally), and the PD version shoots the .45 ACP cartridge. Apparently, it was also available

The Star PD 9x23mm machine pistol

The author firing the Star PD in full-auto mode.

in 7.63mm Mauser and 9x19mm. It comes with either standard fixed sights or a graduated leaf rear unit. The example tested used the standard sights. Full-auto fire is obtained by pushing the selector on the right side of the frame down where it hits the disconnector, depressing it, and allowing the weapon to fire in bursts. The system is simple to make, although perhaps not the easiest to use since it is difficult to change the selector without either using your nonshooting hand or shifting the weapon in your hand. As with all burst-fire, selective-fire weapons, the weapon should be carried in the full-auto position and changed to semiautomatic only if a more distant target is seen. There is usually enough time to shift firing modes, whereas up close the benefits of burst fire will be instantly available.

Many times these weapons are equipped with the extended magazines manufactured for them by the factory, but because of the single-column capacity of the magazines, if any real amount of ammunition is used, they get quite long. In my mind, a better solution would be to carry the shorter 11- or 16-round magazine on the belt and use the standard magazine that is flush with the weapon. With practice, this will give you two, if not three, bursts from the weapon before reloading is called for in combat.

Controllability of the Star MD/PD depends largely on the cartridge used and the shooter's stance. Obviously, no machine pistol can be shot like a conventional pistol because of the rapid recoil; thus, controllability from the traditional firing position is unacceptable. I believe this is what typically causes people to view the machine pistol with such disdain. If better trained and educated about this wonderful type of weapon, the shooter will be much more respectful about its unique characteristics. The Star MD/PD uses a standard steel frame, and the pistol does not ride particularly low in the hand (like a Glock 18 does, for example). Naturally, the PD model in .45 ACP gives more recoil than the 7.63 Mauser example because of the heavier bullet being fired, and thus the PD model is harder to control than the smaller-caliber examples. Additionally, because the Star contains fewer cartridges, the number of bursts will be less by perhaps 50 percent. Still, if a very aggressive shooting stance is maintained, the Star Machine pistol can be shot with efficiency in whatever caliber is selected.

The weapon itself has sights that are small, shallow, and dark. They need to be painted a contrasting color to allow rapid pickup. In the ideal world, a good set of Bomar sights should be installed to help at long range and allow better visual pickup when bursts are fired and the whole sight picture is blurred. Because the Bomars are larger, your eye should pick them up better. As with any such pattern pistol, the magazine release is handy to use and the side safety quick to operate from the holster. Of course, for use as a military weapon, you have all the standard problems that you have with such designs (e.g., failing to clear a round out of the chamber when unloading the weapon, dropping the hammer on a loaded round after removing the magazine, or requiring the weapon to be carried cocked and locked to get speedy firing even though a lot of young soldiers are not very careful with cocked handguns) and no doubt Star MD/PD military users had the same type of accidents with them that ill-educated U.S. GIs had with their Colt Government Model M1911/1911A1 pistols. The design is great for well-trained and alert shooters but a severe hazard for others who are not so attuned to such matters.

The grip safety is missing on Star products of all types, but that is nothing to worry about. It merely prevents dirt from entering there, and people who use a poor grip with a high thumb fail to deactivate the safety, thus tying up their weapon. The Star, of course, like the Colt, should be fired with a low-thumb position to get maximum control over the weapon when rapid fire is called for.

It is indeed unfortunate that the passage of the National Firearms Act in 1934 limited the availability of the machine pistol. I feel certain that if machine pistols had been easily available, a much superior product would have been developed over the years. As it is, the Star MD/PD is interesting, but it represents a development from the mid-1920s. Like a Mercedes-Benz car from the 1920s, it is interesting and fun to try out, but it is not as good as the latest product from the factory in handling, maintenance, performance, or almost anything else. It is unreasonable to expect it to be—what do you think all those engineers have been doing for the last three-quarters of a century?

STAR Z-70

This product of the Iberian region is rather uncommon in the United States, where the prejudice against Spanish handguns is still strong and where interest in wartime guns is high. Since these Star products were not used in any major war, U.S. GIs did not smuggle them home in their duffel bags, and arms merchants did not get a chance to buy them surplus as spoils of war. This is unfortunate because these Iberian SMGs are indeed fine weapons.

The Z-70 has a folding cocking handle that can be used easily with either hand. Since it folds down, it does not catch on vines and limbs, as do the Sterling SMG and similar guns. It also does not move back and forth with the bolt, as is common and quite distracting.

The front sight is a simple post but protected by sturdy ears on either side. Although dropping the weapon hard might damage the sight, given the sturdy ears and the small space involved, it would require an extremely unfortunate choice of landing places to cause much harm. The rear sight is a simple "L"-shaped peep sight adjustable for 100 and 200 meters. There are no false pretensions to being a long-range rifle here. Sturdy ears protect the rear sight as well. Adjustment of the sight is by drift, which I do not care for—although I admit that once sighted in such sights rarely move.

The weapon has a short overall length and a very sturdy folding stock. The stock easily extends from the folded position and just as easily collapses. You do not need three hands to work it as you do with some units. Once extended, it is quite sturdy and rigid. I suppose it could wear and begin wobbling, but my Star Z-70 SMG is still in fine shape despite many such openings and closings. The

The stock on the Star Z-70 SMG will fold and pass over loaded magazines.

stock has a single rather than metal strut that contacts your cheek and thus feels more comfortable than the metal stocks with thinner or rounder struts. No one will ever mistake such stocks for real wood, of course.

The grip is angled nicely and does not cramp your hand, as does the grip angle on the Uzi. There is no grip safety to tie up your weapon at the least desirable moment. The safety is very similar to that found on the Beretta M1951 pistol. As I found on the Beretta when I tested it, those style of safeties may appear difficult to use when you shoot the weapons, but they are incredibly fast. A simple inward pressure with the knuckle of the thumb will remove it, and extending the trigger out slightly more and pushing slightly inward with the knuckle reapplies it. No shifting of the hand is necessary. This is very fast and very secure from accidental bumping or snagging.

The Z-70 is a nicely designed selective-fire weapon. Unlike many designs requiring a lever to be switched to change the mode of fire, the Z-70

The front sight on the Star Z-70 is good sized and well protected. The cocking handle on the left folds down along the receiver to avoid snagging.

The safety on the Star Z-70 is a push-through type that is very fast and snap-proof. A pull at the top of the trigger will result in semiautomatic fire; a pull at the bottom allows burst fire. This fast safety system is excellent but rarely encountered.

uses a trigger mechanism to accomplish it. If you pull on the top of the trigger, you get semiautomatic; pulling on the bottom gets full auto. Again, no shifting of the hand is required, and it is very fast. Some people claim such systems aren't very sturdy, but that has not been my experience (although, admittedly, I have used only one example and that for only perhaps 5,000 rounds). The new Stars have neither the safety nor trigger system found on the Z-70 that I like so much. I think this change is due to popular demand, which is based on the lack of experience with a better system, not a design flaw in the weapon.

The magazine release can be used easily by the left hand when the shooter is right-handed. Since the weapon is held by the weak hand at the magazine housing area, it is convenient. I think it would be less so for a left-handed shooter. A centered magazine release, such as the one on the MP5, is always better for that reason. The magazine housing is not flared to add rapid magazine insertion, which is unfortunate. I suppose a person could file a bevel on the housing, as people do on IPSC match pistols, but it really should be done that way at the factory to hasten loading, especially in the dark.

The magazines are sturdy, hold 30 rounds, and are easy to load without a loading tool because they are double-column-fire configuration. Field-stripping is not as easy as with the Uzi, but at least the barrel comes out of the weapon so you can clean it properly with hot water after a day of shooting corrosive ammunition—a quality you appreciate after doing the same thing with your collector-grade Thompson. The weapon is finished with a tough crackle-finish that appears to be baked on and quite durable. I would like to have the same finish applied to a pistol someday. The parts on the Z-70 all seem to be big and sturdy with none of the numerous small parts and springs common in some of the German SMGs.

Besides being short overall, the Z-70 is both

light (6 1/2 pounds) and handy. Unlike the Thompson and other such weapons, it feels alive in your hands. The cyclic rate is 550 RPM, which is low enough to allow single shots to be fired even if a selective trigger system did not exist. On full auto, the Z-70 is quite controllable even in long bursts. Dumping an entire magazine with one full-auto burst at 50 feet into a chest-sized target may not be tactically relevant, but it does show that this is one very controllable SMG.

I had never really thought too much about Star SMGs until I saw one at my friend Kent Lomont's home. From then on, I had to have one. Once I got it, I determined that my efforts were well rewarded. The Star Z-70 is eminently superior to the Uzi and rivals the Owen in my affections—and on some days surpasses it.

Sweden

M45

During World War II Sweden was sandwiched between potential enemies: Germany was aggressively invading Norway, and the Soviet Union was invading nearby Finland. It was apparent early on to Swedish military leaders that an SMG was needed. Sweden managed to purchase some Thompson SMGs from the United States, but America was far away, and Britain was competing for the Thompsons as well. Suomi SMGs had proven very successful in Finland, but the Finns were too busy producing SMGs for themselves to sell many to the Swedes. However, Finland did

Views of both sides of the Akabar, an Egyptian modification of the Swedish M45 SMG.

This is a Swedish M45B, a variant of the M45, with its bolt in the safety position.

grant a license to the Swedes, and Husquarna produced a variation of the Suomi, the M37/39, for the Swedish military. Although excellent in many ways, M37/39 SMGs were heavy and long and, worse, required a lot of machine time and materials to manufacture. The Swedes wanted an SMG that could be easily and cheaply produced.

Having an opportunity to see all the world's SMGs in operation in World War II allowed the Swedes to develop an SMG that incorporated the good features of all these weapons. Swedish designers took the simple-to-manufacture receiver from the Sten gun and the idea of a folding stock from the MP 40. They developed a very reliable double-column, double-feed magazine from the M38 Beretta. By 1945 the 9x19mm cartridge had become the standard, so the Swedes adopted it, although they frequently used a special loading with greater penetration and velocity. If the Swedes had been a little more farsighted, perhaps they would have seen that the SMG was obsolete once the Ml carbine and the German MP43/4 were released; but at least you can say that the Swedes had looked at all the world's SMGs and planned accordingly.

The front sight of the M45 is a post that is protected by massive stamped wings, so it is unlikely to be knocked out of alignment. Because the wings and the front sight are the same color and nearly the same width, it is possible to pick up the wings by accident and think you have the sights, causing the target to be way wide. This problem can be overcome by painting the top of the front sight for a quick contrast. The rear sight is a three-position "U-flip-type graduated for a sensible 100, 200, and 300 yards. However, given the open-bolt method of shooting, at 300 yards you are unlikely to get hits on 10 x 14-inch targets. This is odd because you are able to do that with the Swedish M37/39 SMG with the same ammunition. Although the sights are probably optimistic, they are not wildly so. Finding the "U"-shaped rear blade is difficult to use, I prefer to convert them to a "V" shape and widen them out a bit. By doing so, I have gotten groups half as big at the same distance.

The barrel is covered with a fairly short and rather light shroud. If you could teach everyone how to shoot an SMG properly and with utmost efficiency, that shroud would be unnecessary. Still, at least it is not too much of a burden and does give you a place to mount a bayonet if you like such things.

The bolt is similar to a Sten or MP 40 in that to put it on safe, you must pull it to the rear and then carefully rotate the bolt handle into the safety notch. I do not believe anyone actually uses a weapon like that because of slowness involved in doing it. A much better feature on the M45 than the other two

This view shows the swivel (which needs to be wrapped to avoid noise) and the locking mechanism of the folding stock.

The author and the test target he shot at 50 feet with an Egyptian copy of the M45. A continuous-fire burst is illustrated.

SMGs mentioned is that the bolt can be locked in the closed position, thereby avoiding the problem associated with inertia-induced discharges.

The weapon is not selective fire, but with the cyclic rate of 600 RPM, it is clear that any reasonably trained soldier should be able to fire founds in a semiautomatic mode by merely pulling the trigger and quickly releasing it. The 600 RPM cyclic rate also results in a very controllable SMG. The stock is a side-folding tubular unit. You must depress the catch and then swing the stock out and away to extend it. Even when covered with leather, such tube-type stocks are difficult to use and produce inferior groups. No doubt the Swedes were greatly influenced by the idea of SMGs as used by paratroopers: with the folding stock the paratroopers did not have to worry about the stock's hitting the plane as they prepared to jump from the C-47 door. The M45 stock is not very comfortable on my cheek. I have seen an M45 with a wood stock attached, but I do not know whether such a weapon was a prototype or not. If an M45 equipped with a wood stock is available, I would prefer to use it for shooting.

The bolt handle is not situated in a place where it can be operated by either hand equally well, although the centrally located magazine does effectively result in this.

Early models of the M45 would take Suomi 50-shot magazines. As they were modified, this was changed so only 36-round M45 magazines could be used, and this was the M45B. As noted earlier, this uses the Beretta-style double-column, double-feed magazine, which has proven to be wonderfully reliable.

The M45 is a fine if uninspired SMG. It is reliable, fairly short overall, and quite easy to control—albeit a bit heavy at almost 10 pounds loaded. I do not believe it had any wonderful design breakthroughs. What it did was evaluate a variety of SMGs that had been used to fight the battles of Europe, avoiding as much as possible the bad things and the parts that actually break in battle and adopting the good points for Swedish manufacturing techniques. Thus it is not the parts of the gun involved but the combination of all of them into this SMG that makes it such a good design.

United States

WINCHESTER M97 12 GAUGE

The Winchester M97 repeating shotgun was the weapon that made the 10-gauge shotgun obsolete as a combat weapon. Certainly before the M97 came out, there were a few repeating pump-action shotguns, including its immediate predecessor, the M93. Another model that comes to mind is the folding Burgess 12-gauge pump, which was made especially for the police market. However, the company that made the Burgess was small, and distribution was spotty. The Winchester M97 was made by a company with a well-deserved reputation for dependability, and Winchester products were sold all over the world. Most important, however, the M97 was a better weapon than the Burgess.

The M97 was available almost from the beginning as a guard or riot gun with a 20-inch barrel. Why they made the barrel so long in those days before the National Firearms Act has always puzzled me. It would seem that a barrel that was cut off immediately in front of the magazine tube would be better, but 20 inches was the selected length.

During World War I when the need for combat shotguns by troops in France and elsewhere was obvious, the M97 was militarized by putting a ventilated handguard that incorporated a bayonet lug on it. Although adding some weight to the weapon, the ventilated handguard was a good idea for a military weapon that might be fired many times in a short time span, unlike a weapon used for a typical police or guard situation. Also a bayonet on the end of the shotgun wielded by a trained individual in the confines of a trench could prove to be very effective.

The M97 has a bead front sight and mere receiver groove in the rear. Nowadays, we know that even with buckshot, a set of good sights is helpful. But for short range, the M97's sights are adequate. No safety exists on the M97 except for the half-cock notch. Additionally, to lower the hammer, you pull the trigger and carefully lower the hammer. With cold-stiffened or wet or bloody hands, I imagine that

The Winchester M97 12-gauge shotgun effectively made the 10-gauge shotgun obsolete as a combat weapon. The author is holding a riot model; the M97 was also available as a guard gun.

the hammer must have slipped more than a few times, discharging the weapon. To fire it, you must cock it manually and then pull the trigger. Again, this is a method destined to cause accidental discharges. I would like to think everyone in 1918 was more careful and weapon-wise than we find today—but in all honesty, I doubt it. The lack of safety and lack of mechanical decocking and cocking are drawbacks.

The M97 also lacks a disconnector. If you hold back the trigger and rack the action, the weapon will fire as the slide is closed. Not having a disconnector allows a fast rate of fire that can be devastating in well-trained hands. Less well trained shooters will forget to release the trigger, rack the slide, and fire a round accidentally.

M97 actions tend to be very smooth as a result of long wear or good fitting perhaps. This helps the rate of fire. The trigger guard is small, making it difficult to put a gloved finger through it. Why it is so small is a mystery, especially given its hunting background. You would think that any weapon that is likely to be used in a duck blind on a freezing day would accommodate a gloved or mittened hand. Naturally, it does not swing to the side or down to allow the use of mittened hands either. This is a serious drawback. The stock angle is low, which allows a greater felt recoil impulse and slows up repeat shots. Buttplates were made of a variety of materials, but none, to my knowledge, offered a butt trap for cleaning materials, a serious drawback.

Other than the typical, pump-action, tube-fed problem that the slow single loading of extra ammunition causes, the worst thing about the M97 from the military standpoint is how difficult it is to clean. For hunting weapons, this isn't a big problem: these weapons are in the field infrequently, and generally the hunter goes back home at the end of the day or at least to a campsite where the weapon can be carefully cleaned. In the military, you are likely to be living in the mud for weeks at a time, so having a weapon that cannot be easily broken down into pieces for a thorough cleaning usually means that maintenance is deferred or ignored, which soon leads to malfunctions.

On the firing range, a session with the M97 loaded with buckshot will soon convince you that you have a powerful weapon. A couple of boxes in the morning makes me feel like I have been boxing with someone bigger than I. If you wear winter-weight clothes and are running tactical courses, it is not nearly as bothersome, but range practice in short sleeves is a chore.

All buckshot-loaded shotguns suffer from the same drawback: lack of effective range and penetration. A shotgun should be capable of placing a load of buckshot on a man-target up to 35 yards in a 12 gauge with current ammunition. You can hit man-targets at 75 yards, but you can also miss, especially with 00 buck. Even if they hit, such loads have very little penetration at such extreme ranges. On the other hand, at night on a trench raid in early 1918, an M97 shotgun certainly would have been a fine choice. Your professional predecessor had a very effective weapon in the M97. Backed up with a .45 Government Model, a knife, and some grenades, I would have considered myself well equipped in 1918 with an M97. Even today with a strict understanding of the potential dangers of the design, the M97 is an effective combat shotgun.

M12 WINCHESTER 12 GAUGE

When the call from the U.S. military for combat shotguns went out in 1917, the Winchester M12 shotgun was a relatively new weapon. Today, we view it as an old and proven design, well tested in countless duck marshes or police cruisers, but in 1917 its value was not so clear.

The M12 was available in guard and riot configurations with a 20-inch barrel, as was the earlier M97. Again, I never really understood why it was not simply offered with the barrel cut off flush with the magazine tube or with the tube extended to the end of the barrel. Either providing shorter overall length or more ammunition would appear to have been a better solution. The M12 Winchester also had a ventilated handguard with integral bayonet lug fitted to it for military purposes, as did the M97.

Obviously, the M12 offered the same performance as the M97 on target because the same load was used. The M12 was a hammerless action with a safety located at the trigger guard. Being hammerless, it avoids all the problems associated with snagging the hammer partially back and then falling onto a loaded chamber, thus

A U.S. Marine in World War II prepares to advance with an M12 Winchester 12-gauge shotgun.

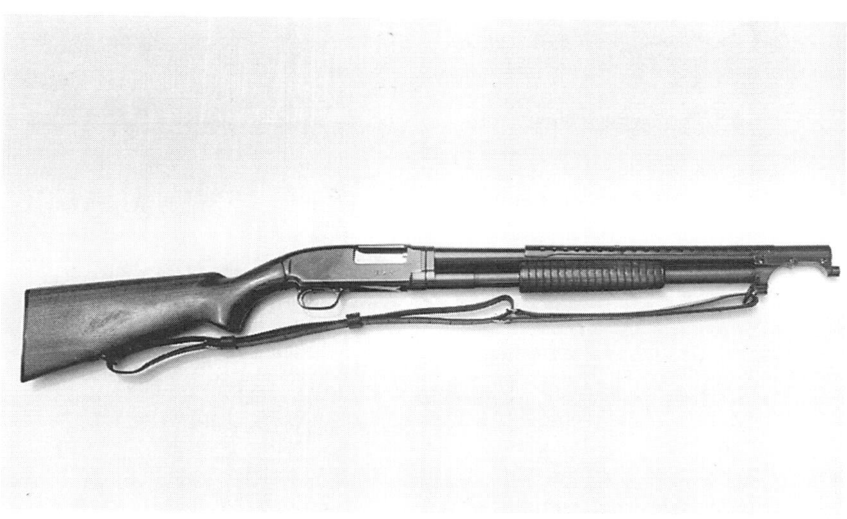

This is an example of a Winchester M12 riot gun as supplied to the U.S. military.

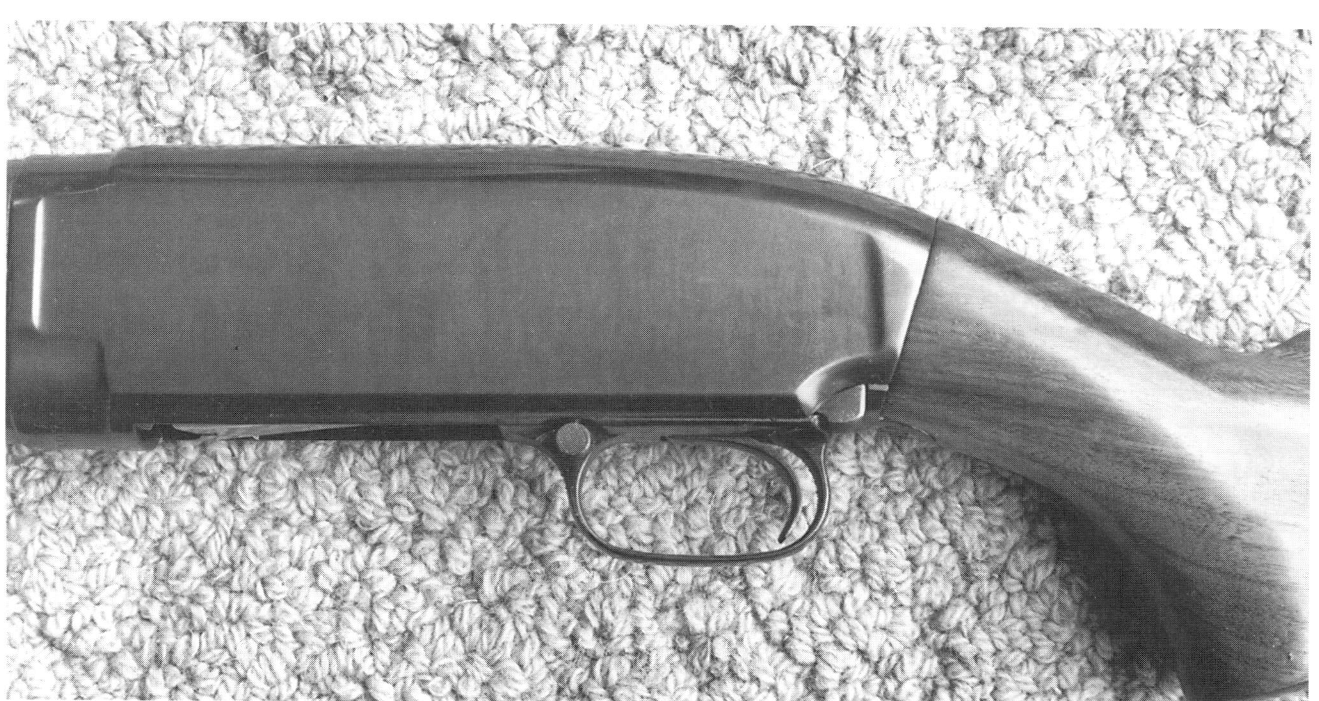

The safety on the M12 Winchester trench gun is small and difficult to use quickly with cold or mittened hands. The trigger guard is also small and unwieldy for cold or mittened hands.

discharging the weapon. However, shooters run into the problem of not knowing whether the weapon is loaded and ready to fire because no obvious hammer exists. Additionally since the trigger guard safety release is a small button, pushing it off rapidly is not easy or certain, especially with cold-stiffened or gloved hands. I would imagine most troops carried their M12s like I did, with the slide slightly out of battering (and closing it when ready to fire) and the safety off.

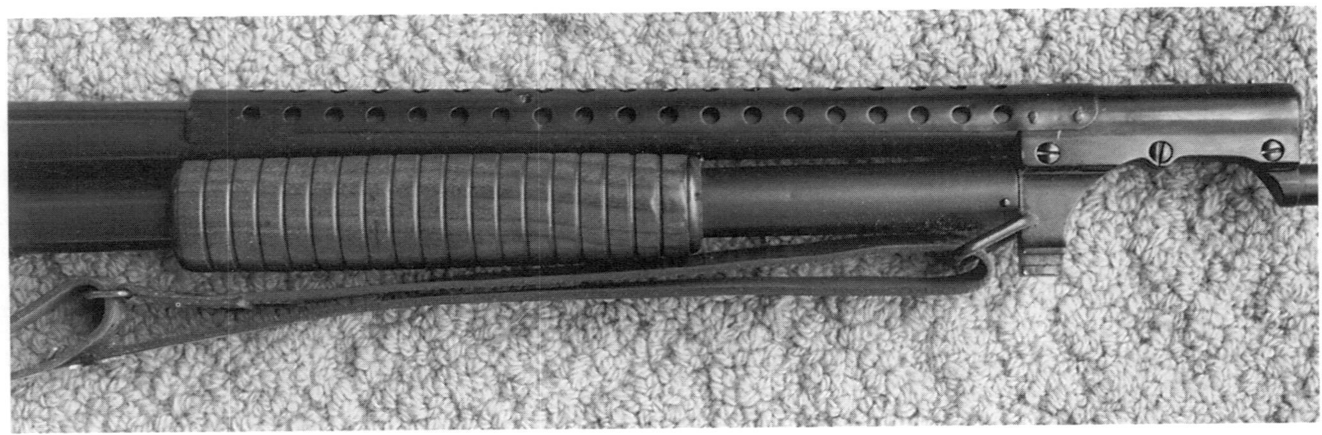

The upper handguard on this M12 12-gauge riot gun was designed to prevent the shooter from burning his hand if he had to bayonet fight after firing a number of rapid shots through the weapon. The bayonet lug on this M12 fits the M1917 bayonet. The ventilated handguard is a good feature for a combat shotgun.

This is much faster and safer in my judgment.

The M12, like the M97, is designed for civilian hunting use and thus does not break down easily in big pieces for cleaning. The parts fit tightly together, giving the weapon a smooth feel but also making it very likely to get tied up if dropped in the mud. Its design makes cleaning it in such a situation difficult.

Sights on the military M12 consist of the standard bear front with receiver groove rear. This substantially limits the effectiveness of the weapon: even when buckshot is used, the shotgun should be aimed like a rifle firing a single projectile. Additionally, different shotguns will throw loads to different points of impact, so a set of sights that allows you to adjust for this so the point of impact and the front sight are in the same position is critical.

The stock of the M12 is made of wood, and the drop is low so the recoil tends to cause excessive muzzle whip, slowing repeat shots. In 1917, a wood stock certainly was acceptable, but today we know they are too fragile. The stock also was attached only to the rear of the receiver by a long bolt, making it inherently weak. I am certain that anyone who ever butt-stroked a German was likely to have a broken stock and that many broke from less exotic things in the trenches.

Like the M97, the M12 lacks a disconnector. This improves the speed at which a well-trained individual can fire the weapon. Simply holding back the trigger and pumping the action allows the weapon to fire when the slide is slammed home. In a well-trained set of hands, this feature allows the M12 to be fired so fast it seems like a constant roar. Less well-trained hands will accidentally fire the weapon when they reload, forgetting to let up on the trigger.

The M12 suffers from a problem inherent in all pump shotguns: it is slow to reload because it requires single-cartridge loading. Although it can be fired as fast or faster than a bolt-action rifle because of the slickness of the pump action, once it is empty, the shooter must pull individual rounds out and insert them one at a time into the tube magazine. This is problematic because the shooter is prone to fumbling, it is difficult to do on the move, and there is no good way to carry spare ammunition. Loose in a pouch, the ammo rattles. On the belt in loops, the rounds are exposed to weather, reflect light (which can disclose your presence), and fall out of the loops as you crawl along the ground. With a typical bolt-action rifle, you merely grab a stripper clip and push the ammunition from it into the action. Better still are box magazines, such as on the BAR, where a fully loaded box is inserted in place of an empty one.

The M12 continued in the U.S. military after World War I and was common up to the early stages of the Vietnam War. By that time, however, the weapon was out of production, and those in the inventory had seen much hard service. Many were scrapped or sold as surplus and replaced with more modern designs that also were cheaper to buy and service. During World War II, the M12 was commonly encountered and, as with all shotguns, well received as long as good, nonswollen ammunition was available.

The M12 offers nothing today that is not available in more modern designs that are easier to service. This weapon is too expensive for military or police use. However, it makes a fine weapon for an individual, given the limitations noted.

BROWNING AUTO SHOTGUN

The Browning long-recoil-action shotgun is included in this volume for two reasons: it was a U.S. military riot gun in its Remington configuration, and, more important, it was used in Malaya during the 1950s "Emergency Days." There the British developed a unique load for it, involving a combination of buckshot and small-sized shot they found very effective under the circumstances they encountered: ranges and contact times were short, skill levels were minimal in many cases (from a lack of background in weapons, I think), and medical facilities were so limited that even a small, light wound inflicted on a guerrilla would get infected, thereby not only disabling the wounded guerrilla but also creating a drag on the entire unit that had to care for him.

Of course, the Browning-pattern long-recoil action shotgun was not designed to be a military weapon. And although it was a rugged sporting weapon, it was not nearly as good as a military weapon because it was used more rigorously and for longer periods in the field. Also its design dated from a period when shotgun cartridge technology was much less advanced (in fact, early models were built around black-powder loads, which is why the action used recoil and not gas pressure to operate). Once a load was selected and the shotgun's spring system modified to function with it, most people found that this modified system was better in the sporting field as well. I assume the military users found the same thing. The action was a long recoil, and many people find that it kicks substantially more than a gas-operated one. For this reason it is harder to use effectively. Further, the weapon is not easily stripped in the field, and reloading via loose cartridges and the tube is always slow. Many times, cartridges are dropped in the mud, which obviously does not improve their functioning.

In Malaya the small trigger guard wouldn't have been a problem, but it is a problem in cold climates where gloves or mittens must be worn frequently. More critically—and this *was* a problem in Malaya as well—the Browning has such a small button that a shooter must be careful not to miss it when in a hurry. I know that people miss the button when startled by quail, and I assume they miss it when startled by guerrillas who pop up out of the bushes at 15 feet. The Browning's push-button safety is easier to use than the bolt-turning system on Sten guns, but it is still not adequate.

The cocking handle is on the right side, which makes cocking it difficult with the left hand and results in the shooter's having to remove his hand

This is the Remington M11 configuration of a Browning-pattern 12-gauge riot gun.

from the shooting position to clear a malfunction. (I assume the shooter will go into action with the weapon loaded.) This will slow up the shooter. The handle is also polished metal, rather than checkered, and slick or sweating hands have a tendency to slip off the handle.

The stock consists of two pieces of wood. The rear stock fits into a tang to secure the wood to the shotgun and can easily break along the pistol grip area if the shooter strikes the buttstock on the ground forcefully. I have seen many with numerous cracks around the grip area as a result of poor fitting and recoil. I would imagine a few weeks in the jungle would cause the wood to swell and make it more susceptible to cracking. The buttstock is not great, but the fore-end is even worse. Its rather complicated design is weak and subject to cracking along the top edges all the way back. Bernat Sutter, a friend, used to repair the fore-ends with epoxy glue, thereby saving the owners a substantial amount of money. However, the fore-ends would later break in another area and need another repair. Of course, today they could be made out of nylon, Kevlar, or fiberglass, and would be cheaper to make and much stronger. However, I have never seen a shotgun of this pattern so fitted.

The U.S. and British military shotguns had bead sights only and no choke tubes. As a consequence, the patterns fired were somewhat marginal and varied tremendously from gun to gun. Because his shotgun lacked good sights, the shooter could not place his loads exactly where he aimed. Of course, if extremely short ranges are involved, such as those encountered in Malaysia, this disadvantage is minimized—but it is still a weakness of the design.

As with all civilian shotguns used in military circumstances, Browning-pattern shotguns mount quickly, which allows the shooter to quickly engage a target, but do not strip easily for ready maintenance in the field. Keeping any piece of equipment in good repair in high-humidity climates is difficult, especially when troops must frequently cross water or go through muddy areas. When the weapon cannot be stripped easily, it is impossible. I can only assume that the Browning-pattern shotguns got very beat up and rusty after a few years in the field.

Other than for its use by the British in Malaysia and as a U.S. pattern riot gun, the Browning long-action shotgun would hold little interest today. However, the British did establish that it could be engaged effectively, that under certain circumstances a special load would work well in it, and that the sporting shotgun was really better than an SMG in certain circumstances. Of course, had the British really been on the ball, they would have chosen an easily stripped gun that used box magazines and had a 14-inch barrel with a good peep sight and ramp front in 20 gauge. Had they done that, they would have had a superior combat shotgun, and all of us would have been able to look at a true combat evaluation of the shotgun. More the pity that they did not do so: Malaysia certainly provided a potential testing ground for such a combat shotgun, one that may never be repeated.

THOMPSON M1921, M1921/8, M1928, M1, M1A1

The Thompson is easily the most recognized SMG shape in the world. The entertainment industry and media have given this weapon so much publicity, starting in the 1920s and continuing to this date, that even people who know nothing about weapons can easily recognize it. When I first brought my M1921/8 Thompson home, my wife, who had never seen one in person, instantly knew what it was. (An M1921/8 is an M1921 Thompson that was modified for a slower rate of fire to fit U.S. Marine Corps specifications. The manufacturer did not make a new weapon but merely overstamped the "1" to an "8," hence the term, M1921/28. Later in the 1940s, Savage and Bridgeport Mills made the M1928 from scratch for U.S. and foreign military orders.)

The Thompson SMG comes in a variety of models made by several manufacturers. As a result, quality changed over time. The earliest models, the M1921 and M1921/8, were beautifully made in 1920 and 1921 by the Colt Firearms Company. They have a lovely blue finish, polished bolts, and nicely finished stocks.

The M1921 and the M1921/8 are the same except for cyclic rate: the M1921 shoots at 850 to 950 RPM, and the later model shoots about 200 RPM less. This naturally will vary among models and ammunition used. Both the M1921 and M1921/8

Early advertisement offering the Thompson SMG as a house gun. Perhaps a good idea that was ahead of its time!

William Fairbairn of the Shanghai Municipal Police and Special Operations, Executive, illustrating instructor-firing with the M1 Thompson .45 ACP.

Winston Churchill inspecting a "Tommy" gun, July 31, 1940. Photo courtesy of the Imperial War Museum.

A British soldier undergoing Commando training early in World War II with his Thompson M1921. Note the foregrip and lack of magazine. Courtesy of Imperial War Museum.

British forces in Italy during World War II clear a building with a Thompson M1928 SMG, an Enfield MK III, and an Enfield .38/200 revolver.

Irish soldier in World War II in Burma armed with a Thompson M1928.

Chinese forces in World War II armed with what appears to be a Thompson M1921 and an M96 Mauser with stock affixed.

A homemade Vietcong submachine gun based on the Thompson. Photo courtesy of the West Point Museum Collection.

These two Thompsons span the production run. Top: Colt M1921 commercial "police model" with finned barrel, vertical forearm, and detachable butt, but no Cutts Compensator. Bottom: M1A1 production by Auto Ordnance. The finish is better on the M1921, but both basically work and feel the same in the field, thus yielding the same results. One difference, however, is that the later model is much cheaper to make. The clamp on the forearm of the M1A1 is a a typical wartime addition to strengthen the design. The author has shot thrown clay birds with this SMG.

A Chinese-made copy of the Thompson M1928.

The final Thompson made: a typical late-production M1A1.

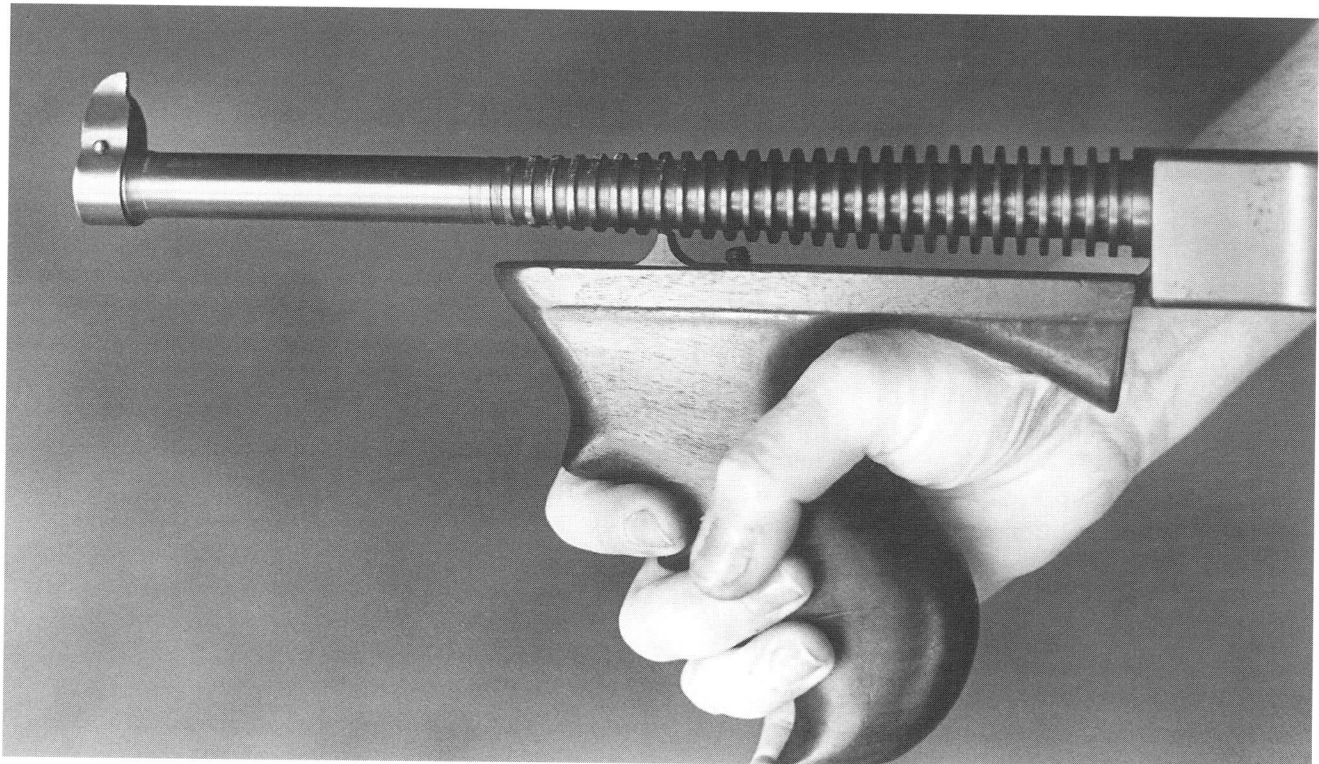

A Thompson M1921 with finned barrel without compensator and a vertical grip that was found on early Thompsons.

come with or without a Cutts Compensator. I remain unconvinced about the real worth of this device, but certainly it adds a distinctive look to a Thompson.

Both models also came with a Lyman multiple-adjustable rear sight, which is far too complicated for the cartridge and combat use of the gun. But if you have it, the weapon can be sighted in perfectly for a specific shooter. I like weapons that are perfectly sighted. Sometimes the springs in the sights will relax so much over time that it becomes impossible for the sights to hold their position. That happened in my M1921/8, and I had to replace the leaf springs designed to give the necessary tension. The cocking lever is easily accessible with either

The simplified controls on the late-model M1A1.

hand but is somewhat smooth. Care must be taken to prevent the knob's slipping out of your palm, which can cause a slam-fire if the bolt is retracted far enough to pick up a round but not far enough to lock into the rear position. Late-model Thompsons did away with the involved, adjustable sight and used a simple peep unit. Some are protected by wings, others not. The wings are better, in my opinion. Front sights are standard, large, thick pyramid units. Painted white on the tip, they are much more useful. The bolt handles on the last models, the M1 and M1A1, were on the side. They work as well as the top-mounted unit, but be careful not to let the bolt handle slip away from your hand or you might have an accidental firing. I have found that the top-mounted bolt guns are easier to use and avoid this problem since you can cock the bolt with your palm, unlike with the side-mounted bolt-handle guns where you pull the bolt with your fingers. The top-mounted units are also easier to use by left-handed shooters.

The buttstock is made of wood but is readily detachable. This same feature causes some wobbling unless you are lucky or fit the buttstock to the back of the receiver. My 1921/8 wobbles so much that it is quite annoying. The drop in the stock is much greater than it should be for best results on full-auto fire. The butt stock does have a space in it to allow storage of oil and a pull-through, which is a nice touch. Sling swivels are frequently missing from Thompsons, although the majority of military guns are fitted with the swivels, which need to be taped to prevent knocking. Also the swivel's location, except in examples used by the British, is not the best when you are attempting to get your soldiers to carry the weapon in the most accessible way possible. British examples are seen frequently with the rear swivel on the top of the stock at the rear and along the side of the foregrip. This allows the weapon to be slung over the shoulder, ready for immediate use when carried in the field. Interestingly enough, this type of carry setup is seen only on military weapons when fighters have used them enough in the field to overcome the parade-

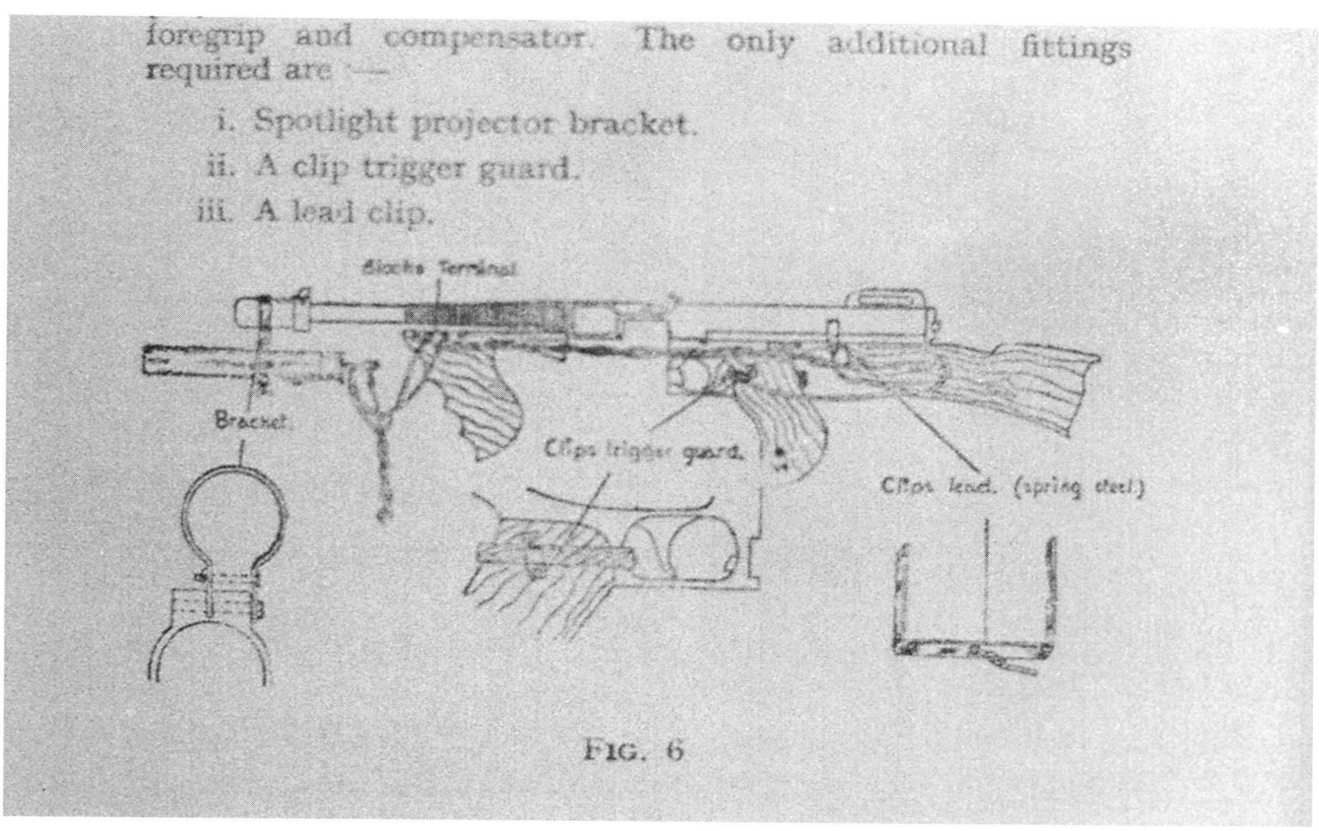
foregrip and compensator. The only additional fittings required are :—

i. Spotlight projector bracket.
ii. A clip trigger guard.
iii. A lead clip.

FIG. 6

This illustration of the flashlight attachment developed during World War II for use by British or Imperial forces was an interesting development. It shows that the use of flashlights on SMGs is not a modern SWAT idea.

ground syndrome. As soon as the campaign is over and the warriors go home to run milling machines, operate businesses, or practice law, it's business as usual in the sling department.

The rear grip on the Thompson is quick, handy, and (because it is made of wood) comfortable even in very cold weather. Of course, the rear grip does tend to crack if dropped and would absorb any gasses it was exposed to, unlike plastic grips, but it is otherwise quite nice. It may be too expensive for today's "modern world." The Owen grip is just as good and made out of a resin material that no doubt is cheaper to make and more durable.

The Thompson's safety and selector system and magazine release are all set up for the right-handed shooter. Unfortunately, unless you have incredibly long thumbs, you cannot flip the releases without breaking your grip on the weapon. Most people tend to ignore the safeties on SMGs anyway because they fire from an open bolt. Cock the weapon when you are ready to fire and keep your finger out of the trigger guard until it is time to pull the trigger. Keep the weapon set on semiautomatic unless you really need full auto and learn to place accurate semiautomatic fire using your SMG: it should be used as a fast-firing, low-recoil, handy semiautomatic weapon in lieu of a longer, more powerful, and slower rifle.

As production increased and the Thompson went through various modifications during the war, the switches got simpler and thus much less elegant in design. It did not affect their functioning, however.

The early versions of the Thompson—the M1921, M1921/8, and M1928—all accept the 50- and 100-round drums. Such drums, however, were found to be awkward to carry and noisy in a battlefield situation and soon disappeared from the scene. Early stick magazines were only 20-shot in capacity, which proved too few. The standard soon became the 30-round magazine, and that is about all anyone could desire.

The magazines are easy to load without a tool,

This photograph captures the actual moment of firing the M1921/8 by the author.

unlike M3 or Suomi magazines, and use the double-column feed lips for maximum reliability. The M1 and M1A1 versions do not accept the drums. This is not a big loss: I have never even put a drum in my Thompson M1921/8 for field carry. The Thompson magazine system does not have a chute to stuff a magazine in rapidly and requires that you carefully align the rib on the back of the magazine with the slots on the weapon. This system is not fast, but it is adequate.

At least the magazine release works efficiently; you can push with your left-hand thumb and pull down at the same time while drawing the magazine with some speed. The controls are all fairly flush on the weapon and do not tend to catch on vines and bushes in my experience. Spencer Chapman, who wrote the classic *The Jungle Is Neutral*, had the opposite experience, so perhaps I just have never carried it in jungle that is thick enough.

The Thompson comes with two types of forearms and two styles of barrels. Early weapons had the vertical foregrip with a pistol-style grip and a finned barrel, and could be had with or without a Cutts Compensator. U.S. Marines found that such grips tend to break easily. I rather like the vertical grip, but perhaps only because I have watched too many TV shows or all the weapons I have had access to on a serious basis had the horizontal grips. Familiarity sometimes breeds lack of appreciation. Barrels on early guns are all finned to improve cooling. This was found unnecessary, as might well be easily admitted, but the finned barrels are clearly more elegant. The same goes for the Cutts Compensator, a doubtful feature but one that all Thompson shooters seem to like because of its familiar silhouette.

The two worst things about the Thompson SMG are its caliber and weight. I like the .45 ACP cartridge and prefer it as a police caliber both for handguns and SMGs. In the military, however, distances are often longer, greater penetration is called for, and—there is no sense kidding about it—the ammunition is heavy. Try carrying eight loaded 30-round Thompson magazines and eight similarly loaded 9mm SMG magazines, and you will quickly see what I mean. In police work, where ammunition supply is not critical and distances are small, this is not a relevant concern like it clearly is in the military. This then brings us to the next point: weight. All Thompsons are heavy. Loaded, you have a 10-pound-plus weapon that anyone who is honest must admit does not feel lively in your hands. It is simply too much weight for too little benefit.

UD 42

The UD 42, commonly called the "Marlin gun" because it was manufactured by the Marlin Firearms Company, is quite rare: only about 15,000 of them were ever made. Most apparently were sold to the Netherlands Purchasing Commission and thereafter lost to history, but some were sold to the Office of Strategic Services (OSS) and used by its agents in occupied Europe when the caliber was desirable (because enemy stocks could be used in the weapon) and when a lack of spares would not be critical (because, as a practical matter, no resupply was anticipated). Perhaps the most famous use of the "Marlin gun" took place on Crete where British commandos and some local assistants kidnapped General Krebs of the German army, transported him all the way across Crete while German forces looked all over the island for

The UD 42 was apparently made available to the Office of Strategic Services and Special Operations, Executive (SO,E) for issue to their local agents during World War II. These three local SO,E guerrillas, armed with UD 42s, helped kidnap German General Krebs on Crete and take him across the island while being hunted by Germans. General Krebs was transported by submarine to North Africa.

Note the bolt is open on this UD 42 9x19mm and the cocking handle is pulled to the rear, although the handle can be pushed forward after cocking and it does not move with the bolt when the weapon is firing.

The lever must be pushed to remove the magazine on the UD 42. This system seems to hold the magazines firmly so that they are not subject to being accidentally brushed off by contact with the shooter's body, clothes, or vegetation.

him, and ultimately took their prisoner back to North Africa aboard a submarine.

The UD 42 is a blowback weapon of limited capacity. Its magazines are much like miniature Thompson magazines and, as a consequence, are easy to load. They were issued welded together in pairs, but such things generally create more problems than they solve—and that was likely the experience here also. Magazine capacity is quite limited, but it does permit a low prone position to be adopted, something not possible with the longer magazine.

The UD 42 weighs 10 pounds loaded and has an overall length of 32.30 inches, yet it is quite handy in your hands and feels alive. Instead of feeling like so much iron and wood, the weapon retains much of the "game gun" feel, which leads to rapid response on targets, good instinctive ability, and fine results when shifting from one target to the next. It is much better in this regard than the Thompson SMG and especially the M3-M3A1 SMG, which were its U.S. rivals.

The UD 42 features a fine, fully adjustable rear peep sight, which permits the shooter to sight in the weapon accurately. The presence of such a capability always tells the shooter that the weapon is capable of accurate placement if he does his part. The knobs are big and perhaps easily shifted by accident, but I would assume that the soldier would memorize his sighting locations and be able to return the sights to that location if the knobs got shifted inadvertently. I know that is what I did with my M14 in the U.S. Army. The front sight is a blade and is not well protected. It should have protective wings around it and be painted white to allow rapid contrast, but it is certainly better for the eye to pick up than the thick pyramid-shaped front sight on the Thompson SMG.

The magazine release is centrally located and can be operated quickly and with certainty even with gloved or mittened hands. However, the trigger guard is small, and a mittened hand would not fit into it. A bigger trigger guard would be preferable.

Hitting the safety on the UD 42 with the trigger finger and pushing quickly engages or disengages the safety.

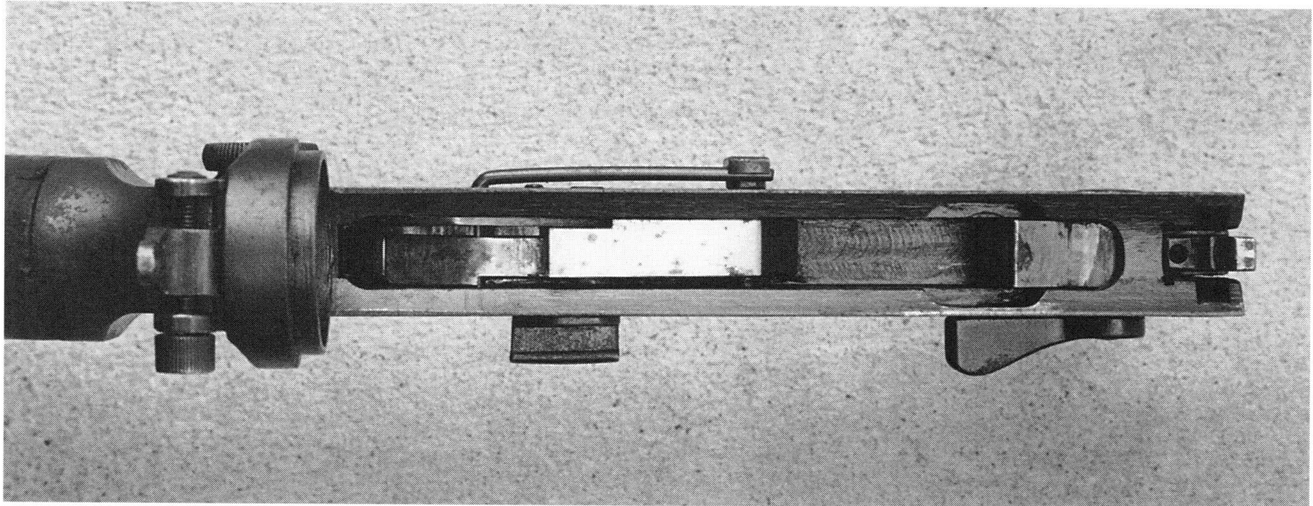

This top view of the lower receiver illustrates the good safety and release lever at the front of the receiver.

The bolt from the UD 42.

Although it is only really accessible to the right-handed shooter, the safety/selector is excellent. It is easily flipped on or off: you can select semiautomatic or full-auto fire by applying pressure from your index finger and operate the whole thing while retaining your firing grip. If the safety is on when the bolt is retracted, the safety is automatically disengaged and the weapon is shifted to the semiautomatic fire position. The index finger can shift the safety off by hitting the top of the flipper and pushing forward, causing the selector to go to the full-auto position. Hitting the bottom of the selector and pushing will rotate the selector to the semiautomatic position. This system is very fast and easy to use. When I tested the weapon on metal plates—with the weapon on safe held down as I would carry it on patrol—I found I could flip the safety off as I lifted the weapon to the shoulder position so that it was ready to fire the instant it hit my shoulder. I could select semiautomatic or full-auto fire with equal ease. The UD 42 safety system is much faster than a Thompson and far superior to such bolt-locking safety guns as the Sten, MP 40, or M45.

The UD 42 has a forward grip that reminds me of that on the Thompson SMG. I am certain that it was originally put there to compete with the Thompson; it was designed in 1939, and that is what people expected an SMG to look like then. Whether such a foregrip actually would break off like the ones the Thompson had or not I do not know. The wood seems sturdier, the screw through it looked massive, and certainly no one ever complained about the Owen SMG foregrip's ever breaking off. Such foregrips allow the shooter to get a firm grip on the weapon. That grip, coupled with the low cyclic rate of 700 RPM and, more critically, the smooth cycling of the weapon, allowed me to fire long bursts and keep them on target. I fired a number of magazine-capacity bursts with Hornady Vector ammunition just to see the bullet pattern and found it resembles a laser beam going down range. I found it quite satisfying to view from the buttstock end.

The buttstock on the UD 42 has an opening for storing a cleaning rod and gear, which is very useful for a weapon carried in the field. The slide swivel on the left rattles unless taped down.

Here the author fires the UD 42 with Hornady Vector ammunition. Note the case to the right of the receiver and the low recoil of the weapon.

The bolt-cocking handle is not fixed to the bolt, so it does not follow the bolt when the weapon fires. Although it is located on the right side of the weapon, I found that I could cock the weapon with my left hand while maintaining my grip on the pistol grip. The handle was smooth-finished metal, which caused some slippage. Putting the handle on the left side of the weapon would have made it easier to cock it. However, locating it on the left would have resulted in the handle's jabbing the shooter while he carried it on patrol. A more practical solution to the problem of hand-slippage while cocking the weapon would have been to checker the handle. With cold or wet hands it would be very easy for the cocking handle to slip out of the left hand before bringing it all the way back. A person might well bring it back far enough to chamber and fire a cartridge but not far enough to lock back, thereby causing a round to fire and either injuring an ally or alerting an enemy to his location. The cocking handle did not stay forward under any type of spring pressure or into a detent once the bolt was cocked, and it did rattle when the weapon was held at arm's length and shaken. Such a device would be a drawback on night patrols, unless a heavy rubber band is used to keep it in position so it wouldn't rattle, yet still be able to perform its cocking function. That is how I keep the cocking handle on my H&K MP5 from rattling, and it seems to work fine—although it does look slightly tacky.

The sling swivels are fitted to allow the weapon to be slung across the body while on patrol, but unfortunately the swivels are metal, and if they hit wood or metal they will make too much noise. They need to be padded with tape.

The buttstock has an opening to carry a cleaning rod, which would more than likely be carried in the field (although it was missing on the test example). The weapon can be rapidly stripped by pushing the large forward lever on the right side near the magazine. The top half comes off, so the bolt can be withdrawn and the barrel cleaned from the rear.

Unlike on the Thompson, hot water can be poured down the barrel to clean out corrosive primers without having to worry about getting the small, difficult-to-clean recess of the receiver wet. You can also clean it from the rear, again unlike the situation with the Thompson. Reassembly is rapid, and there are no small parts or difficult-to-insert parts present that need to be pushed with a third hand while the weapon is closed.

Although the UD 42 has a rather odd look to it, I like it. I found it to be an easy-to-shoot weapon that mounted quickly and felt lively in my hands. It seemed to balance well, so carrying it on patrol or on the march would not be difficult, and it appeared to be reliable and quite accurate. Because the parts are all machined, it was no doubt costly to make, especially in wartime. But as the ultimate end user, I really do not care about such matters. I only care whether the weapon can be carried easily, gotten into action quickly, operated reasonably safely and reliably, quickly cleaned, and, most critically, counted on to put bullets into an intended target rapidly and easily before he does the same thing to me. The UD 42 fulfills all of these requirements for me, and I certainly would not have been adverse to carrying one if I were going to Crete to capture a German general. I would know that I would have been carrying one of the best SMGs that World War II had to offer from a shooter's standpoint.

This U.S. Marine radio operator in World War II was armed with a folding-stock Reising SMG.

REISING M50

In the early days of World War II when U.S. forces were critically short of weapons of all types, the Reising SMG appeared. In some respects, it was a very nice police-style weapon, but unfortunately the tasks it was to perform did not call for a police-style weapon but rather a "tough-as-nails" combat SMG. The Reising did not have a great combat record: in fact, it was bad and it took too much time and money to build. Thus, it has been condemned to the weapons' lockers of police stations around the country, as well as to the back of collectors' vaults.

The biggest problem should probably be mentioned first, namely that the Reising did not have totally interchangeable parts. As a consequence, when men returned from patrols and threw their weapons in cleaning vats, if they did not get the proper parts out, the weapons would not work. This got to be such a problem in the South Pacific that U.S. Marines actually threw the weapons away rather than carry them. A weapon that does not work every time is a liability.

The Reising M50, as well as its folding-stock brother, the M55, fires from a closed bolt, although it is a retarded blowback-locking-system weapon. That makes it easier to shoot accurately than the Thompson and M3, which were its U.S. competitors. Unfortunately, to cock the weapons, instead of a firm pull on a cocking handle, you must insert a finger into the groove in the bottom of the stock and pull the action bar to the rear. This is a slow and uncertain process. The safety selector is located at the rear of the receiver area and cannot be shifted without the shooter's moving his hand from

The Reising M50 fixed-stock, closed-bolt .45 ACP SMG was perhaps ahead of its time for police work given the popularity of the H&K MP5 in the 1990s.

the firing position. It is also slow and none too slick in operation. Unlike on an open-bolt SMG, where you can ignore the safety and merely yank the bolt to the rear when the need arises to fire, the slow and uncertain cocking system of the Reising and its closed-bolt operation mean that you will want to carry it loaded, with the safety on. Removing the safety to the fire position is slow and unreliable, especially with cold or rain-slickened hands.

The stock is wood and one piece. Because of the wood's swelling, I am certain it would become difficult to get the metal out of the wood on some occasions; whereas, swelling wood on a Thompson made no difference. The Reising's wood stock felt good while shooting: it is solid and does not wobble, as happens on the Thompson and M3 SMGs.

The rear peep sight is good, if not very well protected. The front sight was hard to see and not protected from damage. Painted white, the front sight would pick up faster but would still be subject to damage in an environment filled with vines and trees.

The barrel had cooling fins on it, I imagine more to copy the Thompson than from any real need. The weapon was unlikely to get hot enough to need to worry about overheating. Twelve-shot and 20-shot magazines were furnished for the weapon. The 12-shot was totally unsatisfactory, and the 20-shot was not much better.

As soon as more dependable SMGs were available, the Reising went into storage. Most of the examples that you see nowadays were given away to police departments in the 1950s and thereafter found their way into collectors' hands. For certain types of SMG competition, a well-maintained Reising might be just the ticket, but as a combat SMG it falls seriously short of delivering what is needed in the field.

M3/M3A1

When the United States got into World War II in late 1941, it was already apparent to many that the SMG was going to be an important infantry weapon. The M1 carbine, developed in 1940, had undercut some of the need for that type of weapon, yet it was too early to tell whether the SMG was obsolete. Looking at it from today's vantage point, we can now see that the SMG was a technological dead end after the introduction of the M1 carbine and the German MP43/44, but in early 1942 that was not so obvious. What was obvious is that the Thompson SMG was too expensive to make efficiently and that it was too long and heavy for the best combat use. The example of the British with their widely successful Sten gun that violated most of the traditional gunmaker's theories about making weapons also led the U.S. Ordnance Corps to cast about for a replacement for the Thompson.

In one development, the Thompson was modified to become a simple, practical (albeit much less elegant) weapon, resulting in the M1 and M1A1 models. In another, the M3 and later M3A1 SMGs were adopted to replace the Thompson.

Many who have never actually used the M3 series tend to view them with disdain. I think this is in large measure because of their obvious lack of refinement and their low cost. Just as many remember $10 Webley MK VI pistols and may not realize how truly effective these pistols are as combat weapons, there are those of us who remember the $29.95 M3 SMG advertised to individual officers in *Law and Order* and *Police Chief* magazines in the early 1960s. I got my M3 at that time and for that price.

When you hold a loaded M3 in your hand, it feels quite heavy and rather dead. Obviously, this detracts from the handiness of the weapon. You also realize that the .45 ACP cartridge it uses has limited range (because of trajectory problems) and limited penetration when compared with almost any real rifle you would like to name.

The sights on the M3 consist of a fixed ramp-style front, which is integral with the receiver, and a fixed peep rear. I rather like the rear sight, but note that you frequently need to bend the front sight or file it to adjust the bullet impact. A weapon that has been sighted in badly never inspires trust! Unfortunately, the front sight has no protection, so if you drop it on a hard surface, such as the floor of your tank, it can easily bend out of proper position.

To load the weapon you must insert the magazine in the small, nonflared magazine well. This is not something to be done quickly because it must be lined up perfectly. The magazine catch is a button (protected with a shelf on the M3A1 version) on the right side. Although it can be operated while shooting with the weak hand (assuming a right-handed person), it is not as quick as a central-mounted release. The magazines themselves are a serious problem because they are single feed, a design that by its very nature is subject to malfunctions. Further, the magazine is difficult to load beyond 15 or so rounds without a loading tool, and such tools typically get lost in combat. Fortunately, this flaw was remedied on the M3A1 version by having the tool made an integral part of the sliding stock assembly.

A U.S. officer in World War II armed with an M3.

After the magazine is loaded into the well, it is time to cock the weapon because, as is common with most SMGs, it fires from an open bolt. The dust cover operates as a safety on the M3 and M3A1. With the dust cover closed, the projection on it prevents the rearward movement of the bolt.

The lever system on the right side that is used to cock the bolt of the M3 frequently broke, prompting the manufacturer to merely make the ejection port hole larger so the shooter could cock the bolt by pulling back with his fingers. The dust cover needs to be manually flipped up, and it also functions as a safety. The barrel is easy to remove for cleaning. The stock tends to wobble, and the single-column-feed magazine is difficult to load without a special tool.

Opening the dust cover allows you to cock the weapon. The M3 has a cocking handle on the right side. On the simpler M3A1 you simply pull it firmly to the rear with your finger. But you must take care to lock it back into the sear position because the weapon will fire if you pull it partially back and then let it go forward on its own. A round will be stripped from the magazine, and the weapon will go "bang." Similarly, as an aside, take care not to drop a loaded M3/M3A1. The bolt is heavy enough that the sudden halting of the weapon's rearward movement will allow inertia to pull the bolt back far enough to clear the magazine but not far enough to lock the bolt; then it will go forward, firing the weapon. Such an incident happened in Vietnam when a U.S. helicopter brought back a cargo net full of dead Vietnamese soldiers. As the ground forces pulled the dead out and separated the weapons, one particularly dumb GI casually threw a loaded M3A1 that had been carried by the Vietnamese soldier into a connex container. On impact the M3A1 fired, hitting the GI in the leg. He got his Purple Heart and no doubt a fine story to tell all of his girlfriends in the years ahead. After all, you are a soldier for a few years and a veteran forever thereafter.

The stock on the M3/M3A1 is a simple wire unit. It is not very sophisticated, which would be all right, but because of its design and locking system, it is also not very stable. On all the examples I have encountered, the stock wobbles, and effective shooting cannot be done with such a stock. Further, it does not collapse all the way into the receiver, and firing the weapon with the stock collapsed is difficult because your wrist hits the stock. Of course, shooting an SMG without using the stock is not likely to get any real results. Collapsing the unit requires you to push in the catch, as does extending it. The stock tends to bend and catch as you withdraw it, binding it in place. If you push the button and pull to the rear rigorously, the stock will pull completely free of the weapon, leaving you with a piece of gun in each hand. That is not a good stock design. The British did it better with the solid stocks on the Sten, and the Germans did the folding stock on the MP38 better. The United States did a terrible job on the stock. Perhaps the M3/M3A1 is cheap, but that is not a sufficient reason for sending a man into combat with a defective or marginal design.

The M3/M3A1 is made entirely of metal, and the pistol grip has pressed checkering in it. I suppose this is intended to allow the shooter to hold the weapon when his hands are cold or slippery, but in that attempt it fails. Worse, as the weather gets cold, the pistol grip is painful to the touch. I can only imagine how terrible it must have been in Korean winters. Perhaps wrapping it with cloth tape would help. The trigger guard is a thin piece of sheet steel that has sharp edges on it that cut into your fingers if you firmly hold up on the pistol grip as you typically want to do. The edges need to be broken with a file, but I have never seen it done in the field.

Generally, you should never hold on to a magazine in an SMG because it will cause wear to the catch, which causes the magazine to drop down and ultimately leads to strippages. However, with the M3/M3A1 you are supposed to hold on to the magazine housing. As long as you keep your hand on the housing and not on the magazine, all will be well. However, be careful not to bump the magazine release or drop your hand onto the magazine if you wish to avoid a stoppage. The grip is certainly nothing to applaud, but it is acceptable.

The barrel on the M3/M3A1 screws out easily, allowing full access to the weapon and bolt system for cleaning, as well as making it easy to clean the barrel. With the typical corrosive ammunition used during World War II, this was no doubt a very desirable feature. The bolt runs back and forth on a rod system; it does not merely slide into the receiver. This makes for a much smoother operation than would otherwise be the case, plus it provides a large area between the bolt and receiver for the dirt to build up and yet still not affect functioning. The barrel on the M3/M3A1 is short but perfectly adequate to the cartridge and its intended tasks.

I have saved the best thing about the M3/M3A1 for the last, namely its cyclic rate. Because of its very heavy bolt, the cyclic rate with typical .45 ACP standard 230-grain full-metal-jacket ammo is between 350 and 450 RPM. In the last example I shot with a timer it was running 382 RPM. This low cyclic rate allows the shooter to fire single shots easily even though there is no selector on the weapon. More critically it allows you to fire a long, very accurate burst. I seem to be able to pull the weapon out of recoil and realign the weapon between shots with the M3/M3A1, something not feasible with any other SMG. Cyclic rate is always something of a dispute among SMG shooters. Some think the higher the rate, the better: this is the German idea that you fire a burst that goes out the barrel before the barrel has time to start raising up and you thereby saturate the target area. Others think a slow rate is better: you can control the rounds' impact more easily, and the closer you are getting to merely fast semiautomatic fire without the need to learn trigger manipulation the more accurate you are. I have tried both, and I prefer the lower rate, but your experiences may differ.

The author with an M3A1 .45 ACP belonging to John Ross and his test target. The author was unimpressed with the weapon. He found that he could fire a .45 Auto faster than an M3A1. In tests the M3A1 was firing a 392 RPM cyclic rate.

The M3/M3A1 is typically seen in .45 ACP caliber, but a World War II 9x19mm conversion unit took the Sten magazine. These kits used to be common, but I have not seen one for a long time. Factory 9x19mm models are also produced in Taiwan, China, and Argentina. If the 9x19mm model keeps the same cyclic rate, it would be a very interesting test weapon. I have never fired the 9x19mm examples, unfortunately.

As has already been made clear, for standard military purposes, the SMG is obsolete. What's more, the M3/M45A1 SMG was obsolete before the first one was ever issued to a GI. As a bowling pin gun modified to make a sturdier stock, as my friend John Ross did, it makes an interesting "toy." But in the real light of day, I must conclude that the M3/M3A1 does nothing really better than any other weapon of similar blowback design and is in fact a poorly designed weapon that is heavy, ill balanced, difficult to shoot well, and clearly not suitable if you are planning a "long walk through the woods."

SMITH & WESSON M76

Allegedly, the Smith & Wesson M76 was developed because U.S. forces wishing to get Swedish M45s to use in Vietnam were prevented from doing so because the Swedish government opposed U.S. involvement in Vietnam. Unable to obtain the M45s, the military got Smith & Wesson to develop a similar model that would be available without interruption. If this is actually what took place, then obviously there would have been much better ways to get good SMGs than by starting a production line in Massachusetts. Additionally, Smith & Wesson did not just copy a design; it had to make its own design, which is always a source of potential problems. I rather think that the people at Smith & Wesson decided that building an SMG would be a good idea at a time when most SMG designs were World War II concepts and many departments chose not to purchase firearms not made in the United States. This may strike many as odd, but there was a time in the United States when a "buy American" policy was so strong that you could not buy a foreign-made firearm absent extraordinary circumstances. That meant any U.S. producer got the nod for the sale unless there was absolutely no U.S.-made version of the same general type of weapon. Smith & Wesson would, of course, reap the benefit of just such a policy, since at the time it was the only U.S. producer of SMGs.

As an SMG, the M76 is a fairly poor example. It certainly has no unusual features; rather, it is a standard, open-bolt weapon. The engineers were smart enough to realize the double-column, Swedish-style magazine was superior, and they used it as opposed to some in-house design that no doubt would not have been as suitable. Perhaps the finish is better than that found on wartime Sten guns, but having said that, there is nothing else to recommend it.

The stock is a folding unit that tends to wobble a bit when worn and is not terribly comfortable in actual use. Collapsing it is not very fast either, especially with cold-stiffened hands. Although the grip feels good in the hand, the safety/selector lever

Smith & Wesson's Model 76.

Although the safety/selector is available for use on both sides of the Model 76, its location is inefficient because it requires the shooter to break his grip to use it. This is too slow for quick-reaction situations.

is located so far forward that you must remove your hand from the grip to use it or, alternatively, use your other hand. Neither is a proper solution.

The rear sight is a well-protected peep unit but lacks adjustment, which I always find troubling. I prefer to have sights that I can easily adjust to fit the individual shooter, assuming the sights are well protected and will hold their adjustments. The front sight is not well protected and is too dark. A dab of white paint helps quite a bit to allow more rapid pickup, but you would think that Smith & Wesson, which had been making contrasting revolver front sights for years, would have known better and had a similar sight installed on its SMGs.

The rear sight on the M76 is simple and well protected but lacks the capability of altering to meet the demands of individual shooters.

The bolt handle is located on the right side, and, although it can be cocked with the left hand by crossing over the top of the receiver, it would be better if it had some type of dog-leg on it to allow it to be done more easily. As it is, the tendency is to cock it with your right hand, causing you to lose your firing grip. That, of course, is a bad idea. The handle is somewhat small and slick, which can be troublesome in cold or wet weather conditions. In a worst-case scenario, your palm will slip off after you have pulled it far enough to the rear to pick up a round but not far enough to catch the sear and cause a slam-fire.

The weapon can be stripped for cleaning fairly easily. The cyclic rate depends a great deal on the ammunition selected, but it is low enough that single shots can be easily fired with taps to the trigger. Although it has a selector to permit semiautomatic fire, given this feature, the complexity of the selector may be questioned somewhat. However, for law enforcement use, where long campaigns under extreme conditions (as would be expected in the military) are unlikely and where only minimal training and experience with an SMG can be expected, I suppose the selector does little harm and much potential good.

Being developed when it was, I find the chambering for 9x19mm puzzling, but I have frequently been puzzled by the odd timing and developments from Smith & Wesson. Had the developers really been on the ball, they would have made it fire .45 ACP (always the preferred U.S. caliber) from a closed bolt and had it fire semiautomatic only. They would have then had a very nice police carbine. No doubt they would have sold a lot of them, unlike with the M76 SMG, which seems to have had only marginal success.

One way to properly evaluate an SMG is to see whether it is better than its predecessors. Since 1941, the Sten is the weapon against which any SMG must be compared. As a pure SMG, the Smith & Wesson M76 falls far short of the Sten. If we compare the M76 with the Swedish M45, which many claim was a design pattern, we must likewise conclude that the Swedes did a better job. As with many prior attempts by U.S. manufacturers to make an effective SMG, Smith & Wesson came up with what must be viewed as a poor quality copy of a European design.

MAC 10/11

During the late 1960s, the Military Armaments Corporation of Georgia started producing the Ingram-designed M10 .45 ACP/9mm SMG. Coupled with this SMG was a separate suppressor that lowered the noise of the unit. The M10 was unusual in that it used a short barrel and a bolt that was much like that found on the Uzi. The consequence was that a very short overall length was obtained when coupled with the collapsing rear wire stock. This made a very handy (if not terribly controllable) package: the cyclic rate approached 1,200 RPM in some examples.

Although the weapon was equipped with a selector switch, most people who had the open-bolt weapon tended to keep it set in the full-auto mode. As a consequence of that, their ability to control the weapon was extremely limited. The suppressor that was attached by threads on the barrel, which was a common feature of the M10, gave the shooter something to hang on to for better full-auto control.

Sights are very limited. In the front, a set of protective wings protects a simple piece of metal that is mounted on the front of the upper receiver. It is not adjustable except by filing because it cannot be moved. At the rear, a triangular piece of metal comes out of the bottom portion of the receiver. It has three holes drilled in it: the center one is for sighting, and the other two are for attaching slings. Obviously, changing the sights would not be easy. You could bend the sights slightly perhaps or weld the hole closed and redrill it, but for the most part, they are permanently fixed. If they were always sighted in perfectly, they would not be bad. Unfortunately, however, they are generally way off, even considering the effective range of the weapon is perhaps 50 yards.

The bolt is quite heavy, although the weapon still has a cyclic rate in excess of 1,200 RPM. This, coupled with the shortness of the weapon when used without a suppressor, creates a lot of muzzle whip and decreases controllability. However, the bolt does have an interesting and useful feature: the cocking handle is located on the top, which is convenient for all shooters. On the M10, you can turn the bolt handle and lock the bolt in the closed position. By doing that, you avoid the inertia-firing problem that can occur when you jump out of trucks and planes and land on the ground hard enough to cause the bolt to pull sufficiently to the rear to chamber and fire a round. The bolt-locking device prevents this from occurring.

An Ingram M10 .45 ACP with stock extended and folded.

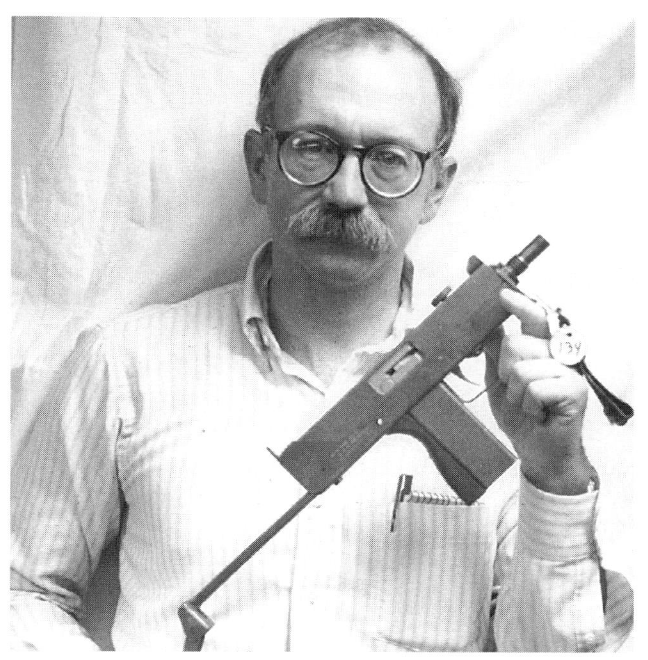

The author found this Ingram M11 9mm small and handy but difficult to shoot well.

The selector is found on the left side of the weapon, but it is so far forward that it is unhandy except to the left hand for a right-handed shooter. Actually it should be kept on semiautomatic except in rare cases: fast semiautomatic is much better for serious work than full auto with these weapons. An exception would be for very close ranges (5 yards or less), where a missed round will pose no risk to bystanders. The safety is located in the trigger guard, but as with most such safeties on open-bolt SMGs, you are unlikely to use it. Instead most shooters prefer to cock the weapon when ready to fire. I suppose it might be useful to apply it when you shoot a few rounds, anticipate further problems, but want to cross an open area at a run. Even then I am doubtful. I would not trust it to work, nor would I trust my ability to push it off quickly enough in an emergency, given its sticking nature and its distance from the trigger. I just am not certain I could push it forward with a single finger to disengage it quickly enough.

The selector on the M10 is slow to operate and impossible to use with the shooting hand while in the firing position.

The grip is quite straight and wide to accommodate the double-column magazines; hence, it is not truly comfortable. The trigger guard is a heavy piece of flat steel with sharp edges that also are not comfortable. As with some handguns, the M10 needs to have the edges "melted." The magazine release is butt-mounted, which makes the magazine release convenient for either hand although the best policy is to use your weak hand to hit the lever and pull the empty magazine out. As an aside, the M10 uses slightly modified M3 SMG magazines in .45 ACP, which has an advantage and a disadvantage. Such magazines are inexpensive to buy, but they are single column, a design that is prone to malfunctions and impossible to load fully without a loading tool. A better two-position-feed magazine should have been used. The M10 is so short that you have very little room to place your hand, and it is possible for it to slip in front of the barrel. It is for that reason that a strap is installed on the weapon at the factory, but most people shoot them with a suppressor or muzzle extension.

The stock is a simple two-spoke unit with a folding wire butt. It wiggles on the weapon, thus reducing stability; is difficult to collapse without pinching your fingers; and can be easily pulled completely out of the weapon frame because it sticks tightly until it suddenly pops free. Then you need to stick it back into the holes on the frame and try to push it home to the locking position. At one time I had a wood stock permanent unit applied to an M10 and found it to be much better, although obviously it made the weapon much less compact. Unless you really need a supercompact unit, however, you always do better to use a fixed wood (or plastic) stock, which is much more stable and a lot easier on your cheek.

The M10 is an interesting development, but as an SMG it doesn't have much to recommend it other than the fact that it is cheap and readily available. About the best thing that can be said of them is that because it was factory threaded for a suppressor, it caused many people to try suppressors who otherwise would not have and legitimized the use of suppressors on SMGs. Also the M10 has been available in semiautomatic form as a "pistol" that is easily converted to fire bursts by trimming the bolt down or inserting a penny in the action. The numbers could be easily drilled out because they were in a noncritical place and a free-market burst-fire weapon was available. Additionally, the receivers themselves folded, or flat ones that you had to fold yourself were available. At one time, a rather flourishing market existed for such items, thereby injecting a large number of such specialized weapons into militia hands.

The M10 has only one real serious drawback: they are not very controllable. They make a great amount of noise and smoke, but you accomplish nothing. I realize that the Israelis used them in Uganda in 1976, but I agree with the SAS, which concluded that the M10 simply was not up to the standard of the Uzi, Star Z-70, or H&K MP5. When it is time to carry a gun and you have the choice, why not take the best and leave the rest? I would not take an M10 if I had access to a better weapon.

MOSBERG 590

This is the standard U.S. Marine-issue fighting shotgun. When the need for a combat shotgun to replace the aging inventory became apparent and the Marine Corps sent out a request for bids in the mid-1980s, the Mosberg Company apparently was the low bidder and got the work. Mosbergs have always been rather dull weapons: well made but not exciting. Although Mosberg had offered bolt-action .22 rifles that were commonly seen as military trainers, this was the first time, to my knowledge, that the company had ever sold weapons to be used for actual fighting to the U.S. military.

The Mosberg 590 is similar in many ways to the combat shotguns adopted in 1917. It is a pump-action 12-gauge that was developed from a sporting shotgun. Unlike the earlier weapons, it does at least have a full-length magazine so it will hold a higher number of rounds in the tube and one in the chamber. Like the World War I-era shotguns, it takes a ventilated handguard with a bayonet lug. It similarly has a mere bead front sight and gutter rear. Other variations of the Mosberg use the ghost ring sights developed originally at Gunsite under Jeff Cooper. Such sights are much better than a mere bead sight on a combat shotgun.

The Mosberg 590 will shoot no better patterns than those shot by the M97 Winchester, so almost 75

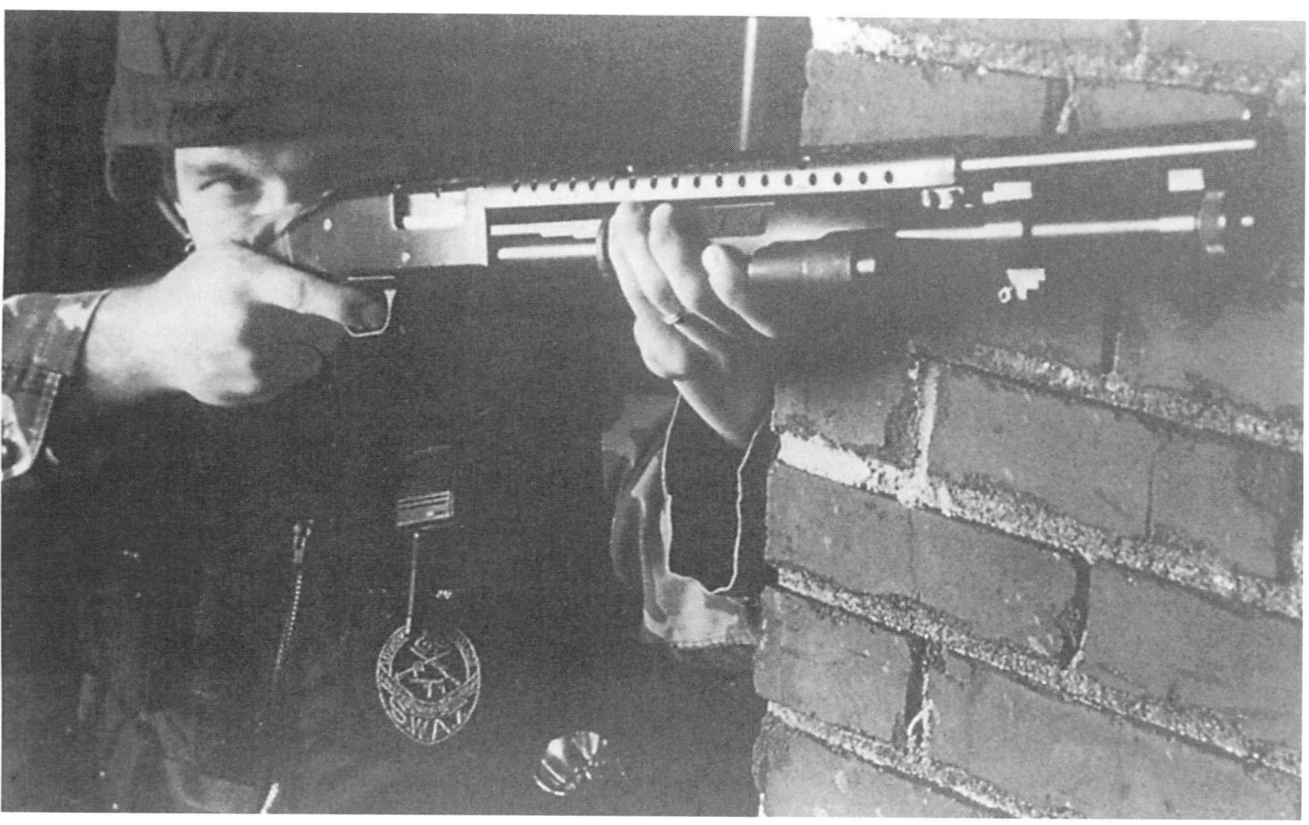

This Mosberg 590 12-gauge shotgun is being used by a U.S. military Special Response Team (SRT) member.

The metal heat shield on the upper handguard of the Mosberg prevents burned hands when using the shotgun with a bayonet. Similar units were fitted to World War I- and II-era combat shotguns.

The Mosberg 590 12-gauge shotgun is really no better than the M97 Winchester made 75 years earlier.

years of time had not given us any real improvement in range or power. Similarly, it loads the same way, which results in a slow process. The stock does hold an extra four rounds to allow the shooter to reload instantly from the contents of the stock. For a police officer or security agent, that may be important, but much less so for an infantry type. The shooter carrying this shotgun today, much like the 1917's infantryman, must carry large, bulky shells loose in his pocket or pouch or in some type of belt loops. With the potential of a large government order at hand, one would think that the Marine Corps at least would have required the weapons to be box fed. Alas, it did not.

The stock and pump forearm are both made out of high-impact plastic. Neither is as likely to break as wooden stocks when they get wet or very cold. For that reason, plastic is a superior choice. Additionally, the forearm has very large grooves cast in it that allow an individual to get a very firm grip on it, far surpassing what was available on factory wood stock shotguns.

The Mosberg 590 is equipped with a top-mounted safety, a much superior location for a safety. It can be used equally well by either right-handed or left-handed shooters and is big enough to flip off rapidly even with cold-stiffened fingers.

The action on the Mosberg tested was not very slick—it seemed to catch and bind quite a bit—but this was because it was not broken in. I am certain that 500 rounds would make it much smoother.

Testing any 12-gauge combat shotgun is never pleasant because they all seem to beat you on the head and shoulders. The Mosberg 590 was no exception; the plastic stock did not absorb the recoil and, if anything, seemed to increase it. I am uncertain whether really short people could shoot this shotgun, and because the butt is plastic, shortening the weapon may be very difficult.

I suppose the Mosberg 590 will make a very suitable weapon to arm marine guards at U.S. embassies or other roles where the ranges are short, the penetration is critical, and the battles are short. In that regard, it is only slightly better than the M12 in 1918: the safety is better, but nothing much else. Perhaps the next time a combat shotgun is wanted, we will start with a clean slate and not merely recycle standard hunting weapons trying to pass themselves off as combat weapons. It can be done, I am certain, and will represent a major breakthrough in a field that seems quite full of excellent designs in other areas of armament.

USAS 12 GAUGE

The USAS 12 gauge is a rarity in the shotgun world: it is a purpose-built police shotgun rather than a conversion or modification of an existing sporting weapon. The USAS 12 gauge is a selective-fire shotgun manufactured in Korea that looks a lot like an M16 rifle. The controls are all similar in that the pistol grip, safety/selector, and magazine release are identical. The USAS 12 uses either a 10-shot magazine or a drum magazine that holds 20 rounds. I find the 10-shot magazine more comfortable to use and carry than

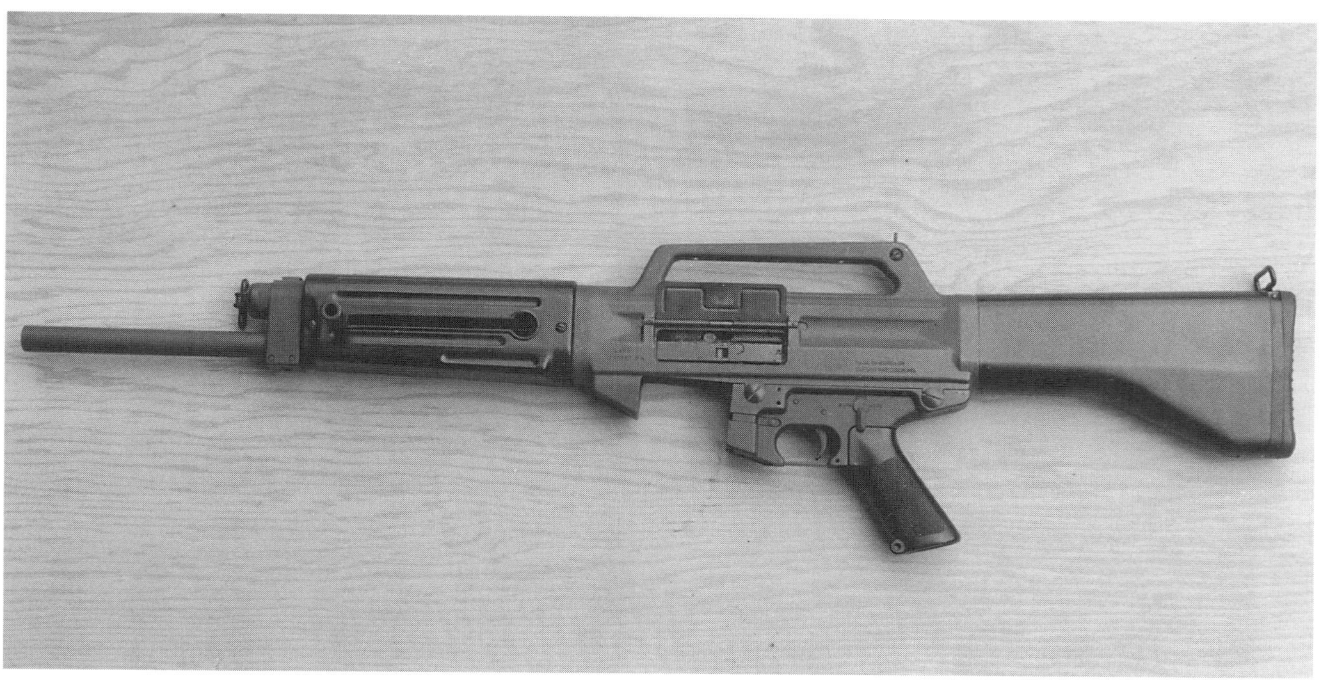

The USAS 12-gauge auto shotgun shares many features with the M16 rifle. The safety is conveniently located, and the bolt handle is handy on the left. The sling swivel on top of the toe of the stock allows the weapon to be slung over the shoulder for field carry, which helps redistribute the burden of the heavy weapon. The folding dust cover is always nice. The front sight was missing on the test example.

The rear sight on the USAS 12 is taller than the one on the M16 and lacks the latter's fine adjustments. Why the Koreans chose to use the M16 carrying handle design is a mystery to the author.

The handy safety on the USAS 12 is similar to the one found on the M16.

The bulk of the USAS 12 is apparent in this photo. the author is 5 feet 9 inches, and the weapon was made and is used extensively in Korea, where the average person is considerably smaller than in the United States. The USAS 12 would have been better if sized for 20-gauge ammo.

the drum, although the latter does work fine and clearly ups the potential of the weapon.

The sights are not very sophisticated, consisting of a post front and an adjustable peep rear. Although it is a shotgun, it is designed to be aimed, and a good set of sights like those on the M16A2 rifle would clearly be a benefit.

The cocking handle is located on the front left side and would be difficult if not impossible for a left-handed shooter to use. It also projects quite a bit from the side of the weapon and would, I fear, tend to get caught easily on brush and trees. In fact, the whole weapon would be very difficult for a left-handed shooter to use because of the location of the safety/selector, but the M16A1/2 also suffers from this handicap.

When I am confronted with a selective-fire shotgun, two questions arise: will it function properly, and how somewhat controllable is it? The USAS 12 appears to be very reliable and somewhat controllable. Prior to my test, the gun had been fired many hundreds of times by others, but it seemed to hold up to the shooting and dirt and continued to work fine. The recoil is quite light, but this is to be expected from its straight line stock and weight. Although the recoil was light and the cyclic rate low enough that I could fire two-shot bursts by trigger manipulation only, I did not find the weapon very useful in full auto. The rate of fire and recoil-climb factors were such that only the first round hit the target. Rounds that are quickly fired but errant are not only worthless, in many situations they are actually a hazard. The shooter issued or using a USAS 12 would be well advised to keep the weapon on semiautomatic and fire rapidly by pulling the trigger each time the sights resettled on the target. Results will be better, and the time elapsed will be only marginally greater.

The biggest drawback to the USAS 12 is its size, which makes it feel awkward. I do not see how any short-statured person could possibly use this weapon, yet I am told it is in use by Korean military and police units. I found it very awkward to use, and I am 5 feet 9 inches. It does not mount rapidly, so tracking a target is difficult. John Ross, the owner of the USAS 12 I tested, took his weapon to Argentina to go dove hunting and found that he got so tired after a day that he could no longer use it and switched to conventional Beretta autoloaders. John weighs at least 250 and stands 6 feet 1 inch.

The idea of a purpose-built police or military shotgun is commendable. Likewise, using magazines or drums rather than tube magazines is an excellent idea. The location of the safety/selector and magazine release is also excellent. But the awkwardness of the USAS 12 and its recoil characteristics are shortcomings in its overall design. The designers should have built the weapon around either the 20-gauge or 28-gauge shell to made it light and handy. A light and handy combat shotgun that will accept removable box magazines, is effective up to 35 yards, and is reliable as well would push all the traditional police or combat shotguns out of the market. Unfortunately, the USAS 12 gauge falls short of the goal, as it is not "handy like a game gun" to quote Lt. Col. R.K. Wilson in his demand for a truly useful SMG in *Textbook of Automatic Pistols*.

RUGER ACF

The Ruger ACF started life as a standard Mini-14 rifle and originally was available only in blue and in semiautomatic-only mode. But apparently Ruger had contracted with some French police agencies to supply .357 Magnum revolvers—France being perhaps the only country in Europe that preferred the revolver to the self-loading pistol. The French police apparently wanted the Mini-14 rifles to fire bursts, and Ruger modified the weapons to do so, ultimately offering a variety of patterns.

The author with the stainless-steel Ruger AC-556 short-barreled rifle he tested. The folding stock is uncomfortable, rattles, and is difficult to both open and collapse.

The modified Rugers were available in selective fire, 3-shot burst, and full auto; in blue or stainless steel; with a short or standard barrel; and with a folding or fixed wood stock. All used the standard Ruger Mini-14 action and were chambered for the 5.56x45mm cartridge. A friend of mine with the Parisian police's RAID unit was very familiar with this version, his unit having used one to kill France's most-wanted criminal in the late 1970s with two bursts from the weapon. He did complain about the excessive penetration of the rounds and seemed quite surprised to hear of the performance of the 40-grain Federal Blitz rounds that, of course, avoid this problem entirely. I would not be surprised to see his Ruger so loaded now.

The Ruger Mini-14 always seemed to me like a

A closer look at the right side of the Ruger AC-556.

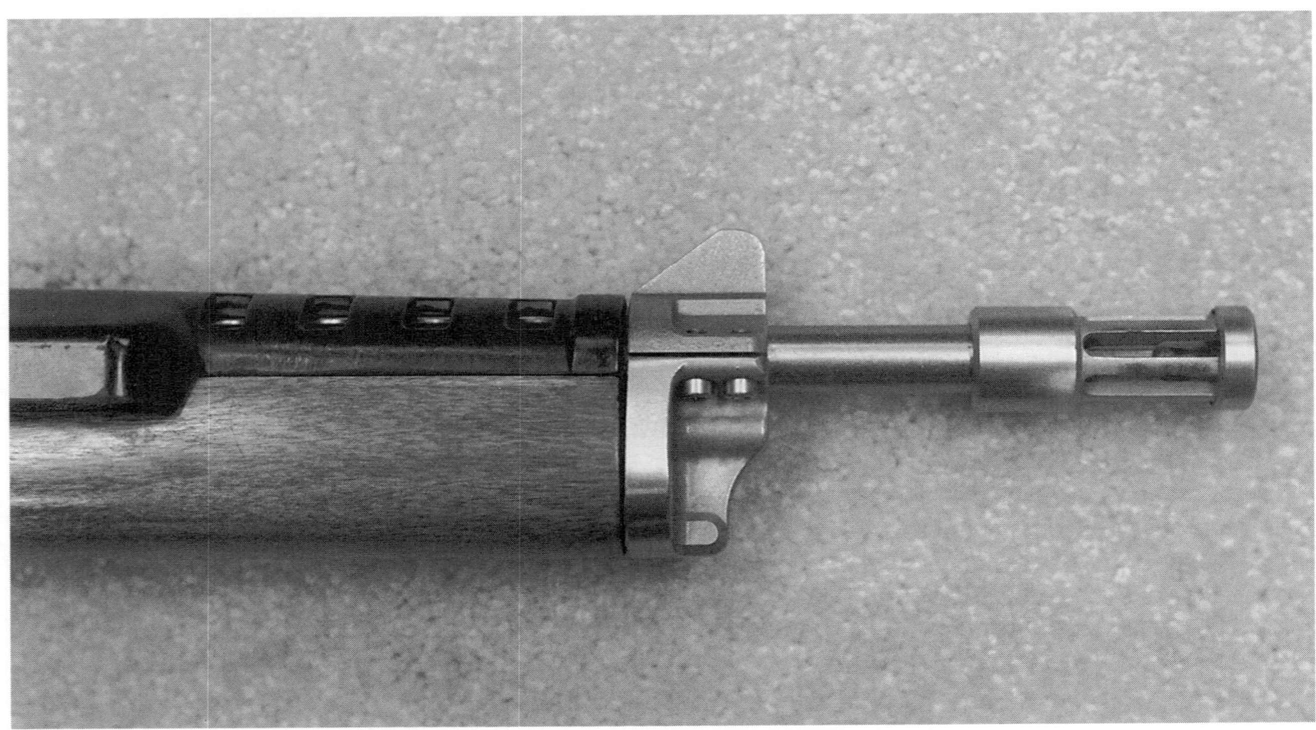

The short barrel on the Ruger AC-556 produces a lot of flash despite the flash hider, which is clearly not up to the task.

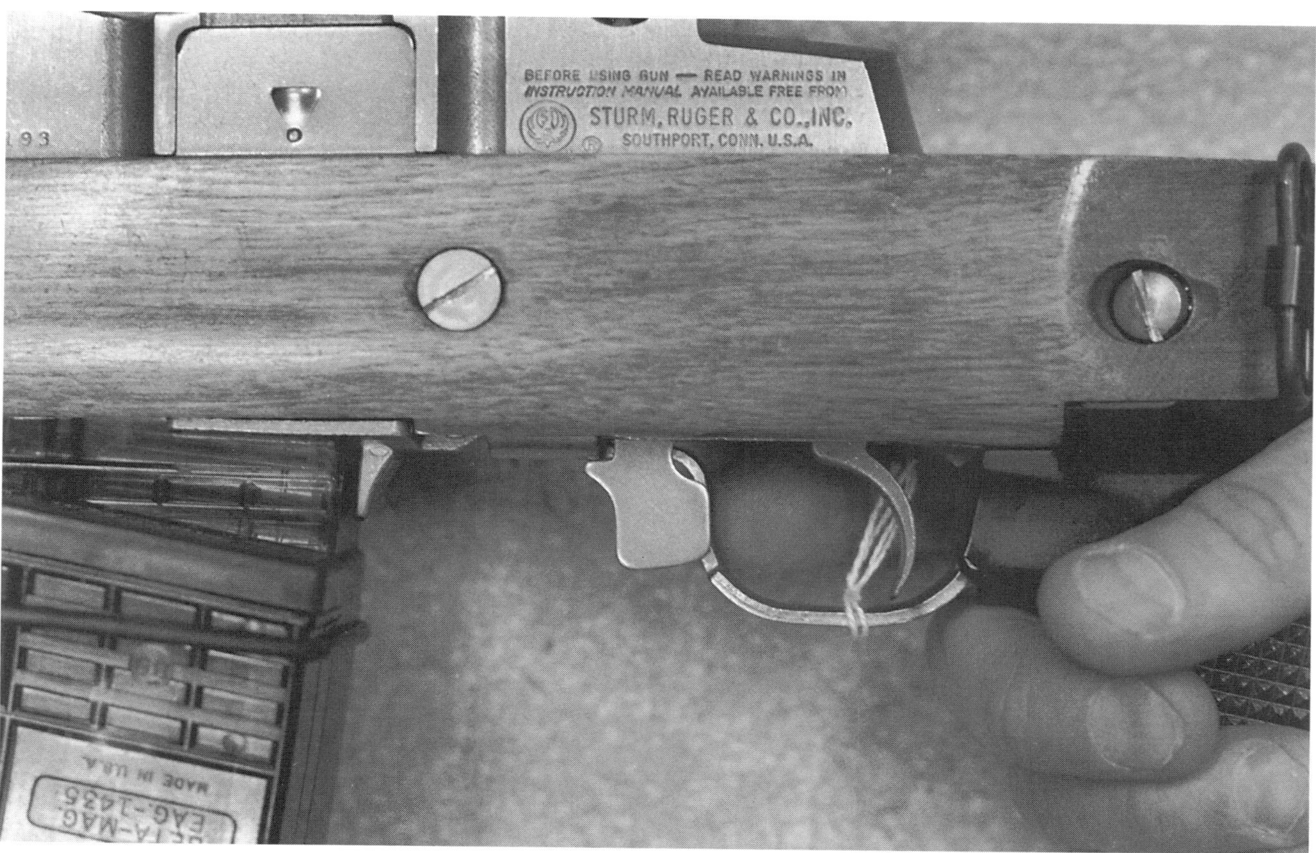

The safety on the AC-556 is centrally located and easy to move.

rather weak design and system, however nice they appear otherwise. The folding stock is slow to extend and awkward to close. The strut is not very comfortable to use, often hitting the shooter's cheekbone. With the shorter barrel of the ACF model tested, blast is quite a problem, as is the fireball unless care is taken in selecting the proper loading.

Fortunately, the sights on this model are better than those on the commercial Mini-14s, which were totally unprotected and prone to movement. On this model, they are adequately mounted and protected. They do need to be painted a good contrasting color to allow quick pickup as well as to avoid confusing the ears of the sight protector with the actual sight blade. The rear sight is a good peep unit.

The magazine release and safety are copied off the M14 U.S. service rifle, and, being an old M14 user myself, I rather like it. You must remember to tilt the magazine in and rock it back, however, not simply push it in place, which makes prone loading somewhat troubling. The trigger guard is too small and does not fold down or to the side to permit winter use. On the M14, a winter trigger system was developed (although I admit I never saw one in the field), but you would think Ruger would have made arrangements for the guard to fold down or to the side, knowing these rifles might well be used in the field where a deployment might extend over a long period in hostile weather.

I rather doubt that the Ruger M14 is as durable as the Colt M16 rifle because of all the development that has gone into the latter, but I will admit that the Mini 14 mounts quickly and is pleasant to shoot (except for the short-barreled models). About the worst complaint I have heard is that it sets the wood on fire when long bursts are fired. Do a lot of bursts and you definitely will set the stock on fire. But you can do that with an AK-47 as well, and, frankly, this problem is really one for the recreational machine gunner, not the practical user.

Pushing the selector on the AC-556 requires the shooter to break his grip.

When the Ruger was available for less money than the Colt or Galil, it made sense for police agencies to adopt it. Also perhaps it was less frightening than a "black military rifle," but this always seemed like an inconsequential concern, given the weapons being used by SWAT or other special-response teams. With the price differential gone, I think law enforcement users might as well choose the M4 Carbine instead. Military users should always select the more battle-tested M16 or Galil. The plinker can use the Ruger to advantage, however, because of the large number of transferable guns in the system.

COLT 9mm

The Colt 9mm SMG was designed to compete with the H&K MP5, which had become a driving force in U.S. law enforcement circles. Among many police agencies, especially in federal service, there is a requirement to "buy American." When I used to work for the federal government, we had to go through all sorts of hoops to order Uzis because they were not made in the United States. Perhaps it is easier today, but 20 or more years ago, all sorts of certifications and explanations had to be provided. The arrival of the Colt 9mm, no doubt, was greeted by many with enthusiasm.

The Colt 9mm is, of course, merely a modification of the Colt M16 rifle to accept the 9mm cartridge. The Colt 9mm fires from a blowback system rather than by means of gas operation, as does the M16. But like the M16 and its main competitor, the MP5, the Colt fires from a closed bolt. Of course, the barrel is shorter than even the shortest on the M16 series, and it uses the standard M4 carbine sliding stock. Interestingly, the Colt SMG that I tested, which belonged to my friend Ken Hackathorn, had a rubber inner tube slide over the sliding stock junction. When I asked Ken why, he replied to keep from catching his mustache in it. I had the same problem in 1973 with my XM177E1 5.56mm version. I wish I had thought of the inner tube trick. I used tape.

The Colt 9mm is short and well balanced. The controls are like on the M16 and easy to operate for a right-handed shooter, but slow for a left-handed shooter. The long reach makes for a long flip from safe to auto. The magazine release is like that found on the M16 and is quick to operate.

A Colt engineer who was present when I tested the Colt 9mm (and who shall remain unnamed for obvious reasons) noted that the biggest problem with the weapon was the magazine. Apparently, when looking for a magazine, Colt engineers chose an Uzi magazine, but it would not fit into the magazine well; rather than cutting out the magazine well on the receiver (which required two $5,000 cutters), they modified the magazine. As a consequence, they introduced a defective magazine design into the system. At the time of the testing, Colt had an engineer on the problem full time, but no fix was in sight. As a consequence, malfunctions resulting from the defective magazines are common. The most important part on a self-loading weapon is a proper magazine, so it is hard to understand why this series of misadventures took place.

The Colt 9mm SMG fitted with the Ultra Dot sight unit.

The example tested by the author was a loaner from Ken Hackathorn. Note the three cases in the air in this photo.

Changing magazines is not as fast as with the M16 because the Colt's magazines are smaller than the magazine well and a spacer is fitted to the magazine well. This means that you cannot simply dump the magazine and shove in a new one; you must take care (and time) to insert it properly into the magazine well. This slows up reloading substantially.

Sights are the same as on the M16 and are well protected and have good adjustments. The front sight needs to be painted white to allow rapid pickup, however.

The Colt 9mm SMG is not up to the standard of the MP5 primarily because of the defective magazine system. Unless budget restrictions require that you absolutely have to have a closed-bolt 9mm SMG of U.S. origin, keep looking.

CALICO M955A 9x19mm

About the time you get used to the M16 rifle and it starts looking normal, along comes something like the Calico, which looks like it is a prop weapon from a Buck Rogers film.

The interesting Calico has one real drawback: it does not feel like a weapon; it feels like a toy. Lest you think I am just prejudiced, French customs issued an alert to watch for these weapons because agents had mistook them for toy guns and let them into the country. The Calico simply does not feel like a weapon.

The stock on the SMG feels too long when holding and mounting it, but actually it is quite comfortable when mounted.

The magazine is one of the major improvements on the Calico: it holds 100 rounds, and since it can be loaded and left unwound, the shooter can wait to put the springs under pressure until he is ready to fire. Certainly, loading the magazine is time consuming, in spite of capacity. The magazine is also not the usual large box-type configuration that makes it almost impossible for the shooter to adopt a concealable position. The magazines seem reliable, although I did not give them an extensive test for durability, and I did manage to break a spring on one by overwinding it. The magazine is marked "23" for, I assume, 23 turns—but if you try 24 either by accident or design, something inside

The futuristic design of the Calico M955A 9x19mm makes it long, light, and flimsy looking, almost toy-like. This target was shot by the author with 2-shot bursts fired at 10 yards off-hand. As illustrated the SMG pulled high and to the right.

The front sight on the Calico, painted white for better pickup, is a far better sight than that found on most military-issue SMGs.

The grip section on the Calico features a safety that can be flipped from either side. The selector is with the safety lever function and is handy to use. The top-mounted magazine, shown in this photo, is rather odd and takes some getting used to. It is difficult to replace quickly, but its 100-round capacity limits the number of magazines that has to be replaced.

will snap and you will have a nonfunctioning magazine on your hands.

Ejection is to the bottom, much like on the Owen SMG, and a bag can be installed to catch the empty cases on low-profile missions. The bottom-ejection system also enables the shooter to take a very low prone position.

The weapon tested had a muzzle break/flash hider on it, but it seemed to do nothing of any significance. The pistol had a front pistol-type grip, like on the early Thompsons, which gives the shooter something to hold on to but also is something likely to break when the shooter rapidly assumes the low prone position and bangs the grip on the ground.

The front sight is good sized, white, and fully adjustable. The rear sight has white dots on it and a square notch. The only things that disturb me are that it is an open sight rather than a peep and that the rearward sight is affixed to the magazine. I am troubled by sights mounted on detachable magazines because I believe it is possible that the sights will be in a different position with each magazine. But the nature of close-range encounters may be such that the slight aiming error has minimal consequences. Also the comb on the stock is quite high, and I found it necessary to push my head down firmly to see the sights.

The safety, which is quite convenient for the right-handed shooter, is rather odd. To put the weapon on safe, you push down—all the way down. The middle position is semiautomatic, and the last position is full auto.

The rate of fire is supposed to be adjustable down to 400 RPM, but the model tested had a rather conventional 720 RPM. As a consequence, recoil impulse was both heavier and less controllable than it would have been at 400 RPM.

The magazine release consists of levers on each side of the receiver that must be pressed in to release the magazine. They are slow to operate and would be especially difficult in cold weather with mittens on. Similarly, the trigger guard is small, so the safety would be difficult to flip if wearing mittens.

The Calico M955 represents an interesting development, but it does not appear to be a serious weapon. It has a noteworthy magazine system that might well merit further research. It may be a fine weapon for the recreational shooter, but it is not something I would care to carry with me on a 40-mile jaunt, nor would I want to have it issued to me to be carried day in and day out for a year. It is not in the same league as the AK-47 or M14 by any means.

RUGER MP9 9x19mm

Every U.S. manufacturer of SMGs has ultimately gone broke attempting to sell them in the United States. In 1939 Auto Ordnance still had its original stock of SMGs built in 1920; Adolph Hitler's actions allowed the firm to sell off its remaining stock to the French and British militaries, which were both desperate for something to counter their enemies' MP38 SMG.

Later, Gordon Ingram designed the various Ingram SMGs, with the Models 6 and 10/11 being the most popular, and Ingram went broke attempting to sell them. Only the availability of parts kits for M10/11s (that could be made into untaxed SMGs at home) and the semiautomatic pistol version (that could be quickly modified to SMG specifications) prompted as many M10/11s to be built as were, I am certain.

Recently, Colt modified its M16 rifle to become a closed-bolt 9mm SMG, and although Colt has sold many to various law enforcement agencies, most would agree that it is merely a modified rifle, not a true SMG design. And at that, making a cheaply modified rifle for the magazine used to save cost has done nothing but cause trouble for Colt.

The latest entrant into the SMG market is Ruger with its MP9 9x19mm. Ruger is trying to see if it can do what has never been done before: successfully develop and market an SMG in the United States. Only time will tell. Firearms are frequently the subject of whims and fashion, so it is possible. However, whether the weapon is a commercial success may be more a matter of marketing and fashion than the inherent qualities of the weapon. In this volume, we are concerned with the weapon and its qualities as opposed to whether or not it is a commercial success.

The first thing you notice about the MP9 is how much it resembles the Uzi. This is hardly surprising since it was designed by Uzi Galil for the Ruger Company and thus follows a familiar Israeli pattern. Unlike the Uzi, however, the MP9 is a closed-bolt weapon. In that regard, it reminds me of the closed-bolt Uzi carbines. Although open-bolt SMGs are commonplace, closed-bolt guns typically are easier for most to shoot accurately, and the problem of "cook-offs" in a police SMG (or military SMG, for that matter) always seem overblown.

Loading the MP9 is interesting and quite convenient. After inserting the magazine, pull the bolt to the rear, and it locks into position. To close the bolt and chamber a round, strike the top of the cocking handle forcefully with the left hand, and it will close, thus chambering a round. Unfortunately, the MP9 follows the German practice of not locking open when the last round is fired. Although probably not a real problem for police agencies that are unlikely ever to fire it enough to empty the magazine anyway, it is a weakness for a military weapon because it will ultimately result in a weapon being triggered on an empty chamber. World War I combat taught the Germans the importance of a bolt hold-open. Nothing they have done since World War II ended has given them similar real-world experience, and the designers have failed here. With an open-bolt gun, the bolt goes forward when the last round is fired, leaving the bolt forward on an empty chamber and alerting the shooter to the fact that it is time to change magazines. But there is no such alert with a closed-bolt weapon like the MP9.

The MP9 has good, well-protected front and rear sights. The front is a nice, square-faced post that is yellow—what a relief after trying to see so many black sights over the years! It is nice to see it done at the factory rather than requiring the shooter to paint his front sight a contrasting color. The rear sight is a two-position peep and perfectly adequate to the task at hand. Although it naturally blurs out on full-auto fire, a good peep sight allows the shooter to engage

The Ruger MP9 9x19mm with folded stock. Note the trigger guard that is also a forward grip.

Ruger MP9 with stock extended.

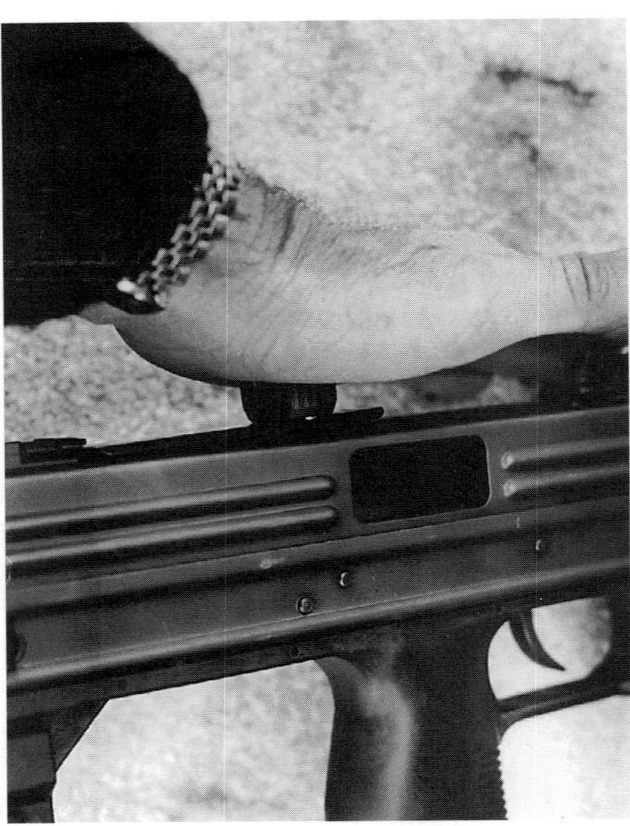

The Ruger MP9 fires from a closed bolt. After pulling back to cock the weapon, close the bolt by firmly hitting the top of the bolt handle with your palm.

The front sight on the MP9 is a well-protected, square-faced blade with a factory-painted yellow dot for good contrast.

targets easily at 200 yards. Even though the sight radius was short, I found I could hit chest-sized plates on semiautomatic at 300 yards about 50 percent of the time, thanks to the closed-bolt operation and good sights.

The MP9 offers an ample trigger guard, so gloves can be used. However, I would prefer a fold-down trigger guard like on the M16 or a side folder, as on the SIG Stg. 90, to accommodate mittens. The furniture on the lower receiver is all plastic and is comfortable to the touch, even if the metal on the receiver is hot or cold.

The stock folds open and closes quickly and efficiently. It is locked at two points, and I found it to be quite stable and rigid. With the stock folded, the MP9 is quite compact and could easily be carried under an overcoat, much the same as an Uzi. I noticed, in fact, that it draped across my body exactly as does the Israeli SMG. Although not as compact as a micro-Uzi, the MP9 has a cyclic rate that is much lower, making the weapon easier to control. I did not get a chance to time the MP9, but it seemed only slightly faster than the Star Z-70 SMG that I shot that same day with the same ammunition, which was timed at 525 RPM.

The safety located in the pistol grip area is easy to flip off to permit firing. It goes from off to semiautomatic and then on to full auto, showing a proper appreciation for how such weapons should be used generally—as a semiautomatic pistol-powered carbine. The bottom is smooth to the touch, works easily, and both flipping it off and returning it to the safe position can be done quickly. I found it very similar to the safety on the Uzi, except that it is easier to operate than any I have encountered on any of the various Uzi SMGs I have shot over the years. I prefer the cross-bolt safety of the Star and Beretta SMG because it is quicker to use, but the MP9 is quite good. Certainly, it is better than that found on the H&K MP5.

The design of the MP9's trigger guard permits the nonfiring hand to grip the trigger guard to improve control.

The controls on the MP9 are easily operated.

To test the MP9 for mud and water resistance, the author submerged the test weapon in a muddy pond and dragged it along the bottom. He then shot it without cleaning it and experienced no malfunctions. The MP9 passed the "pond test" with flying colors!

Of course, the real proof of any weapon is how well it stands up under abuse over time, and only extensive use by a wide variety of people will tell this. However, within my limited ability, I tried to see how well the MP9 would stand up to mud and water. With the kind permission of David Kennedy, the weapon's owner, I threw it out into my pond about 15 feet then dragged it along the bottom in the mud and pulled it out. As soon as it was out and the tape removed from the muzzle (to keep the mud out), I ran an entire magazine in rapid burst through it without missing a beat. I was pleased with the MP9's performance, and even more so when we cleaned it later and found very little mud had penetrated the weapon's interior. I would be willing to carry the MP9 in the field after the "pond test."

The MP9 is a nice weapon, but I must admit it did not excite me. It is rather heavy for its caliber, and the weight gives it a "dead" feeling, at least in my hands. A lively feel for a weapon is always important, in my opinion, for best results and the heavy, blocky Ruger MP9 simply lacks that quality. Otherwise, it appears to be an adequate SMG designed especially for the police market. Whether it will be a commercial success remains to be seen, but it appears to be a design success for now.

PART III

Conclusion: Surprising Findings and Rating the SMGs

This volume dealing with SMGs and combat shotguns has taken me, and hopefully the reader, on a long and interesting voyage of discovery. Much has been learned along the way.

Perhaps the most obvious, yet most alarming, lesson is how difficult it has become to do research on firearms because of the constraints imposed on my Constitutional (and *your*) rights. If a scholar researching a historical period found that much of the research material was locked up in archives and off limits to him without his getting the express permission of the government and paying a very high tax to view it, I am certain a loud outcry would be heard in the academic community. Yet in my area of scholarship—what I view as firearm archeology—it appears acceptable to chill all investigation, levy oppressive taxes, and make the research as difficult as possible. Perhaps scientists who deal with chemicals think the same thing; I do not know. On some level, I hope they do—I do not like to think my chosen academic field is the only one attacked in this manner.

I have discovered that many fine SMGs have been made over the years in places where they were not widely seen or encountered, and yet those weapons exhibited many fine design features. Their relative obscurity makes such SMGs unappreciated, or at least underappreciated. On the flip side, some widely known and popular designs turned out to be surprisingly inferior. An example of this is the Thompson, which is heavy, slow, and unwieldy. Other weapons I tested were made in large quantities and were widely used at a certain time or in certain countries, yet are rare in the United States, so testing was difficult to for me to arrange. The best examples are the various Soviet designs, such as the PPSh-41 and PPS-43. Both were made in large quantities and were frequently given away by the Soviets or Communist Chinese to countries around the world, yet finding examples in the United States is difficult. Most tend to end up in museums beyond the reach of the weapon tester.

This problem will become even more acute in the future, to the point that those who wish to evaluate SMGs will be in the same position as a black-powder shooter who can only look to a fixed pool of Hawken rifles and Colt Dragoon pistols to test. My project here would have been much easier if I had started in 1950—and certainly a lot easier if done before the black month of May 1986. Prior to that time, I could at least have made one improvised example of a firearm that I couldn't get my hands on to test. Today that is not feasible for the nongovernment-sponsored firearms scholar.

SURPRISING FINDINGS

I also discovered a number of things in my research—many of them quite surprising—that were invaluable in rating the SMGs. The following are the most significant.

1. *A fixed-stock weapon always provides a better shooting platform than a folding or sliding stock*. They may not look as neat to the gun store commando, but they are actually better fighting tools.

2. *Cost means nothing in evaluating a combat SMG.* Quality and reliability are the key elements of an SMG, not how much it cost to build. The cost of deploying a soldier or police officer far outweighs any weapon costs.

3. *Caliber is important, but the purpose for which the weapon is used is also essential.* For military use, the .45 ACP is probably not a good choice because of the cartridge's weight and low ranging ability, but the 9mm or .30-caliber SMG is frequently too light. The hot-loaded 10mm would be ideal.

4. *Sights are best if they consist of a good contrasting front sight and a large, well-protected peep.* However, optical sights may be something to be looked at in the future with greater interest.

5. *The SMG should be shorter than a conventional rifle if it is to be handy.* I suggest deleting ventilated handguards because they simply make the weapon heavier and are unnecessary, given the few rounds fired in an SMG as opposed to an LMG.

6. *Compensators are unnecessary given the cartridge intensity level and the weight of the weapon.* A suppressor, however, makes a very fine addition.

7. *Selectors can be handy, although if the cyclic rate is low enough, it does not matter.* Still, handy ones—such as the dual triggers on the Beretta M38 series or, even better, the single but dual-function trigger on the Star Z 63/70—are certainly useful and quick in comparison with flipper-type selectors.

8. *Better safeties, such as the cross-safety found on the Star Z 63/70, are far superior to those encountered in bolt-locking safeties on the Sten or MP 40.* It should be noted that I seldom use a safety on an open-bolt gun, however.

9. *No SMG offers the type of finish consumers have come to expect on handguns.* But the better models, such as the Star, Sterling, and Uzi, offer a good painted finish on top of a parkerized finish that, although not up to the better finishes applied to up-to-date handguns, is far superior to the traditional blue. (It goes to illustrate, I suppose, how the free market has been artificially restricted in SMG development. No doubt if a large consumer [*not government*] demand existed, a better finish would be applied to SMGs. One can only wonder what other features the free market would have caused to appear on the SMG, as has apparently been the case with handguns—better sights, safer actions, lighter weapons, more ambidextrous actions? All have occurred with handguns in the 50 years since World War II, while SMG development has effectively stood still because of a lack of free-market, consumer-driven demand.)

THE WORST SMGs

Picking the best is always difficult because a lot depends on our past experiences and future expectations. Picking the worst is generally easier because certain things are really quite obviously bad to almost anyone, so let's start with the worst.

The Australian Austen, for instance, had a lot of poor features: bad sights, cramped handguard, poorly designed shape, slow safety, single-feed magazine that was subject to malfunctions, and overly long stock. And the added insult: it was not particularly cheap to produce.

The British Lanchester, likewise, had a poor magazine system, bad sights, and was both heavy and expensive to produce. But it was a reliable piece of equipment, which makes it better than the Austen.

I like the Finnish Suomi in both M31 and M37/9 configurations, but I will admit the trigger guard is too small, the front sight is too big and shaped wrong, and the magazine housing is difficult to use quickly. Still, I like the way it shoots enough to overlook the problems.

I find the American Thompson heavy, awkward, slow to reload, and slow to operate the safety or selector, yet I admit I would feel I had missed something if I had not tested one, and I have to say its distinctive silhouette means SMG to most people.

THE BEST

The easiest SMG to shoot accurately is the German H&K MP5 because of its sights, closed-bolt operation, and stock. The trigger is nothing to cheer about as a rifle, but as an SMG it is great. Still, you are always left feeling that if you are going to use an H&K design, you should use the H&K 53 and get the advantage of the 5.56x45mm cartridge, which is almost always better than a 9x19mm except for certain limited functions. However, the H&K MP SD model is no doubt the dog or cat gun of choice!

The Australian Owen is very effective, easy to use, quick to load, easy to shoot, fairly safe to carry within the limits of an open-bolt gun, and a good shooting platform, and it has a good peep sight system.

The British Stens are interesting if only for the fact that they proved to be very effective and cheap. If a modern designer cannot make an SMG that works better or offers better features than a Sten SMG, he might as well stop because he clearly will never beat the price.

The U.S. Ingram M10/11 is only worth considering because of its availability in kit form, which gives the shooter certain benefits that otherwise do not exist but with a Sten SMG parts kit.

SUMMARY

If pushed to the wall, I would rate the American Ingram M10/11 as the worst SMG tested and the Australian Owen the best. The reasons for both conclusions are more fully detailed in the chapters dealing with the weapons. If I were limited to one SMG, the Owen would be my choice, although I admit it probably would not be the best choice for a left-handed person and it is heavy. Still, its reliability and other design features make it stand at the front of the line in my hopefully educated judgment.

About the Author

Timothy John Mullin comes from Scottish-Irish stock and traces his family's arrival in America back to 1690. As his ancestors would no doubt agree, he views individual firearms ownership as a critical component of liberty and democracy.

He was a member of Phi Beta Kappa at St. Louis University and graduated magna cum laude. He received his juris doctor degree from the University of Chicago Law School.

Mullin served seven years in the U.S. Army, first as an infantry officer and later with the Judge Advocate General's Corps, assigned to the Criminal Investigation Division. He was awarded a Meritorious Service Medal upon leaving the military with the rank of captain.

During 1976 and 1977, he served as chief of police for the St. Louis Area Support Center and as a deputy U.S. marshall. Since that time, he has served as training officer with local law enforcement agencies, establishing a modern firearms training program that emphasizes legal and tactical aspects.

Mullin has written numerous articles for a variety of firearms periodicals and law journals and is a frequent speaker on such topics.

Mullin is married, and his wife, Eleanor, works with him in his St. Louis law office. They have one daughter, Catherine, aged 14.